Pitt Latin American Series

KINGDOMS
COME

Religion and Politics in Brazil

ROWAN IRELAND

UNIVERSITY OF PITTSBURGH PRESS

Published by the University of Pittsburgh Press, Pittsburgh, Pa. 15260
Copyright © 1991, University of Pittsburgh Press
All rights reserved
Eurospan, London
Manufactured in the United States of America

Library of Congress Cataloging-in-Publication Data

Ireland, Rowan.
    Kingdoms come : religion and politics in Brazil / Rowan Ireland.
        p.   cm. — (Pitt Latin American series)
    Includes bibliographical references and index.
    ISBN 0-8229-3696-8
    1. Religion and politics — Brazil.   2. Afro-Brazilian cults —
Brazil.   3. Pentecostal churches — Brazil.   4. Catholic Church —
Brazil.   5. Brazil — Politics and government — 1985-   6. Brazil —
Religious life and customs.   I. Title.   II. Series.
BL2590.B7174   1991
322'.1'0981 — dc20   91-19448
                                                          CIP

CONTENTS

LIST OF ILLUSTRATIONS

PLATES

FIGURES

PREFACE

"Don't write for just the eight of them," was a commandment that one of my mentors urged me to display prominently on my desk as I drafted chapters for this book. Eight, she imagined, was the number of experts for whom I'd be tempted to write. And this would bring out the worst of the academic in me, so that, anticipating every criticism, I would dare nothing — I would keep my unruly informants severely in check and would write in the obscure argot of an elitist learned tribe.

I had many motives for obeying the commandment. One, it must be confessed, was ambition — which, the book now finished, I recall wistfully. This was to be no mere ethnographic monograph, reporting fieldwork in a Brazilian town for a select few; nor was it to be just an adroit critical appreciation of the literature on religion and politics in Brazil, for another select eight. It was to be all that and more. Reaching beyond those readers interested in the religions and politics of a town in northeast Brazil, my book would show all students of Brazilian politics that they must take note of the religious kingdoms constructed at the grass roots. Reaching beyond students of Brazil, my work would contribute to the great project of Max Weber and Clifford Geertz — to understand the construction, in religious life, of cultures informing development of political economies. Reaching beyond academic study, my book would speak to those working in the tense, difficult frontier land where the quest for justice rises out of religious vision.

Ambition may be base, but another motive for addressing more than the select eight is surely less so. As I reflected on my research journals and interview transcripts, my commitment to writing for, if not to, my many informants grew. Information was the least they gave me. They gave me that and much more: the insight into the various ways religions may be lived and communities of the faithful developed, and this not just to satisfy the visitor from Australia who was always asking questions. Very often they told me the history of Brazil, the story of a particular place, an autobiography, an account of political intrigue, a religious myth, a tale of political heroes, because they believed me to be a storyteller. They entrusted me with stories so that I would tell those stories again – and so much the better if in places where they would not usually be told and to audiences who would not usually hear them. I want to fulfil that trust, not just because it was given me, but as a small return for the generosity and friendship extended to myself and to my family in more than a year of fieldwork in the town of Campo Alegre. And to fulfil the trust that commandment must be obeyed.

In the end, academic ambition and execution of trust may well get in one another's way. I have tried both to give voice to the Afro-Brazilian spiritists, the Pentecostals, and the Catholics who shared so much with me, and to contribute to debates on the religious factor in the construction of Brazil's political economies. If I have succeeded in any measure, much is due to the help, inspiration, and encouragement given me by Mary Aitken and my La Trobe University colleagues Inga Clendinnen (the mentor of the commandment) and Rhys Isaac. My colleagues in La Trobe's Institute of Latin American Studies and in sociology have helped equip me with the knowledge and theoretical insights that gave me the courage to enter debates on the making of political economies.

Beyond home and university, the network of those who must be acknowledged extends far in time and space. David Maybury-Lewis at Harvard introduced me to Brazilian studies and helped me find my feet as a young academic in Recife, Brazil. With infinite patience, professional wisdom, and humor the sociologist Heraldo Souto Maior of the Federal University of Pernambuco guided my first efforts in research in Brazil and introduced me to the social science community of Recife. Clóvis Cavalcanti and Helenilda Wanderley Cavalcanti, dear friends of the family for over twenty years, have not only made us feel that Recife-Olinda is our second hometown, but, in their professional capacities within the Fundação Joaquim Nabuco, have directly helped us in our researches.

This book, although based on fieldwork in one town close to Recife, seeks nonetheless to say much about religion and politics in the whole of Brazil. That enterprise could not even have been contemplated were it not for the extraordinary richness of comparable case studies from many other regions of Brazil. There is a special debt, then, to the ethnographers of religion and/or politics who saved me from being locked in to the local. There is a special debt, not only for comparative data but for intense intellectual stimulation, to Carlos Rodrigues Brandão, Rubem César Fernandes, Colin Henfrey, Renato Ortiz, Francisco Cartaxo Rolim, Yvonne Maggie Velho, and Emílio Willems. A similar acknowledgment must be made to Thomas Bruneau, Ralph Della Cava, and Scott Mainwaring. I have been free to focus on the local and cultural aspects of Catholicism in Brazil, because I know that the institutional and national aspects have been so carefully described and analyzed by them.

Research, of course, does not thrive on inspiration alone. I am grateful to the Ford Foundation for a small grant in 1973. La Trobe University through its overseas study program and the School of Social Sciences at La Trobe through its research grants have made the fieldwork possible. Writing of the first drafts of several chapters was made possible when the Woodrow Wilson International Center for Scholars, Washington, D.C., awarded me a fellowship in the fall of 1982.

So, very slowly in between teaching and administration, the book was written, assuming legibility as Jill Gooch, Therese Lennox, Barbara Matthews, Beth Robertson, and Elaine Young have, over the years, transformed my ragged drafts into clean printout. That it came to be published is due to Albert Hirschman who helped guide me to a sympathetic publisher, to the anonymous reviewer who not only recommended the book but made many helpful suggestions for its improvement, and, of course, to the University of Pittsburgh Press. That it might be readable is in no small measure due to my editor Kathy McLaughlin and the free-lance editor, Pipp Letsky.

May at least eight hundred times eight enjoy the fruit of the labors of all I have thanked and may no blame for any shortcomings be attached to any of them but only to the author when he missed the point or did not take good advice.

KINGDOMS COME

CHAPTER ONE

Starting Again

ON 17 DECEMBER 1989, Brazilians elected their president for the first time in twenty-five years. With the victory (in the second round and by a narrow margin) of the conservative populist Fernando Collor de Mello over the socialist unionist Luís Inácio da Silva, the period of transition from a lengthy period of military rule (1964–1986) to full civilian democracy was formally at an end. But the parameters of transition are difficult to establish. Did the transition begin with the concessions of *distensão* (distension) under the fourth military president, Ernesto Geisel, or with the indirect election of a civilian president in 1986? Was the end of transition in the elections of 1989, or in October 1988 when the new constitution for a full civilian democracy was proclaimed?

In this book I investigate the politics of transition without any concern for these questions. I examine continuing transitions that are not marked on the calendar of great ends and beginnings. I look for transitions (and for the making of Brazilian politics) in places unfamiliar to most students of the political: at the grass roots, in everyday life in poor neighborhoods, and in the so-called popular religions. From statements about the Constitution made by major political actors and from the rhetoric of the electoral campaigns, I could have documented the range and depth of conflicts that continue beyond their formal resolution. But that is not the tack I have taken. I do not pursue the narrowly political, and the dicta of known political virtuosi, when I investigate persisting differences about the criteria of legitimate authority and continuing contests between opposed visions of the Brazil of the future. Rather, I delve into what is sometimes called civil society, to find sources of, and constituencies for, the rival political-economic projects that are seen when political virtuosi clash in the public arena.

I start with one neighborhood, a town on the periphery of Greater

3

Recife in the northeast of Brazil, and attempt to plot the constructions of everyday life that, I will argue, at once enter into the making of Brazilian politics and also affect the realization of those political-economic projects that remain in contest in Brazil. And I plot outward, toward the central political arena, from churches, temples, and cult centers — the living popular religions, where (I believe) I can show that the various rival Brazils are most evident and most dramatically enacted.

My concern with the multiplicity of Brazils emergent at the grass roots may seem quixotic to those social scientists who focus on the political arena and who are absorbed in the intricacies of the present-day realpolitik, or with the economic relations that are often presumed even more real than the political. Surely, in Brazil, the notorious distance between ordinary citizens and political-economic elites and the extraordinary manipulative skills applied by the latter to maintain hegemony have rendered irrelevant the inchoate political projects of the politically amateur masses? And what significance can popular religions at the local level have (though it would have to be conceded that the Catholic church must be included in any study of transition — even continuing transition)? Are Brazilians so attuned to those otherworlds of religion that religious beliefs and practices should be turned to in a search for their this-worldly concerns?

Satisfactory answers to these questions, I hope, emerge in the course of this book. Here I can only assert my conclusions after twenty years of research on religion and politics in Brazil. I have seen, and I record in this book, how Brazilian Catholics, Protestant Pentecostals, and spiritists interpret and modify political-economic realities they cannot control, how they set up as much as they can of their religiously inspired Kingdoms in the free spaces available to them, and how they live patterns of citizenship that they themselves construct. And I open a case that these constructions do, in fact, make a difference in the unfolding of Brazilian political history.

There is a deliberate tension in my title. *Kingdoms Come* is redolent of the future-in-the-making, according to models proposed by religious faith and vision. *Kingdoms Come* refers to Brazil-emergent, potentially accessible to description and understanding but also elusive, because categories for the description of its lineaments must be discovered in the discourse and practice of daily life. The subtitle, *Religion and Politics in Brazil*, connotes institutional solidities — at least to those schooled to assume solidities in political and religious life. The subtitle refers to a Brazil that can be mapped according to the conceptual matrices of social scientists, a Brazil that is describable: as a political and economic system (genus — democratic capitalist, species — savage); as a demographic structure (third-world pyramid rather than first-world bell-shape); as a matrix of institutions; as a class structure. In my placing *Religion and Politics in Brazil* in the context of *Kingdoms Come*, I ask for a willing suspension of the taxonomic skills that become, all too easily, a trained inability to hear the sounds and see the shapes of political economies in the making at the grass roots. In particular, I ask that standard notions of the boundaries of the political be suspended for a while.

I ask the reader to consider that the millions of Brazilian Pentecostals are acting politically, when they assert, celebrate, and argue about their images of legitimate authority and righteousness, and when they organize this *vida passageira* (life of passage) for the Kingdom the Lord will bring. Similarly, I ask the reader to consider, when the million or more Catholics engaged in their church's base communities proclaim and plan the future they are called to by their Christ the Liberator, that they too are acting politically (probably more consciously than the Pentecostals but usually not with any intent to be "politically engaged" in any narrow formal sense). Again, when Afro-Brazilian spiritists call their spirits down to earth, I invite the reader to consider that they might be reconstituting patronage politics or, alternatively, acting politically as they reveal to one another that Brazil in which the poor teach, heal, and empower one another, as they contest the Brazil of the *cultura alta* (high culture) of the professionals and the experts.

My asking readers to make a fresh start — to broaden categories of political action, to deconstruct institutions, and to listen for the Brazil that is emergent at the religious grass roots — warrants an explanation. I hope this explanation will unfold as I describe my own starting again (and again), in my attempts over twenty years to study religion, politics, and finally transition, in Brazil.

During my first period of residence in Brazil, from 1968 to 1970, I started to study what seemed to be sea changes in the Catholic church in Brazil and the bearing those changes had on church-centered opposition to the increasingly repressive military regime. I was Catholic in religion, an idealistic liberal in politics, and a temporary resident in the archdiocese headed by Dom Helder Câmara, then the leader of the "progressives" in the Brazilian church. I had just completed my Ph.D. in sociology (although it had nothing to do with religion and politics), and at first I studied the changing church as an interested amateur, drawn in by personal orientation and circumstance.

In my last six months before returning to Australia, I turned to a more academic study of the church as I prepared a chapter for a book, edited by Riordan Roett, on Brazil as it entered the seventies.[1] Influenced by Michel Crozier's *The Bureaucratic Phenomenon*, my focus was on the church as a complex organization, and I tried to draw out tensions between the progressives' project of a church of and for the poor and the church's structure as a clerical centralized bureaucracy. Unlike Crozier's work on French bureaucracies, my analysis was based on documentary evidence and personal observation rather than on action research, which starts from engagement with protagonists in situ and attempts to reconstruct their experience and strategies in their own categories.

In 1973, when I returned to Brazil for three months, I attempted to make that start on action research. I interviewed some bishops and some lay leaders of movements in the progressive church, asking for their reactions to my reconstructions of their projects. In Recife, I interviewed a random sample of diocesan priests about their use of working time, their pastoral activities, and the problems they encountered. I learned a lot and wrote a paper, which other students of church and politics in Brazil found helpful.[2] But, as so often happens in social-science research, the main lesson concerned something I, as yet, did not know enough about. The priests, especially those who were enthused by the Medellín Documents (which defined a new church for Latin America), saw themselves as engaged in the formation of a new grass-roots church for a more democratic and equitable Brazil. But they emphasized the difficulties involved in community building and in communicating the new Gospel at the base of society. Government repression, the resultant fear, and the ponderousness of ecclesial institutions were all part of the problem. Above all, however, the priests were aware of a certain resistance from the poor themselves: popular Catholicism had scant space for the new priest and was resistant to his calls for a new communal order; or the poor were so immersed in Afro-Brazilian spiritist cults that they were unavailable for church community life (even though they might regard themselves as Catholics); or one or other group of Protestant fundamentalists had converted the nominally Catholic poor so that they were unavailable for Catholic clergy-led causes of justice and peace.

What the priests and some of my readings at the time were telling me was that I should start again on my investigation of the Catholic church and politics in Brazil. And starting again meant starting with new notions of church, of religion, of politics, and with a host of new questions. In the case of the church, this meant conceiving of the church, not just as a formal organization pursuing proclaimed goals, but more as a set of shifting networks and diverse complexes of myth and symbol, all of which orient church members as they negotiate lay-clergy relationships and take on or reject the projects of the new priests.

In the case of religion, starting again meant that I must investigate the whole range of popular religions – the themes and variations in popular Catholicism, in the Protestant groups, and among the Afro-Brazilian devotees. It was not just a matter of taking in the full range but of conceiving of religion in a different way. Religion would come to mean religion-in-use, the religion that inflects daily life: those stories and images that define transcendent order, that are used to legitimate or criticize one's own and others' actions in everyday life; those prescriptions for right and wrong, for attaining the good and avoiding the evil, that are passed down by exemplary saints, or in the Bible, or through mediums from the spirits; those enactments of right order and the good life that take place in rituals not only of church, temple, and cult house, but also outside, in the streets and the town square. And of each item in the range of religions-in-use, I would have to ask a question relating to a specific use: how does that particular myth, symbol, or ritual, which engages believers in their everyday lives, predispose them in relation to the projects of the new Catholic clergy?

In the case of politics, notions of politics would also have to be reworked. The stories the clergy told me in 1973, and the accounts of popular religion that I read, showed me that ordinary citizens at the grass roots were contesting a range of issues much wider than those presented by the political agenda of the military state or the activists opposing it.[3] Ordinary citizens were themselves protagonists: for particular models of patron-client relations; for different notions of what should be regarded a public issue; for diverse conceptions of the good past and the desirable future. I would have to find a definition of *the political* that was broad enough to include at least some of these issues on the people's agenda. My point of departure in 1976 was that positions taken by ordinary citizens on items on the people's agenda were indeed political, in the sense that they affected the chances of the more overtly political projects of the Catholic progressives.

By the mid-seventies, as the totalitarian controls set up during General Garrastazú Médici's presidency relaxed, the boundaries between the political and the religious could be and were contested. The sense in which religious and political institutions were fields of contest (rather than mere elements in a matrix of social control) became increasingly apparent. This was a time in which important political issues were being fought, dramatically and with increased self-consciousness on the part of key actors, in what had been regarded by church, state, and social scientists as the religious sphere.

In 1976, when I set out with my family from Australia for fieldwork on religion and politics in the northeast of Brazil (making yet another start on my study of the Brazilian Catholic church), setting the boundaries between spiritual and political realms had become an issue to be contested in religious groups and an element of conflict between church and state. Accompanying this shift in location of the political were significant changes in the Catholic church and the state. It was still possible in 1976 to characterize the church as a centralized hierarchy, although the projects of its leaders had diversified, and in some areas the outlines of a "new church" growing out of the *comunidades eclesiais de base* (CEBs) or grass-roots ecclesial communities were very visible.

In 1973 I had interviewed Dom Helder Câmara. He had just returned buoyant, but defeated, from the biennial assembly of the National Council of Brazilian Bishops (CNBB). In a series of votes, the large majority of bishops endorsed episcopal control over a church that was both committed to maintaining good relations with the military regime and also, to that end, anxious to stay within the boundaries of spiritual activities set for it by the regime but disputed by the progressives. By 1976, however, Dom Helder was a member of a majority that endorsed the CEBs and challenged assigned boundaries. In a few years, two tendencies had become well defined. One was the internal tendency for the church to become rather flatter in structure: with more two-way communication, and some members of its clerical elites oriented more to forming communities at the grass roots than to forging alliances with political elites. The other tendency was to jump the boundary, enjoined on it by the state and the more conservative groups in the church itself, between political and spiritual concerns.

At the same time, as already noted, there were some changes at the level of the state. An authoritarian national security state remained in place, but a regime policy of gradual *distensão* had been initiated, and free spaces for the projects of "justice and peace" were being discovered or created, though often at tremendous cost to the pioneers. These historical developments themselves invited a new start on religion and politics in Brazil.

I made this new start when I went to live for a year in the town I call Campo Alegre.[4] I chose this town because I believed it to be small and isolated enough that its political and religious life could be comprehended in a year of residence. But it was not so isolated that its citizens were cut off from the choices and dilemmas, the opportunities and constraints, the contests for hearts and minds that are integral to modern Brazilian social life. These citizens were marginal to power in Brazil as a structured political economy; but they were not disengaged from Brazil-under-construction.

I will describe Campo Alegre in detail in my next chapter. Here we need only note the ways in which it is unrepresentative of towns in Brazil and the one sense in which it is representative. Local customs, ethnic de-

1. The Ireland family finds a home and is put on the map by neighbors.

mography, and the life-chances of its citizens are still marked by Campo Alegre's minor functions in a traditional sugar-plantation society. A coastal town about eighteen miles from the center of Recife, in the northeast of Brazil, Campo Alegre has a history very different from the history of similar-sized towns on the periphery of large southern cities like Floria-nópolis or Porto Alegre. Unlike in those southern towns, Campo Alegre's culture and local economy have not been shaped by the great European migrations (from Italy and Germany in particular) in the late nineteenth and early twentieth centuries. Unlike in the cities on the periphery of São Paulo, growth in recent decades has not primarily been a function of rapid industrialization.

On the other hand, Campo Alegre shares much with these towns and cities from supposedly more modernized Brazil, and particularly an as-pect of in-between-ness. Just like the residents of *favelas* (shanty towns) and settlements on urban peripheries all over Brazil, many of its residents locate themselves in between their immediate past life as farm workers and the future prospect of permanent urban residence and occupation. Like the scores of towns incorporated into creeping São Paulo or Vitória, Campo Alegre, as urban space, seems oddly in between a focus on its past (expressed in the church and market squares) and its future (expressed in the now dominant physical feature, the busy main road that cuts the town in two as it wends its way to Recife). Culturally and politically in 1976, the town, even on superficial acquaintance, seemed in between a remembered and memorialized coherence (in which the lay Catholic brotherhood had been the dominant institution) and a sort of hotchpotch of competing religions and rival, institutionally disarticulated, political allegiances. This was another dimension of representative in-between-ness that I hoped to explore.

The Ireland family, including two daughters aged eight and ten, rented a house in one of the poorer neighborhoods in Campo Alegre. While my wife worked on her own research project, I set about provoking, gathering, and recording the various sorts of data that would allow me to represent how particular groups of Brazilian citizens constituted political cultures, in and through the living of their several distinctive religious traditions, and how they variously endorsed, rejected, negotiated, inverted, subverted, or enacted the political-economic projects of the rich and powerful in Brazil.

I conducted long biographical interviews with Catholics, Protestant Pentecostals, and Afro-Brazilian spiritists and observed their rituals, along with as much as I could of their everyday lives, hoping that, as I put biography and observation together, I would learn about religion-in-use in the negotiation of everyday life and life's decisive passages. I attended as many religious rituals as I could and I attempted to "read"—from use of religious space, repeated gestures of status, enactments of religious myths, and exhortations to the exemplary life—the moods and energies that were being celebrated by, enjoined on, and communicated to participants. As I interviewed and observed, I tried to test, then revise or reject, a number of hypotheses about particular religious traditions and the realization of particular political projects. (Later, some of this testing will be made explicit as I try to place my case study of Campo Alegre in the context of other studies of religion and politics in Brazil.)

One useful, and final, way of redefining the project of this book is to log the changes in my focus on religion and politics in Brazil over the last twenty years, up to the point of ceasing to start again so as to write the book. First, I have moved from the study of the Catholic church as a rapidly changing formal organization to the study of a variety of catholicisms and other popular religions, as lived at the grass roots. Second, my conception of politics has broadened: from an exclusive focus on the struggle for liberal democracy against military dictatorship to the inclusion of that broader contest between paradigms for living, as expressed in the practice of everyday life and in representations of the good in social, economic, and power relationships. Third, the study of religion and politics has become, for me, less an investigation of relationships between organized institutions (the institutions of church and state) and more an attempt to examine the construction of paradigms for living where this construction is most explicit and visible in Brazil, in the several great religious traditions that engage millions of Brazilians.

So far, I have shown these changes arising from my pursuit of answers to academic questions, from the lessons of the field, from the discipline of writing. But my move toward a study of the religious constructions of politics in Brazil has been accompanied by changes in my general theoretical orientations as a sociologist (or anthropologist) of religion and politics. The influence of Clifford Geertz will be obvious to all who know his work. More general has been a gradual move from systems thinking toward action perspectives in the social sciences.[5] My perspective on Brazil — as a national society continually under construction as its future course is contested — owes much to theorists as diverse as Alain Touraine, Erving Goffman, and Marshall Berman, who have alerted us to the unclosed, nonsystemic aspects of complex modern societies. They have encouraged me to move from describing a static Brazil, molded by its most readily identifiable institutions (the military, the Catholic church, the various components of the state), to describing Brazil in motion, emerging from rival visions of Brazilian society and projects for living in it. The action-perspective theorists have provided conceptual space in which to see Pentecostals, Afro-Brazilian spiritists, and Catholics as constructing politics in a Brazil essentially in transition.

In the writing of this book, in the production (or reproduction) of the narrative, Geertz's works on Islam and religion in Java have provided me with rich inspiration. I have attempted to show the religious constructions of politics in Campo Alegre, as its citizens act, and reflect, on what they define as the social, political, and economic problems of the day. In chapters on each of the religious traditions, I follow a certain method. On the assumption noted earlier (that patterns of political construction are most easily discernible in Brazil as the religious traditions are worked on in everyday life), I start off with religious virtuosi in each of the three major traditions, noting their constructions of faith and experience in the stories they tell about Brazil, themselves, their religious heroes, and their neighbors. Then I widen the focus to bring in the less, or more intermittently, committed, the less religiously articulate. On the assumption that the intertwining of religion and politics must first be grasped at the level of the socially palpable, as it were, I try to show the religious traditions as they are lived in Campo Alegre. Only later in the book do I try to relate the Catholics, Pentecostals, and spiritists of Campo Alegre to their co-religionists as presented to us in other community studies.

Chapter 2 opens the narrative in two senses. It presents the social, political, and economic realities of Campo Alegre that are worked within and worked on by its citizens. The Campo Alegre of Chapter 2 is, of course, my reconstruction, but it attempts to incorporate the reconstructions of the past and the visions of the future through which the citizens of Campo Alegre constitute the present. In great part, my reconstruction of Campo Alegre is achieved through what Geertz calls a "thick description" of the making of the feast of the town's patron saint.[6] The Catholic priest's attempts to organize the feast according to his memories and dreams, which are often in conflict with the plans, memories, and dreams of members of his flock, are central in my thick description of the town. The story of conflict between Catholics, obviously enough, gets the book going in a second sense. Through that conflict I can introduce some of the divergent projects for Brazil that are emerging from the Catholic tradition. Those Catholic projects are further investigated in Chapter 7, after two chapters each on Protestant Pentecostalism and Afro-Brazilian spiritism.

But let us first see what a Catholic priest's engagement in the politics of a saint's feast may reveal of a Brazilian town and of the religious factor in the Brazilian politics of the future.

CHAPTER TWO

Religion and Politics in Campo Alegre

COMPETITION FOR A FIESTA

WHEN THE TIME of the saint's fiesta came around, Padre (Pe.) Eduardo had to devise his own script. Ten years ago, or thirty, or a hundred years ago, as far back as the foundation of the brotherhood of the saint in 1870, the priest's script was quite clear.[1] Living ten kilometers away in the next town, the seat of the municipality, he would be invited by the leading laymen of Campo Alegre, who comprised the board of the brotherhood, to officiate at certain ceremonies of the fiesta. A fee would be offered (and sometimes disputed), transport and lodging arranged. The priest would come to say an agreed-upon number of masses, to bless and officiate at designated points in what was essentially the brotherhood's fiesta. There were variations in the script: one year, a priest, disgruntled at the low fee, performed minimally and perfunctorily; another time, a young priest, fresh from Belgium, used the occasion to conduct a campaign to regularize marriages and berate those wayward sheep lost in the immoralities of the day. But most priests recognized their place in things and performed as expected. The board of the brotherhood, too, knew its place in things and, with variations according to the acumen and energy of its judge and treasurer, supervised the ritual, display, and merriment of the fiesta, knowing that its rubrics were a matter of common knowledge and common sense.[2]

But Pe. Eduardo, in 1977, could not abide by the old rubrics. He was young and had been taught in the sixties in Recife seminary by José Comblin, one of the leading formulators of the theology of liberation. In his eyes, the old script would lock a priest into blessing the remnants of a corrupt order and subvert the building of a more just order in Campo Alegre. That could not be allowed to happen. True to his training, Pe.

13

Eduardo regarded his incumbency in the town as a requirement to go well beyond the functions of a traditional rural parish priest. It was part of his brief to challenge traditions — especially those through which the Catholic church sanctified the institutions of power and patronage that oppressed the poor.

As he pondered an alternative script for the fiesta, to include a new role for himself, his reconstruction of the town's past corresponded with the memory of old-timers who hoped to restore an old order in the name of the saint. They hoped the saint's processions around the town might open the hearts of the patrons who, in the past, provided food and drink during fiestas, and jobs and occasional handouts during the year. The saint, they hoped, would look on the blocks of land that were still part of his patrimony, and open the eyes of his trustees to the real-estate bargains they might bestow upon the brothers. There were still members of the Amorim family around and other well-off members of families who had provided officers of the brotherhood over the generations. The fiesta might draw their heirs back from jobs in the city, from their new preoccupations with state politics and administration — draw them back to remember old responsibilities, and the old times that had been better for all.

There were still sufficient traces of a remembered past to sustain hope in a return to old times. A fisherman with a hernia would still ask a *dono* (owner) of boats and nets for help in his sickness. Old modes of exchange and traditional social relations might be seen when a poor man bargained over credit for manioc flour and soap in a *venda* (stall); or when a sharecropper negotiated a rent or, having lost his land, solicited odd jobs from the landowner. Old ways of arranging livelihood and striking bargains were not as ubiquitous and taken for granted as in the twenties or even the forties, when the commercial elite of the town, assembled as the executive of the brotherhood, had jobs, land-use privileges, and small construction contracts to dispense. But at fiesta time the old ways might be given a new lease of life and the saint, the patron of patrons, might have a hand in their rejuvenation.

The fiesta would not be that way without a battle, however. Pe. Eduardo wanted the old ways to die. Leading a small band of the most educated and urbane members of the brotherhood, he had — by 1972, not long after his arrival — engineered the defeat of the old guard, the Amorim family network. He had taken personal control of the finances of the brotherhood — the rents and the proceeds of the quarterly coconut harvests would no longer be the lifeblood of brotherhood patronage. Then the priest and the new guard in the brotherhood refused to act as patrons — at least of the kind an old-timer might recognize. Every transaction was recorded, and rules, rather than ties of friendship or kinship, henceforth determined how the resources of the patrimony were collected and disbursed. The priest arranged the renovation of the church building. The cleaning and the painting perhaps justified his claim that this was a "restoration" of the church. But he also removed so many statues of patron saints and Virgin Marys that the new bright bareness made the church as chill and newfangled as the *templo* of the Protestant Assembly of God. The beautiful old painted wooden statue that had been the real saint for so long was removed to the sacristy and could no longer be taken out for processions – the priest was keeping the patron for himself in the building he had made his own, old-timers said. Now it was a larger, pink-faced, black-and-white-robed, plaster saint, new and factory made, that went on parade with the priest's blessing. It was this substitute saint into whose hands or crevices one might put – a little doubtfully now – the request for the end to a daughter's illness and the vow, should the request be granted, to follow barefoot in the steps of the saint at the next fiesta.

Perhaps it is understandable that the priest should do so much to abandon and discourage the ways of Campo Alegre. He was still young, not long from the seminary, and he had come from another town, way in the interior of Paraiba where things were surely different. Sometimes such a person could do a lot of good, like the legendary Padre Cícero of Joaseiro, the politician-saint who had, by the time of his death in 1934, won order and prosperity for the people of the northeastern backlands. But Campo Alegre had always managed without such a priest and Padre Cícero was probably the last of his kind.

In all sorts of ways, not the least in the way he sought to shape the fiesta, Pe. Eduardo seemed to reject the role of local politician and eschew the games of local politics altogether. But there were other roles ready for him if he chose. If not the role provided in the old brotherhood script, then there was a somewhat newer, populist politics script for a priest during a fiesta. Local politicians knew the script and tried to cajole, then manipulate, the priest into adopting it. Pe. Eduardo also knew the script and refused to use it. It required him to do some blessing even before the fiesta began. He would have to choose one political group over others and allow that group exclusive rights to the entertainment side of the fiesta. He could agree that the opposition party (the Movimento Democrático Brasileiro [MDB] at the time) could hire the Ferris wheel for the church square and publicize its subsidy for cheap rides. An MDB commentator might announce the return of the saint and the boat races on MDB sound equipment – if he gave his blessing to such an arrangement.

There were many reasons why he might. A clear, public alliance between priest and MDB politicos would lend strength and credibility to priestly support of the sharecroppers, who had recently been served quit notices by the new owner of the big estate adjoining the town. Without such an alliance the landowner had things sewn up. A retired military man, he could influence the deployment of military police should there be trouble. Smaller things could be handled through the local magistrate, who had accepted a parcel of land on the estate, or through the municipal president of the rural union, in a similar situation. In the town itself, the submayor was an employee, as was the primary school principal, who was the landowner's lawyer. In the municipal seat, the government party (ARENA) was in power (with a variety of ties to the landowner), and on the council a still-resident member of the Amorim family (which had so recently controlled the brotherhood) was ever ready to attack the priest or embarrass him by calling on him to hand over patrimonial land to the poor.

An alliance with the MDB would give Pe. Eduardo counterweight to the landowner's network – a voice in council meetings, a say in the alternative patronage network of the party. He could be seen as delivering a sure majority of votes for the MDB in the next election and, as an important powerbroker, would be thought about twice by police chiefs, magistrates, lawyers, and union bosses, perhaps even landowners – the persecutors of those whom he felt as a priest called upon to protect. Allied to the party, he could also lobby effectively on behalf of the growing number of townsfolk who depended on the jobs or the meager social services provided by the municipality. He had chosen not to be a town patron – a substitute Amorim, recognizable as one with whom a deal could be done. He could choose to develop a constituency among the commuters: those whom old-timers had a hard time recognizing as neighbors, who commuted regularly to the city to work, the lowly state and federal government employees, people who came and went and came again, adrift from old patrons, without roots in the new industries nearer town.

Pe. Eduardo was no fool. He saw these possibilities; though he was inclined to think the MDB stood to gain more from him than he from it. That was not the main reason he rejected the politicos' script for the fiesta. What he wanted was a completely different fiesta. Not the old fiesta of local patronage for locals – not a fiesta for the shifters who sought patronage and protection in the statewide and nationwide institutions of *populismo* (as he put it) – but a fiesta that would celebrate and rehearse a New Order. The priest's fiesta would be a fiesta of the people and a sort of sacrament, at once celebrating and strengthening the authentic grassroots communities (CEBs) in the town. For example, the small group of women who, with the help of a nun, seemed to be really connecting their management of a fishing cooperative, their discussions on the meaning of the Bible stories, and various self-help projects – the fiesta should be theirs. The fiesta should express the fragile but growing solidarity of the small farmers resisting expulsion, who were beginning to meet together up in the manioc shed at the other end of town. The fiesta should be a call to all the poor — isolated and competing in a struggle for the crumbs from the rich man's table — to discover what might be achieved in neighborhood associations and through group solidarity.

But clear aims and principles do not make a priest's fiesta script. They rule out scripts surviving from the past. Newer scripts are incompatible with them. Apart from the populist script, there was an even newer one available in the next town. The old priest in the municipal seat was content to accept his role as a purely religious functionary blessing a new-style saint's festival that centered around a parade advertising its industrial financiers and its military choreographers. The younger Pe. Eduardo had already made it clear he would have no part in that sort of tableau for a new Brazil. He had refused to take his seat in the town square for the National Day parade when the children of the employed, who could afford appropriate uniforms, stood to well-schooled attention to hear the mayor and a local military commander declare the achievements of the military coup of 1964. He would resist offers from the metal extrusion factory to underwrite a fiesta in the image of another National Day, despite the fact that the factory was the largest single employer in the area, and many a new, wage-earning family in town would be proud to display its children marching to the Brazil of the future.

In the absence of a script prepared for him, the priest could still help to nudge the fiesta into a shape compatible with his hopes for the fledgling grass-roots communities. Though rather solemn in personal disposition, he knew that a fiesta must be fun, and that meant music. So he would provide music. Not the pop music that artful politicians had blaring forth at their rallies; not the cacophonous brass band that the brotherhood used to subsidize; still less a more tuneful military band. The priest had in mind a group that used instruments of traditional folk music and that seemed to be having some success at making folk music popular again.

Since everyone expected clerical sermons during a patron saint's fiesta, why not bring in a skilled orator, who might persuade people that the true celebration of unity around the saint involved working together for justice — for land and fishing rights in particular? The priest had a colleague, a priest-lawyer, who could preach and also, during the fiesta, advise on justice achieved through legal communal struggle.

Band, visiting colleague, and extended hospitality for the three weeks of the fiesta would amount to a fair sum of money. In the old days, the brotherhood would call in debts, solicit gifts even in the capital city, and sell off bits of the patrimony, to provide a good fiesta. The priest was not prepared to spend like that. He would underwrite only specific parts of a full fiesta — greater spending would be an immoral waste of patrimonial resources and would probably provide support for activities incompatible with his vision of a New Order.

Limiting the budget placed limitations on the priest's definition and control of the fiesta. In the capital city, the TV, the newspapers, and the government tourist bureau would announce that one of the state's biggest and brightest town fiestas would take place. Outsiders would come, expecting to be entertained, in the way they had heard the saint always entertained. Insiders, too, would gather for the fiesta of their memories. Crowds would gather, expecting an event, and there was nobody quite in control of how to make it happen — here was irresistible investment opportunity for the politicians and bigger businessmen of the municipality.

They were accustomed and willing to collect money and channel it into advertisement, increased sales, greater public support. The best sound equipment, donor-named prizes for festival contests, food-and-drink stalls, decorative lighting, bunting, the cleaning of selected streets — these could all be provided, as the structural shell from which a fiesta would emerge. Donors of the shell would be acknowledged. As this structure turned the fiesta into spectacle, the radio announcer could not only advertise but also play his part as the loudest choreographer of all. The fiesta was a time when echoes of the country-town past might be heard, and a time when everyone would expect to see the priest do something special. But it was also advertising time for a modern urban happening — a happening waiting to be produced and directed, its meaning told. The priest would be director only if he were prepared to pay.

He was not. He rejected available scripts. Others were ready and knew how to choreograph urban happenings to their own ends. And so it was that Pe. Eduardo, at one point literally and at other points figuratively, almost missed the boat. The great happenings of the fiesta offered him only ill-defined roles. Around and in the church, and through a visiting band, something like a priest's fiesta took place. But it merely coexisted with other fiestas. One was a fiesta of landowning *coronéis* (colonels) and the ghosts of sharecroppers almost incapable of resurrection because there were so few around who knew their world — even though the boundaries of that world might be retraced in the processions of the saint. Another was a fiesta of erstwhile commercial patrons of the town, vanquished in battle with Recife retailers or glad to have won lucrative office in city-located state bureaucracies: this was the fiesta that many gathered there would try to recreate, as they had done before, within their own living memories. Another was a fiesta of those who knew how to transmute memories into the currency of urban go-ahead Brazil of the future-that-has-arrived. Another was a fiesta of sheer diversion. Another was a fiesta of private pacts with the saint, for those who had learned despair of earthly community but still hoped in a communion of saints. Another was a fiesta to be avoided, the children forbidden to attend because it was a Catholic farce, parading idolatry, a time when Satan could more easily move the town to drinking, dancing, and whoring.

THE FIESTA

The saint had little say in what would be the real fiesta, because almost no one knew his story, and the few old people who did disagreed about the details. Even the priest, like the Protestants, seemed to think the saint was only a plaster shell enclosing nothing at all. But once a businessman provided a truck, and the crowds turned out to set him on his way, the saint played his part in the opening procession according to the doubtful and often conflicting memories of those who gave him passage.

The first procession in the first weekend of the fiesta was the *levada* (taking the saint out of town), through the municipal seat, and around to a resting place in a small town on the coast, twelve kilometers by sea south of Campo Alegre. If anyone controlled this comparatively unadvertised beginning of the fiesta it was Pe. Eduardo. He had called together the committee that had arranged the donation of the utility truck for the saint, together with several other trucks, and a bus to provide free transport for those who wished to follow the saint on procession. He and the lawyer-priest were co-celebrants of the Sunday farewell mass. The purple-vested members of the saint's brotherhood who carried the saint on a palm-decorated palanquin were the priest's men. Seven years before, they had welcomed the priest as leader in their bid to defeat the Amorim family.

Pe. Eduardo could not have everything his way, however. He would have liked the mass to have had a congregation representative of the town, or at least including respectable numbers from the farmers and fishermen. And the small church was packed, but with a larger-than-usual number of the usual Sunday faithful, four-fifths of them women, neither the richest nor the poorest, with the middle-aged and elderly far outnumbering adolescents and younger adults. More men and boys came along this Sunday, but most remained outside. The nun who worked with the fisher-women knew that some of the poorest stayed away because they were ashamed to be seen in church in their rags and worn sandals. The small church was packed, with nearly two hundred people, but that was about the number that turned up at the Assembly of God *templo*, and they managed to draw in a much better cross section of the town's twelve thousand inhabitants.

Nevertheless, the priest could have his say. In the sermon he told the congregation that the fiesta was, among other things, a time for achieving unity in the struggle for social justice and a time for discovering one's brothers and sisters. After mass, dressed casually in open-necked shirt and slacks, he hovered around adding his word in last-minute planning for the motorcade. Almost two hundred and fifty people, in overloaded trucks, cars, and the bus, processed with the saint. Pe. Eduardo took visitors in his car, but most of the processants were townspeople who liked a festive outing. Passing through the municipal seat, some of the better-known beauties of Campo Alegre on the trucks drew enthusiastic catcalls from men in the small crowds that had assembled to cheer the saint on his way. There was more cheering in the third largest town on the main highway. Then the parade turned back toward the coast, passing estates that still bore the names of *engenhos* (mills) that had once produced sugar for the first executives of the brotherhood of the saint.

Eventually the saint arrived in the fishing village and was unloaded from the truck near the first tiny houses on the main street. Pe. Eduardo joined the procession to the village chapel as a member of the crowd. He stayed close to the saint but had nothing in particular to do — not even when the saint was taken into the chapel to loud applause and installed in the sanctuary. There the saint was to stay for a week, amid memorial plaques for members of one of the great landowning families that had dominated the brotherhood from the 1870s into the early twentieth century. Fishermen and retired crew of the coastal trading vessels had their stories about why it was appropriate for the saint to stay in the village, but perhaps only the saint could remember why the chapel should seem a home away from home.

It was the next week, during the *buscada* (bringing the saint back to Campo Alegre), that Pe. Eduardo almost missed the boat. Campo Alegre priests had never had anything to do with the proceedings in the fishing village that led up to the saint's departure by boat to Campo Alegre. The priest's job had always been as part of the reception committee in Campo Alegre: he would wait on the quay there and then accompany the saint on the procession back to the church, the chapel of the brotherhood. But this priest was no longer an employee of the brotherhood, and he had his own car to take him to the fishing village; and if the fiesta could be shaped for commerce, or for politics, then it could also be shaped for religious vision. So, Pe. Eduardo decided to go to the village, lead the procession there, and then embark with the saint on the launch for Campo Alegre. He would then be seen as bringing the saint back to the town.

2. The saint arrives back in Campo Alegre.

This bid to achieve a more central role in the rituals of the fiesta almost foundered. The first problem was with the good ladies of the fishing village, who were looking after the saint and decorating not only his palanquin but another, on which Maria das Dores (Our Lady of Sorrows), their saint, was to be borne in procession as patroness of Campo Alegre's patron. The good ladies were going to determine when the procession should begin, when they had finished their decorating. Neither owners of launches nor a rather tentative priest dressed in a sports shirt would hurry them in the name of crowds awaiting the saint in Campo Alegre.[3]

They finally released the saint, the band tuned up, the chapel bell clanged, and a procession of about one hundred and fifty headed through the village to the boats. There, at the point of embarkation, Pe. Eduardo encountered his second problem. He was unable to negotiate his passage, with the owner of the launch that was to carry the saint, until almost the last minute—just ahead of many others on the quay struggling to put their case for a place on the accompanying boats. And in the midst of all the shouting and jostling, he had to find someone who could drive his car back to the town. And so it was that, in all the confusion, he almost missed the boat.

Then the priest was to encounter another problem on arrival at the quay in Campo Alegre, where the well-amplified commentator, hired by municipal authorities, had established himself as master of ceremonies. During the couple of hours it took the boats to make their way up the coast, booming loudspeakers enabled the commentator to turn a motley crowd on the quay into a responsive audience. At increasingly frequent

3. The brothers accompany their saint back to what was once the chapel of the brotherhood and is now considered to be the priest's church.

intervals, he interrupted assertive national pop music to tell the crowd who they were waiting for—the miracle-working saint. He welcomed the tourists, especially those from their beach houses on the island opposite the town; and the welcomes were so frequent and profuse that even townspeople were drawn in as tourists, waiting to have their fiesta described. Eventually some motor launches, then the sails of *jangadas* (fishing rafts), and finally the launch bearing the saint appeared. The commentator boomed excitement, artfully laced with production credits. The names of the owners of the finer launches, the shops that had sponsored aspects of the program of the day, the mayor, and other donors of prizes for the boat race on the following weekend, all became patrons of the saint.

Pe. Eduardo had no microphone, and his contribution to the practicalities of unloading the saint on the quay and handing him over to the robed members of the brotherhood for the procession to the church went unannounced. The commentator called *Vivas* for the saint and led the crowd in singing a hymn he presumed everyone would know, the nineteenth-century devotional "Ave Ave Ave Maria." As the procession moved toward the market square, then back to the church square, a competition developed between the discordant brass band, which the brotherhood had established fifty years ago, and the folk band the priest had brought in. Whenever Pe. Eduardo could manage it, the brass band would march in disconsolate silence, and his pipe-and-drum band would take over. When he accompanied the statue into the church, however, the brass band struck up again, victoriously loud. Even in the church, the commentator had the microphone at first and called *Vivas* for the saint and Our Lady. Pe. Eduardo eventually took the microphone and led the singing of a special new hymn to the patron saint; but he was only rather weakly followed. After he announced his program for the fiesta that evening and next weekend, the commentator regained the microphone and enlivened the packed church again with *Vivas* and *Aves*.

Then the fiesta took off. For those with spare cash, there were all sorts of things to buy—rides on the Ferris wheel, pictures of the saint or of other great patron saints, popcorn from the fatman's handcart, meat on a skewer, drink from one of the *vendas*. The proprietors of the *vendas* complained, once the tourists had gone home, that there was less money around this year than last year—the local factories had not advanced payday, so workers from the town did not have money to spend. The fiesta in the municipal seat was the one the factory managers really set their minds to, it was said. The fishing folk were not spending either. The older fishermen and their women would say that things were better in the town now because there was more money around, less survival through barter. But the fishing was bad at the moment (some said it was because there were no fish, others blamed the boat and net owners and the market intermediaries). In any case neither factory workers nor fishermen had much to spare.

There was a street theater though (a *bumba meu boi* performance). The performers seemed to know whom to hand the hat to, so the out-of-pocket could watch for nothing. Then, whenever Pe. Eduardo managed to prize the musicians away from the bar, there was free music and dancing around the pipe-and-drum band. There was an air of festivity to be enjoyed, the night was *movimentada* (lively), worth dressing up for, even if one could only get to the edges of the fun. In a number of the more affluent houses, including the priest's, there were private parties; but they were for well-heeled guests, often family from out of town, invited for the fiesta.

Even this phase of the fiesta was a cluster of different fiestas—of family parties in private houses, of buyers and sellers of fiesta commodities, of those out to take the festive air. These elements of the fiesta constituted a single category of *festejantes* (festival-goers) mainly in the minds of those who stayed away. And not even the absent were of a group.

The Protestants of the Assembly of God and the Baptist church stayed away because this was an occasion of Catholic idolatry ("God only is God; a true Christian has nothing to do with images") and an occasion of the great sins that proceeded from drinking and dancing. Others, who would say that their "law" was Catholic, stayed away out of disappointment of one kind or another. Some were disappointed that the fiesta was not what it used to be. Now the saint was accompanied by launches owned by out-siders—up to twenty years ago, the *buscada* had been beautiful to see, as the saint had been brought back by the *barcaças*, the coastal trading boats that had made Campo Alegre a commercial center in the old days. The fiesta was neither beautiful nor Campo Alegre's as it had been; so it was best ignored. Those who felt the saint somehow diminished, or who blamed the priest for dishonoring him and the other saints, also stayed away. Others, who remembered how fiesta street patrons had provided barrels of wine in the old days, could see nothing worthwhile in going down to the church square.

So the third phase of the fiesta, the *encerramento* or laying to rest, was itself disappointing—at least to the priest when he reflected on the small numbers present at the more religious activities and a certain lack of enthusiasm. The Saturday afternoon boat race drew good numbers, including a reduced number of tourists. Electrical goods (donated by ad-vertised businesses) were presented to the winners, some of whom had no electricity supply. The entertainments of the evening drew more towns-folk than the previous weeks. And the final procession of the saint, from the church and across the streets that not long since had marked the pe-rimeter of the town, was suitably noisy and thronged.

But only a few heard the visiting colleague deliver Pe. Eduardo's mes-sage, after the saint arrived back in church. Religion was not just the fi-estas, he declared in high hortative style, but giving to those who had less than ourselves. The fiesta, with everyone cooperating and enjoying themselves together, should continue—everyone attempting to live united, sharing, perceiving, and attending to the needs of others whose need is greater. . . . But, in terms of the numbers who heard and their immediate response, the priest's message about the fiesta did not take. And the pre-sentation of the saint's flag did not carry the message far enough, either.

Until a few years ago, the flag had been taken in procession to the house of the man who would be the patron of the next fiesta. Pe. Eduardo had thought of two ways to modify that tradition. One was to select by lot from among those who were interested in the honor, no matter how poor. That was difficult for the priest to arrange—he found he was not in good enough contact with the men among whom he wanted to adver-tise the honor. So he adopted an easier ploy, which was to present the flag, once again, to the son of the recently deceased patron (who had received it for some years before the priest arrived in town and who had been one of those members of the brotherhood against the corruption of the Amorim family network).

This year there was an added point to the strategy of change through continuity. The son, Pedro Faró, was owner of the manioc processing house and tenant of one of the larger plots of land about to be enclosed by the new landowner. He was shaping up as something of a leader among the other threatened tenant farmers. His manioc house had become a meeting place for what the priest hoped would become a united community of farmers, and he had led the group to ask the priest for aid when the quit notices had arrived. Presenting him with the flag would surely extend the message of the meaning of the fiesta beyond the church.

To a few it might well have done. But the town did not gather for the presentation. Fishermen and those who lived at the other end of town, the church and market end, did not come along. And even in the neighborhood there were many who had to go to bed long before the midnight presentation if they were to be up for out-of-town work on Monday morning. The young patron's Protestant friends and neighbors would have nothing to do with even that part of the fiesta, sober as it might have been.

With a priest without a script, a saint without a story, ghosts from an imaginary golden age of the brotherhood bearing scripts, politicians bearing gifts, a department of tourism advertising an event with commentator but no director, the fiesta was bound to disappoint all but those who wanted fun and spectacle. It was bound to disappoint anyone who wanted it to help fashion a better Campo Alegre — a town for a Brazil dreamed by modernizing technocrats; a town of memory reconstituted; a solid political base rather than a town of feckless shifting voters; a town of vibrant communities; a building block for a new Brazil.

THE TOWN AS MÉLANGE

If would-be scriptwriters and directors of the fiesta were disappointed, none could be to blame. Each had only a constituency-in-the-making to mobilize for the making of his fiesta; and constituents, gathered as audience, processants, anticipating crowd, were fickle. Then, increasing the difficulties of priest, politicians, and businessmen, the various potential constituencies assembled constituted a mishmash, a mere gathering; not a *community* in any sense of that overloaded word. Neither priest nor his rivals had a town-as-community to work with. The disappointment engendered by the fiesta showed a town that had become little

4. Saint Severino is powerful even in politics. Among the grateful commemorations of successful *promessas,* two ARENA party candidates in municipal elections (HE and SHE) have left a framed copy of their campaign literature. They promise industrialization.

more than a space demarcated by high residential concentration, its inhabitants having no focal point of association. The jostling of factions to shape the fiesta enacted the town's incoherence, its polymorphous culture, and its segmented social structure.

Perhaps the saint himself could take some blame for the fragmentation of fiesta and town. Though the commentator called him a *santo milagroso* (a miraculous saint), and some locals made *promessas* (promises in return for favors) to him, he does not have sufficient reputation to rally his people. The town has ceased to be the center of anything, becoming a mere outer suburb full of refugees from somewhere else; even the produce for the Sunday market being brought in on trucks from the central city wholesale market. So also the saint has failed to hold his own as other saints of higher reputation and new accessibility appeal more to those who still believe in making *promessas.* He might help draw crowds on the days of his feast, but unlike Saint Severino he cannot draw busloads of pilgrims from all over the state and beyond, week after week. Unlike uncanonized Padre Cícero, the saint lacks the power to remake a dismantled town.

Nevertheless, many of the older brotherhood critics of the fiesta excuse the saint and blame priest and politicians for advancing the disintegration of their town. The town's better past is recalled with memories of better fiestas, when the fiesta belonged to the town and was not a spectacle for tourists or a vehicle for the priest's fancies. Old-timers remember different pasts and sometimes conflate them. But the better town of the past was always a viable center — a center for coastal trade, a commercial center supplying locally owned sugar plantations, a market town where local fishermen and sharecroppers could sell and exchange their produce — not least, a center for trade in patronage, focused on the dealings of the brotherhood.

Most old-timers are discriminating in their praise of the past. In the old days there was not enough money around, travel out of town was difficult, some patrons could not be relied upon, conflict between residents was often bitter and bloody, old age for the poor often meant beggary, too many children died and adults, too, when the smallpox swept through. But there was more cooperation, more loyalty, more friendship, more contact with the powerful, more knowledge of the exact status of anyone you might meet. The fiestas of the past — not only the fiesta of the patron saint but the fiesta of Saint John and the other June saints — were better then because these virtues were evident.

The history of the town vindicates these memories.[4] If there is any delusion, it is that Campo Alegre has ever been other than a dependent appendage to regional and even international political economies. But the forces that produced its dependence allowed (we might even say required) that Campo Alegre have boundaries and that its inhabitants have a certain homogeneity of purpose and identity, up to a time within living memory.

From the nineteenth through to the mid-twentieth century, Campo Alegre's fortunes waxed and waned with developments in the sugar-plantation political economy and the burgeoning of the Brazilian state. By the 1890s Campo Alegre had emerged as an entrepôt for one of the weaker clusters of plantations in the state of Pernambuco. Roads and railways developed by the state government passed this cluster by, though it was only twenty-five kilometers up the coast from the state capital, Recife. So Campo Alegre, with its quay on the channel separating it from an island with no well-protected harbor of its own, became the port for a peak number of ten sugar mills on the island. It was also the trading center for up to five mills and their surrounding lands that were close to the sea but without easy access to the state capital by road or rail.

The bustle of the port and the substantial size of the major warehouses and commercial establishments around the town square and in front of the quay suggested prosperity. There was indeed a prosperous elite — not only the mill owners or the better-off estate managers, who came into town to attend to their business or the business of the brotherhood, but also, by 1890, resident businessmen owning bakeries, warehouses, the drapery, and general stores.[5] It was this elite of businessmen that supplied most of the members of the board of the brotherhood, as they began to out-number the mill owners who had dominated the first board commissioned by the Archbishop of Recife-Olinda in 1870.

The minutes of the brotherhood suggest that prosperity did not ex-tend far beyond the town square and the small elite.[6] Though top posi-tions on the board were fought over, some positions were hard to fill — especially those to do with the treasury. The collection of rents and other monies was a thankless task. The whole town was built on the brother-hood's patrimonial land, and there was land left over for renting to farm-ers. But most residents were so poor (many almost completely outside the money economy) that it was difficult to get land rents from them. And though most members of the town wanted to retain membership of the brotherhood, payment of small dues was difficult. The demands on the brotherhood for charity and patronage always outstripped its regular in-come. At times members of the board clearly wondered whether it was worth supplementing funds with special donations, squeezing rent pay-ers, and keeping books that would pass inspection by the Curia of the Archdiocese.[7]

But despite financial troubles, despite the disparity between the re-sources of the board and those of ordinary members, the brotherhood seems to have provided a sort of institutional focus for town life — a focus that is still remembered by longtime residents in the rituals of fiestas, funerals, and the excitements of electoral intrigue. The board of the brotherhood was the visible, recognizable elite, controlling and maintain-ing what were regarded as the amenities of civilization. Above all, a de-cent Christian burial attended by the berobed brothers was guaranteed and, in case of indigence, paid for by the brotherhood. The benefits of the one true religion were received in the brotherhood chapel and financed by it. The brotherhood provided charity to the indigent, and its board controlled access to an increasingly scarce resource that might allow the recipient to rise above indigence: patrimonial land.

Well into the twentieth century, the wider world of sugar allowed the maintenance of that urban coherence. Even as momentous change took place in the sugar industry elsewhere in the state, the small world around Campo Alegre remained relatively undisturbed.[8] For a variety of reasons (including ecological and land-tenure factors), most of the sugar mills of the area were not worth taking over by the large firms that were consolidating mills and setting up modern central refineries able to produce white sugar and alcohol at lower costs. For the same reasons and for a time, the area was not worth incorporating into the growing network of land transportation. As long as the area was allowed to be a backwater, mill owners required Campo Alegre as an entrepôt. As long as mill owners required a port, its inhabitants, rich and poor, could still require that the mill owners help maintain it as a civilized town, without the aid of state and industry.

So the *barcaças* that brought the saint back to town continued to carry sugar out from the mills, even though that sugar received a progressively lower price than sugar from elsewhere because it was only crudely refined and suffered water spoilage. And if a certain autonomy is a benefit for being a backwater, vulnerability is the cost. By the mid-twentieth century, the sugar economy and incursions of state and federal government agencies had commenced the disintegration that old-timers recognized in their fiesta, a fiesta that was bigger and better than ever before but no longer belonging to the town.

By 1950, two great sugar refineries of the new type and the owners of the large textile factory in the next *município* (municipal town) had bought up a large proportion of the best land in the hinterland, and the rationalization of land use had a number of effects on Campo Alegre. Sugar production in the old mode became steadily less profitable, and some owners decided to sell out of sugar and take their money elsewhere. An early sale of this kind was to the state. In 1934 one of the old properties on the island became a prison farm. There was a steady exodus of the rural elite: a new elite of managers and administrators unbeholden to Campo Alegre took over. At the same time, the population of the town swelled: rationalization was translated into eviction, and expelled tenants took refuge in and around the town. Cheap or nominal rent for town land administered by the brotherhood meant that Campo Alegre was chosen by many refugees as a place of residence and as a base from which to seek fishing or laboring jobs. The new land investors were not interested in taking over the lands still available for farming that immediately surrounded the town, because of their sandy soil. So some refugees were able to negotiate sharecropping — rental and labor-exchange deals with smaller local landowners for tiny plots where they could grow manioc, corn, beans, and other vegetables for subsistence and sale in local markets.

By the fifties, not only had the elites become more diverse and less locked into Campo Alegre but the town's population was newer, and the range of relationships with the central institution of the town was much more varied than in previous decades. The inner coherence and the outward boundaries of the town were becoming less well defined, the degree of integration with the outside world much greater. These processes were enhanced when the bridge linking Campo Alegre to the island was built, with the subsequent, if slow, development of roads and bus service to Recife. The bridge was opened by the president of Brazil in 1940; and Campo Alegre could be bypassed as a trading port, if with some difficulty, after then.

By 1970 the bus trip to the capital took an hour, instead of the day it had taken in the fifties. So Campo Alegre could easily serve as a satellite town for people who wanted to commute to Recife on a daily basis and who wanted Campo Alegre only as a place of cheap residence. Recife, also bursting with refugees from rationalization in its rural hinterland, had grown out along the new roads toward Campo Alegre. Although still separated from the municipal seat and the main highway by a nine-kilometer band of open farm country (with the aluminum factory in splendid isolation), Campo Alegre was already, in the mid-seventies, on the outer limits of planners' maps for the development of a Greater Recife.

Not only planners plan to catch up with the times. Before planners had decided what was happening, astute members of the town's commercial elite read the signs and decided their future lay in incorporation into city-centered bureaucracies. They left poorer or older relations to contend with newcomers for control of a brotherhood that was no longer at the center of a world. But the town, adrift from its connections to a superseded sugar economy, abandoned by its commercial elite, continued to grow and grow — to about twelve thousand by the mid-seventies.[9]

Data from a small survey that Mary Aitken and I conducted in 1977 provide some indications of how variably the new population was related to the older Campo Alegre, where the brotherhood had been a central and focal institution. As Table 1 shows (all tables are in the Appendix), only a quarter of Campo Alegrenses sampled in the survey had always been resident. Another quarter had come from other urban areas, including the capital city. Almost one-half of the sample had come into Campo Alegre as refugees, from rural rationalization or as a consequence of the sale of properties on which they had plots.

Few of those who came to Campo Alegre chose it for the opportunities it offered, other than a place of residence. As Table 2 shows, a majority of economically active heads of households had to change their type of employment in the course of their work history. The changes reflect increasing urbanization (over one-third had moved from farming occupations to urban service occupations or industrial employment) and shrinking opportunities in the rural sector. Table 3 helps communicate a sense of the diversity of occupations among Campo Alegrenses. Over half of the working population reported in the sample is engaged in urban work;

5. Through the 1970s and the 1980s, Campo Alegre kept growing, houses sprouting along unmade streets like this.

and the greater number of jobs reported in these sectors involve work with individual employers, companies, or government agencies located outside Campo Alegre.

Clearly, by the seventies, there was no one institution, and certainly not the brotherhood of old, that could articulate or coordinate the urban diversity Campo Alegre had become. It is important to recall that, though slow, the processes contributing to this end point were not, and probably could not have been, controlled from within. No one person, institution, or local elite was able to select the changes Campo Alegre should absorb or dictate the meaning of what took place.

Social Mélange

The consequences of these changes were the dismantling of a previous coherence (not necessarily a harmony) and the production of a residential conglomerate that is probably best described as a social mélange. If change had been designed and managed from within (that is, by the citizens of Campo Alegre), the dismantling of past power structures would have been more complete and the shape of the new more coherent. The dismantling of Campo Alegre, because it was not contrived from within, did not involve the rapid obliteration of previous social arrangements but rather the destruction of institutional focus, so that a variety of social arrangements (a variety of modes of being Campo Alegrense and of being Brazilian in Campo Alegre) remained juxtaposed and in rather untidy interaction (disorder in the new not being implied any more than harmony in the old). Clifford Geertz has described the social structure of a somewhat comparable Indonesian town of the fifties as "a mélange of factions representing different modes of integrating past and present, the local and the cosmopolitan."[10]

In the case of Campo Alegre, the term *factions*, with the connotation of self-conscious identification with an interest or ideologically based group, would be misleading. But the term *mélange* will do nicely. What I am referring to is, in part, the co-existence of distinct, though not entirely exclusive, types of social-exchange networks. There is the type of network, with origins in the old world of sugar, that links patrons and clients in local patronage systems — the Amorim family is still a node in such a network, and some Campo Alegrenses spend considerable time and energy patching up or trying to build similar structures around owners of boats and nets, for example. Like these in local focus, but without the patronage, are the mutual aid or communitarian networks, of the kind the priest encourages among threatened farmers and fishermen. Other types of networks, made possible or necessary in a larger-scale diverse economy, draw Campo Alegrenses, economically and politically, out and away: to personal patrons who employ them for domestic service in the capital city; to municipal, state, and federal government agencies located out of town; to construction companies operating in the greater metropolitan area; to transnational industrial enterprises.

It is not difficult to put a name to the types of networks — what is more difficult is to specify how Campo Alegrenses actually figure in relation to these networks. For the moment (and in anticipation of the complications arising from consideration of individual cases), my brief outline of the incomplete urbanization of Campo Alegre makes it plausible to speak of Campo Alegrenses being engaged in four types of social-exchange network. (1) There are the traditional local patron-client networks involving some fishermen and a small number of farm workers on older properties. (2) There are municipal- and state-services networks with participants in jobs as diverse as prison warden and street cleaner. Campo Alegre's various categories of pensioners should be included here, since they, like government employees, depend for their livelihood on their ability to negotiate networks of bureaucratized patronage. (3) There are those whose diverse and shifting employment might attract the label lumpen proletariat. These are perhaps less plausibly consigned to a type of social-exchange network. But Campo Alegrenses who survive by hawking their

6. Mending nets. Fishing provides a meager living for many Campo Alegrenses.

unskilled labor in the city and countryside are certainly intent on building and maintaining networks of short-term wage-rewarded patron-client relationships throughout an extensive metropolitan area. (4) Some of these hawkers of labor, in more recent years, have succeeded in developing somewhat more stable employment in modern industrial enterprises. Related impersonally to a large private bureaucracy and receiving a set wage for unskilled labor, they have become participants in a kind of network — that modern urban industrial complex in which, at the highest levels, civilian technocrats, military brass, and company directors claim they are creating a Brazil-of-the-future that has already arrived.

At any given moment Campo Alegrenses may be frozen, as it were, in a photograph, and separated according to network type. But the movement provided by biographical detail calls for a more complex and dynamic picture of social structure. As a member of a household, and very occasionally of a functioning extended family, a fisherman linked to a local patron will also be linked to a transnational industrial enterprise: his calculations for survival and advancement will include vicarious knowledge of how the factory managers relate to their employees and estimates of the viability of the enterprise. Then, in the course of a working life, as Table 2 suggests, any one citizen might move from one type of network to another. The moving picture would also show that membership of religious groups and informal friendships will modify (or even, though very rarely, supplant) work-determined social-exchange networks. So the structural mélange of Campo Alegre comprises something more complex than mere juxtaposed layers reflecting stages in modern Brazilian political economic history as Campo Alegrenses have responded to it. Structural mélange includes indeterminacy of social-exchange networks, for individual Campo Alegrenses move between different types, not only over a lifetime but sometimes even within a single day.

Cultural Mélange

This complexity is compounded when we add, to a work-focused description of social structure, an account of cultural mélange. If the fiesta reveals and constitutes structural mélange, it also shows us Campo Alegrenses interpreting and negotiating that mélange with myths and metaphors related to, but in no simple way merely reflective of, their location in social-exchange networks. As we shall see later in some detail, members of the Assembly of God, who through involvement in patronage networks have every reason to derive benefit from participation in the fiesta, stay away not only out of narrow moral considerations but because almost all aspects of the fiesta symbolize contradiction and even subversion of the world they are trying to construct. Some farmers, whom

7. Bringing in the coconut harvest from the patrimony of the saint, now administered by the priest. The saint still provides an income for some.

the priest would have drawn into the fiesta-for-community-building, would have nothing to do with it, persuaded by the myths and symbols of the *regime militar* that a different Brazil-of-the-future was good and inevitable and best celebrated on other occasions.

These points of view of the fiesta, we shall see, are often parts of more or less coherent and more or less explicit worldviews that Campo Alegrenses enact not only in fiesta but in everyday life. The factors that created structural mélange in Campo Alegre allowed cultural mélange, that is, the profusion rather than the synthesis of sets of "symbols in terms of which men think about and attempt to regulate their collective behavior."[11]

What is referred to by such sets or cultural paradigms may be illustrated by a story: In 1946 one of Campo Alegre's cosmopolitans, a literate man (who : 1976 was serving as postmaster), became known as a communist. He attracted several other members of the brotherhood to his persuasion. Other members of the board and the parish priest in the municipal seat were disturbed by this development. The priest was especially appalled that anyone should imagine that the Catholic way of life and the communist way were compatible. At his insistence, an extraordinary meeting of the brotherhood was called. At this meeting, the judge of the brotherhood quickly called on the priest, and a lawyer whom the priest had invited along, to instruct the brothers on the evils of communism. In rather folksy and ungrammatical Portuguese, the secretary recorded his version of the priest's words: "Having been apprised that within this brotherhood there are some communists and communism cannot stand next to Catholicism and given that a brother in this brotherhood has fallen deeply into communism and that he is a member of the board . . . he cannot remain in that position."[12] With many repetitions, the point conveyed to the brothers was that communism was, like Catholicism, a set of beliefs and hopes that constituted a way of life, a *sociedade*, but that this way of life was totally incompatible with Catholicism and the way of life that the brotherhood successfully maintained in Campo Alegre. The brotherhood could not be faithful to its constitution and its own history if it allowed avowed communists to continue as brothers.

The priest and the lawyer won the day. The communist members were expelled. The priest, clearly enough, had seen in communism not just a political party opposed by his church but a cultural paradigm incompatible with the type of Catholicism that was symbolized in the brotherhood. So he exerted himself decisively to convince the apparently bemused brothers of the danger they were in.

Communism was never reassembled in Campo Alegre as anything like a working model for social life and individual career, but in succeeding years other paradigms were. Curiously, as the last mills closed down and the old *coronéis* died or sold out, *coronelismo* (the reassembled model of the old world) arrived in town.[13] Refugees came, with their stories of the good patrons they had worked for. Then, from the sixties onward, new messages from the church proposing a more just Brazil set up *coronelismo* as a way of life to which it was all too easy to regress. For many Campo Alegrenses of recent rural origin, the way of life *da rua* (of the city street) — its disorder, the lack of public respect of young for their elders, sexual immorality flaunted in dress and gesture — induced a redefinition and reaffirmation of the way of life of the *sítio* (farmer's plot), the old market town, and the good patrons who presided over both. Disappointments endemic in newer ways of life — unemployment, families without men, priests and politicians messing in fiestas — vindicated hope in a restoration of things remembered. Criticized, or nostalgically recalled in image and story, *coronelismo-paternalismo* (which not too long ago had been the only way of life) became yet another model of life, in contention with all the others, in the mélange that was now Campo Alegre. The priest found that he jeopardized the success of his own enterprises if he ignored the ability of this nostalgic ideology to move and motivate the people. Politicians had long since learned to accommodate to it.

Gonçalo

Gonçalo, an underemployed farm worker (fifty-five years old at the time of the interview), may help define the power of that paradigm. He also alerts us to a major theme of this study: the interweaving of religious elements and models of citizenry in the cultural paradigms found in Campo Alegre. I first met Gonçalo when I was conducting a random survey of households in the town. My question about religious affiliation triggered a long and bitter critique of the modern Catholic church, in particular, and of the modern world, in general. Gonçalo's critique was set against images and stories of his lost world of *coronéis* and populist politicians.

When I asked his religious affiliation, Gonçalo replied he was Catholic: "I remain *na lei* (in the law) in which my parents brought me up."[14] He never goes to mass or participates in any other religious activities. But that, he hastens to explain, is because the church in which his parents raised him has left him. That was the church that administered a law under which each man knew his rights and duties. In return for obedience, poor agricultural laborers like himself could turn to a priest for protection (he spoke of a particular German missionary, the parish priest in his hometown over thirty years ago). The priest even looked like a protector. His home was one of the public buildings in the town square — "just like a *quartel* (military barracks)." The priest moved easily as a protector among the powerful, so that he was able to "arrange" things for the poor who came to him.[15] The good priest also organized fiestas and conducted liturgies with pomp. "In those days religion was so fabulous. Today it's so simple." To Gonçalo, the new priests, less interested in ceremony and in taking their proper place in a social hierarchy, disqualify themselves as protector-patrons and as agents able to establish contact between the poor man and his miracle-working patron saint.

Gonçalo's religious stories are of two kinds. There are stories about priest heroes, some of whom, like Padre Cícero and his successor Frei Damião, are miracle-workers themselves. And there are stories about the miracles — stories of hope in which health or money or some other just reward is given to the poor man through miraculous interventions of power greater than the greatest earthly powers. The theme of these stories, emphasized by Gonçalo himself, is that in religion (as preached and celebrated by the good priest and embodied in him) the normal life of suffering for the poor might be quite regularly overturned. Good priests prepared the ground for miracles.

But the new priests do not teach about the saints and do not seem to believe in miracles. They call people together to discuss problems, says Gonçalo, but there is no point in that, "each man knows his own problems." As priests fail in their duties, he laments, miracles happen less now than when he was young. This is disastrous for the poor, for, as Gonçalo understands it, the world stays the same, and the poor may hope only in miracles and the protection of patrons. His critique of the new priests asserts the links that must not be broken between the obedience and loyalty of the poor man, the good priest, and the hierarchy of patrons — from those on earth to the saints in heaven. Once the links are broken, and especially by the priests who are pivotal in the whole system, then all the poor can do together is to talk about the wreckage.

Gonçalo had much more to say about the wreckage. But the lineaments of a mode of citizenship — and justification for referring to a cultural paradigm — are evident enough. Gonçalo's expression of the paradigm of *coronelismo* emphasizes religious elements, but his stories of religious heroes, his images of priest-centered community, and his myths of hope in patron saints contain a model of citizenship. He draws it out, especially in his critique of Campo Alegre. The good and sensible citizen accepts inequality and a lowly position in a social hierarchy; but, in return for respect and loyal service, he expects protection from the insecurities of poverty and inclusion in networks of personally distributed largesse. When the sources of largesse are remote, intermediaries (with whom personal exchanges are possible) will establish the links. The humblest citizen, as due reward for loyalty and astuteness, can expect inclusion in a visible, manipulable community through which material resources and the amenities of civilization flow.

Orientated by the ideals, images, and stories of *coronelismo*, Gonçalo is an anguished critic of Campo Alegre's new priest and of many neighbors. He is as astute as the anticommunist parish priest of thirty years ago in spotting and dismissing the paradigms that, he believes, prevent the realization of his own. He will have nothing to do with Pe. Eduardo's communities — not only because it seems absurd to think of communities of the poor adrift from patronage but also because the attempt to establish them was destructive toward the good order and correct behavior that remained. For Pe. Eduardo, Gonçalo reserved the bitter anger and contempt due to one subversive of all that was good and true. As I see it, he recognized in Pe. Eduardo the agent of a hostile paradigm (he gave this formation no name but he, and the priest, would understand my label), the grass-roots communitarian paradigm.

In his critique of his neighbors, who themselves had nothing to do with the priest, Gonçalo alerts us to a third paradigm. This one has several names in Campo Alegre, but I shall use the name most commonly understood in Brazil, *populismo*.[16] Like *coronelismo*, the word may designate a type of political economy, but it may also refer to a way of life, and to the myths and images that orient that way of life. When Gonçalo is contemptuous of neighbors who devote themselves to the pursuit of individual advantage, who enthuse over distant politicians, and who celebrate heroes of gamesmanship in their victories over life's problems, he is setting up *populismo* for dismissal.

Gonçalo is well aware that he might share some of the same heroes (Padre Cícero, for example) and some of the same assumptions about patronage with his errant neighbors. But there is difference enough for mutual critique between the paradigms of *coronelismo* and *populismo*. Where the *coronelismo* heroes are local landed chieftains, who showed what a good patron was, the *populismo* heroes include national figures, like Getúlio Vargas, and populist politicians of regional fame, like Paulo Guerra.[17] Where the *coronelismo* myths of hope might tell of a relationship with a good patron who provided more than any union, the *populismo* myths of hope tell of the lowly jobseeker landing a job or obtaining health care through an attentive politician or a benevolent institution with connections. *Populismo* stories draw out the virtues of competitive individualism in an essentially insecure world of wide scale, while *coronelismo* stories enjoin acceptance of one's place in a stable local hierarchy.

I cannot use Gonçalo for the brief introduction to a fourth cultural paradigm found in Campo Alegre, since he did not allude to it in my conversations with him. This is the paradigm of the *regime militar* or, in a phrase familiar to students of Latin American political economies, the paradigm of bureaucratic authoritarianism. (Individual variations on some of its main themes will emerge when we see the thought and biography of a Campo Alegrense called Severino, later.) In this paradigm, which was insistently nurtured in educational institutions, military parades, and radio broadcasts during the period of military rule, the heroes of *populismo* and *coronelismo* are scorned. The new heroes are more remote — generals and civilian experts in high office — but they get things done without the hoopla and corruption of democratic politics. In return for hard work and the acceptance of necessary disciplines, these men will make Brazil a better place for the poor. Hope resides in a strong authoritarian state, which can get things done (witness the new factories spreading out from the city) and protect the poor from the avarice, corruption, and backwardness of the local rich. Campo Alegrenses who carry, speak, and work on the paradigm of the *regime militar* contrast their everyday world with stories and images of a more ordered, more technologically sophisticated world.

The labels used here to describe the various paradigms constituting cultural mélange in Campo Alegre focus attention on the political strand in each paradigm. But (as Gonçalo suggests), in any Campo Alegrense cultural paradigm, there will be religious strands woven into the political. This weaving of the religious and the political produces very complex patterns indeed: real life challenges the academic's parsimonious construction of cultural paradigms. Nevertheless, we may start with some simplicities, proposed by Gonçalo and by the account of the fiesta: that a traditional form of Catholicism, under the sacred canopy of the world of sugar, is woven in with the myths and ideology of *coronelismo;* that *populismo* emerges as Campo Alegre gradually enters a society of larger socioeconomic scale and as the traditional Catholic religious monopoly crumbles and other religious options become available; that the paradigm of communalism emerges from Catholic critiques of bureaucratic authoritarianism and of the old and the new forms of patron-clientage. Clearly enough, constructing the cultural paradigms of Campo Alegre involves review of its religious mélange.

Religious Mélange

The contemporary diversity in religious affiliation is reported in Table 4. There has been great change since 1940. National census figures for the municipality in 1940 report a nominally Catholic world. Of 26,278 inhabitants, 25,558 were listed as Catholic, only 672 as "others."[18] These statistics obscure many things, including the variety of modes of being a Catholic and the extent of participation in Afro-

Brazilian spiritist cults by those who considered or advertised themselves as Catholic. Despite this (and despite the fact that we cannot make a direct comparison between census figures for the municipality and survey data from Campo Alegre), the contrast with the religious profile reported in Table 4 is dramatic. Families identified as Catholic are down to 60 percent, compared to above 90 percent in 1940. By 1976, families linked to the Catholic church by at least moderate attendance at mass by one or more members are outnumbered by families similarly linked to the Assembly of God or to one or more of the fourteen Afro-Brazilian cult groups in Campo Alegre. Though most members of Afro-Brazilian cults would continue to report themselves Catholic in the national census, a noticeable 19 percent of my survey interviewees classified their families as attached to the Afro-Brazilian traditions even though some members might attend rituals infrequently.

Mélange in religion has become patent in several ways. From the forties through the fifties, the small group of the Assembly of God could easily gather in the tiny living room of a private house on the main street. By 1977, the Assembly *templo* was the largest hall in town, but it was unable to contain all the three hundred people who would turn up for the open-door service, the *culto,* on Sunday evenings. During May, the month of Our Lady, and at fiesta time the Catholic church might attract as many to mass; but on a weekly basis, the Assembly of God was plainly the largest organized religious group in town. Catholicism had not been replaced in any simple sense. Its liturgical calendar still marked out the year for many Campo Alegrenses — July might be referred to as "Sant'Ana," June as "São João." Its priest was still the religious leader best known by name in town. But the square outside the Catholic church could no longer be referred to as *the* Church Square, because the square in front of the *templo* up the street was the busier square. The noise of solemn assembly came louder and more frequently from the highly amplified services in the *templo* than from masses in the church.

Perhaps not quite so patent to a casual visitor to the town, but still insistent to residents, is the presence of the Afro-Brazilian spiritist cults. Lauro, born locally of extremely poor parents, has his *centro* in his own house, the finest house in town. Day after day clients stream through his door and throng his ample waiting rooms, hoping that the renowned medium will draw a remedy for life's sicknesses and troubles from the spirits. Dona Paula, in her large *salão* (salon) at the back of her comfortable house on the main street, attends to her scores of clients, and on the nights of her special *toques* (ceremonies with chants and dance to the sound of drums) in which African Indian and street spirits descend, the drums can be heard all over town. Out near the edges of town, Pai Fuló, the old leader of the Xangô cult, draws his clients, trains his "sons and daughters in the saint," and presides over *toques* for the African spirits where the drums are loudest of all.

The cults, with leaders often competing for clients, challenge the Catholic church and the Assembly of God for dominance in the town's religious life. Their claim would be that in any week they draw the largest number of Campo Alegrenses (and outside visitors) to participate in some sort of religious activity (albeit, most usually, a consultation about an errant husband or an ailing liver). If the cults do not regularly compete with *templo* and church in sounds of assembly, the presence of their spirits is broadcast ubiquitously, if more softly. They are heard in the susurrations of stories told to children about the *caboclo* (Indian) spirits of the forest that might draw them away from home, and in stories told among adults of powerful African spirits, causing harm to those who fail to pay them homage and helping those who learn what they might teach.

Therein lies a point of method: the religious element in cultural mélange is apparent not only in census statistics and survey results and town squares. It is there to be heard — in bars and on doorsteps, in the early morning when transistors are turned high for the hour of the Assembly of God, late at night when the drums of a *toque* might keep angry Protestants awake. It is comically insistent when trumpets and drums for dances celebrating the feast of Saint John compete with blaring messages from the loudspeaker of a visiting evangelist's truck. Cultural mélange is in the air, to be heard, as well as in assembly, to be seen and quantified.

THE POLITICS OF MÉLANGE

A large part of this book will be devoted to the description and the elaboration of cultural and structural mélange in Campo Alegre. Motivating this investigation of local and individual cases is my concern to understand aspects of Brazilian national politics, as it emerges from religious life at the grass roots. So, for example, the investigation of links between political and religious strands in Campo Alegre's cultural mélange leads on to consideration of Pentecostalism and Afro-Brazilian spiritism, as they affect the chances of a military national security ideology taking hold at the Brazilian grass roots. Or, in the same mode, the examination of forms of collective life — the structural mélange of Campo Alegre — will generate questions, and some conclusions, about the Catholic communities and other social structures at the grass roots, as they affect the fortunes of participatory democracy in Brazil.

In this shuttling between the local and the national, my primary focus is on the relationships between political and religious strands in cultural paradigms at the grass roots. Within each of the religious traditions, we may formally distinguish the several elements of political culture. First, there are beliefs, images, and stories that define the boundary between private concerns and those public matters that must be addressed politically. Second, there are beliefs, images, and stories that define rights and responsibilities with regard to public issues — the role of the citizen, for example, or expectations concerning leaders. Third, there are assumptions, embedded in myths and symbols, about what constitutes legitimate authority in dealing with public issues. Fourth, there are ideas and myths that map where it is possible and desirable to go on public issues — these include ideas about material progress, both individual and social, and assumptions about the efficacy of human action.

The separation of political elements from the religious arises from an outsider's analytical concerns and is not a normal process in the way Campo Alegrenses understand themselves. Gonçalo's ideas about the legitimate authority of the good patron are bound up with his more general religious myths of cosmic order and salvation history reconstituted in the ritual that was "so fabulous." To appreciate the depth of his political definitions and convictions is to draw out the dialectic between religious and political elements in his cultural paradigm.

In my chapters on the Pentecostals, the Afro-Brazilian spiritists, and the Catholics, I will investigate this dialectic. I will ask a number of questions of each of the religious traditions as it is lived in Campo Alegre. (1) To what extent and in what manner does that religion enter into the defining of problems experienced in everyday life and the location of these problems as private troubles rather than public issues?[19] (2) How do different religions predispose believers toward accepting or rejecting hegemonic ideas (for example, ideals promoted by ruling groups with the intention of inducing compliance to a regime)? (3) How do different religions shape responses to claims of legitimacy and to different types of leadership? (4) How do the different religions affect the sort of political alliances that will be congenial to adherents?

In putting and receiving answers to these questions, I have found that attention must be given to a wide range of factors. Relationships between the remembered political-economic experiences of individuals and their changing religious commitments require examination. The forms of religious ritual and images of political processes demand attention. Experience of religious organization must be seen in relation to expectations of political participation. In the following chapters, the focus and emphasis is always on culture, however — on the dialectic of religious and political elements within cultural paradigms. Only in the last chapter of this study, after we have seen this dialectic in each of the religious traditions, will the group life that those elements generate be compared. Throughout this study, I hope, the dialectics of social structure and culture — of individual and group dynamics — are respected and allowed to emerge without any reductionism.

The dialectics are further explored as we move from a schematic reading of Campo Alegre's history to one based on biographies of some of its citizens. A schematic reading would rest happy with the simple patterns and relationships suggested so far. It would note cause-and-effect relationships between Campo Alegre as a backwater in a small-mill sugar economy, the locally centered patron-client networks, the cultural paradigm of *coronelismo,* and an intact Catholic world integrated around the brotherhood of the saint. In the contemporary period, this schematic reading would prompt us to conclude that there are direct causal relations between a comparatively dismantled Campo Alegre, in a political economy of ever-widening scale, and its variety of multicentered patron-client networks; between the competing cultural paradigms of *populismo,* national security authoritarianism, and communalism, on the one hand, and the emergence of a sort of religious marketplace in which Catholicism, Protestant Pentecostalism, and Afro-Brazilian religions compete for hearts and minds, on the other. Diachronically, the schematic approach would focus on explaining how each of the religious options related to each of the cultural paradigms and how these arose out of the processes of political economic change.

The risk involved in staying with schematic simplicities is that of confining forever a more complex reality to the terms that arise in the first attempt to understand it. There is a further danger: that in resting with the real affinities between economic bases, relational networks, cultural paradigms, and religious options, we should obscure the creativity of Campo Alegrenses as they construct their own lives and social relations. To avoid the risk of reducing religion and politics in Campo Alegre to schematized relationships, I propose to focus on citizens like Gonçalo, who will show us how they weave a social world out of visions of the past and of the future and out of their experience of the social, economic, and political systems that constrain them.

I hope also that Campo Alegre will not be reduced to a representative case as I move from the local to the national scene, any more than any of my individual cases should be reduced to representative examples of religious traditions or political stance in Campo Alegre. Campo Alegre is not representative of towns (or as it is now, peripheral suburbs) of Brazil or even of Brazil's northeastern states. It is no more representative in any statistical sense than its elaborate three-stage fiesta is typical. But just as the fiesta (and the priest's problems concerning it) may be read met-onymically, as revelation of the town's social and cultural heterogeneity, so Campo Alegre as mélange provides images that may help us under-stand the current social and cultural history of Brazil.

It is not for their representativeness but for their representations of linkages between the local and the national that I advance case studies of Campo Alegre and its citizens. Through them we may assess or reassess the plausibility of a number of hypotheses about religion and politics, in general, and about specific religions and Brazilian politics, in particular. Hypotheses have been developed in abundance and will be reviewed in some detail throughout the book, but some examples bear listing here. (1) Popular religions, it is said, are religions of alienation. (2) Folk Ca-tholicism contributes to the politics of despair. (3) The Afro-Brazilian reli-gions restore broken patron-client systems in urban areas. (4) Alternatively they are said to be replacing Catholicism as a prime means for establish-ing the hegemony of ruling classes. (5) All grass-roots sects and cults tend toward "the seduction of the innocent."[20] (6) Pentecostalism restores broken patronage systems in urban areas, or (7) it predisposes its devotees to ac-cept authoritarian military rule. These are just some of the hypotheses about the conservative possibilities of grass-roots religions. There are hypotheses that consider popular religions in general as a religious de-fense of class interests and of lower-class ways of life against invading manipulative modern Brazil.[21] But the list of hypotheses claiming religious input to creative and radical political transformations at the grass roots is much shorter than the list of those proposing a reactive and conserva-tive role for the popular religions.

Campo Alegrenses have taught me that most of the simpler hypothe-ses just will not do; that few neat conclusions can be drawn even about particular religions and particular political paradigms. They have also taught me that their religions, their experiences of power and economic forces in the struggle for survival, and their political constructions inter-act in a constant and fascinating dialectic. The attempt to understand that dialectic is, I believe, of intrinsic worth. By the end of the book, I hope to have established that such understanding is also necessary for any se-rious student of the jostling political economies of Brazil in continuing transition.

In this chapter we heard Catholic voices in the dialectic. Pe. Eduardo attempts to shape the feast of Campo Alegre's patron saint so that it will be something of a sacrament, symbolizing and achieving his religious vi-sion of justice and peace in a communitarian Brazil. Part of his struggle is with Catholics like Gonçalo, who would restore in the fiesta that other Catholic patronage world of saints, *coronéis*, and priests mediating between heaven and earth. We will go deeper into this conflict between Catholics later; and as we go deeper we shall also go wider, beyond Campo Alegre, to examine the claim that the contestations described are local manifestations of national jostling.

But the full values of the stakes in a continuing national transition cannot be understood by paying attention exclusively to the dialectics of religious vision, political-economic experiences, and construction of the political among Catholics. First I will explore that dialectic in the individual and collective life of Protestant Pentecostals, at first in Campo Alegre, and then, through discussion of other studies, in Brazil at large. After that I shall pursue the same sort of investigation with the Afro-Brazilian spiritists.

CHAPTER THREE

The Crentes

SEVERINO

THROUGHOUT BRAZIL members of the Assembly of God, together with Baptists and other Protestants, are called, and call themselves, *crentes* (believers). In Campo Alegre, by far the largest group of *crentes* constitute the Pentecostal Assembly of God. In my description of the fiesta, the *crentes* were passed over as a mere absence from an important happening in the life of the town. But, as the story of their increase and the signs of their presence suggest, they cannot be dismissed as a mere absence from a Catholic world. Dispersed across the several segments of Campo Alegre's social-exchange networks, they constitute a powerful presence in the cultural mélange. Although there is no one clear *crente* political voice in that mélange, there are distinctive *crente* accents in the dialectic of political-economic experience, religion, and political culture.

I did not choose Severino in my attempt to gain access to that dialectic because he is the typical *crente* but rather because he is unusually articulate as a religious and political man. With little formal education, but with verve, insight, and fluency, he presses toward coherence in his beliefs in a way that would make him exceptional in many a group of university-trained members of the intelligentsia. Precisely through his exceptional abilities and proclivities, he presents the variations that help me begin a definition of some *crente* themes. In his subtle internal dialogue, he lays out and populates the domain of a distinctly *crente* dialectic of religious meaning, experience, and politics. His resolution of that dialectic is not typical, but his presentation of its terms and possibilities are exemplary.

Right from the start of our relationship, Severino challenged my understanding and my initial stereotypes of *crentes.* I first met him when we

8. Severino (third male from left) with wife, brother, a *crente* neighbor and several of Severino's children.

were both trying to help a mutual neighbor, a municipal laborer like Severino, who was crippled and dying of neglected kidney disease. I offered transport to the hospital in the state capital; Severino explained rights and procedures within the rules and regulations of Brazil's social security program. Five minutes into our first conversation, Severino established his intriguing complexity as religious and political man. He was a *crente*, a convert to the Assembly of God, but not a churchgoer. He was a stern, self-centered, Puritan moralist, but his God required him to help others and build community. Democratic politics was the Satan's playground, in his opinion, but military governments, like all governments, served basically to defend the interests of the rich and greedy.

Even on first acquaintance, the man himself, as much as his views, challenged my understanding. Highly intelligent, articulate, energetic, clearly skilled in negotiating Brazilian bureaucracies—he had all the qualities of a successful businessman, one would say. But Severino was (and was still, in 1989) a municipal street cleaner—his job, by 1989, for twenty years. He has found it difficult to feed his family, and the health of his wife and two of his five children has been permanently affected because Severino has never been able to afford a house with a sealed roof and dry floor in the rainy season. Extracts from subsequent taped conversations elaborate the problem presented to understanding, even as they begin to resolve it.[1]

In my initial encounters with *crentes* in Campo Alegre, I often tried to move too quickly: from drawing out detail of religious belief and practice to eliciting political ideals and beliefs. I was anxious to try out models of the *crente* as political economic man. Perhaps *crentes* were latter-day Puritans of the type described by Max Weber: driven by anxieties arising from their faith, they strove to achieve upward mobility and to opt for economic and political individualism in pursuit of salvation-assuring success. If that were so, then we might expect an elective affinity between *crente* religion and the cultural paradigm of bureaucratic authoritarianism (*regime militar*). On the other hand, the *crente* religion might be more of the Holiness type, providing psychic compensation for intolerable political and economic repression — compensation through immediate gratification of the feeling of being assured salvation and investiture in the powers of Jesus and the Holy Spirit. If that were so, then we might expect *crentes* to have given up on any action for political-economic change, and to conform, reactively, to the political economy of the day.

Severino — in long, usually taped conversations in 1977, 1982, and much more briefly in January 1989 — demonstrated the limitations of my initial models and challenged too easy a move from the religious to the political. He liked question and challenge in his long monologues. He would set a time for me to meet him at his house (on one occasion having arranged with his foreman to finish work early so he could be interviewed by the Australian professor). With a Bible close at hand he would sit us down at the one table of his house, his family bidden not to interrupt. A few pleasantries might be permitted: my hair was greyer since our last meeting, he noted in 1982, while his, though receding, was still black; that was because my white blood was weaker than his African blood. That sort of introduction over, Severino would hunch his stocky shoulders and lean across the table in eager anticipation of the first serious question. Putting me right might take us hours, well beyond lamp-lighting time.

One of the first things to get right was the primacy of religious knowledge and doctrine:

> Doctrine is like school. At first you go to school without understanding. But the way you learn opens little by little and the pupil begins to understand. If he doesn't understand he asks questions and the teacher sets him right, the answer enters into the mind. And so he is able to improve his position — improving, improving, and after all that confusion he ends up as you've ended up, a teacher or even something else higher. So with religion here. If we go to the pews — there we have to go in with Bible in hand — there they explain completely. And that explanation becomes part of our living. Because if our

tendency is to live in error, then, once we take on religion, we have in some manner to raise ourselves up and away from that side and follow a correct and sure path. That is to say, our own religion is a part of our lives because if we were to live without religion, without doctrines, we'd lead a dissolute life — a life that is *ignorada* [base]. A man without principles is a man without upbringing.

Like Weber's Puritan, and contraposed to Weber's and his own similar image of the Catholic, Severino believes that doctrine, entering into life, requires asceticism:

> In this life, there's the part of the flesh and the part of the spirit. Many times, when it comes to a conflict, for the spiritual part to be satisfied, the flesh must be denied. You know that the *crente* leads a *vida privada* [a life of self-denial]. He has to deny himself everything. At every moment of temptation he has to *dar a chave* [turn the key on himself] so as to contain his desire.

But Severino is also something of the Holiness enthusiast. He describes vividly and defends with warmth Baptism in the Spirit and subsequent possession by the Spirit. He values the immediacy and the transcending emotion of possession:

> It's not something that you can pick up; that seeing, you might imitate. Nobody can imitate it, nobody can stop it happening. There you are in a meeting in the church and the Holy Spirit comes and makes you move in such a manner that you appear drunk, that you have a demon, that you're mad. But it's none of those things. It's because when the Spirit of God enters into a man that man is so deeply moved and so stirred that he becomes like a child and loses comprehension. And though people doubt that a man who eats meat and manioc flour can receive the Spirit of God, through Him we are all shown that we can. God was a man, Christ was a man on Earth and God made that promise to man: that an animal may not receive the Spirit of God but a man may.

Together with Holiness enthusiasm there is the trustful spontaneity of Holiness religion. This theme, on first hearing, seemed to me to be in tension with the planned asceticism in Severino's more Puritan statements and, indeed, in his biography.

> And if we pray to God in the spirit of truth, God is completely with man and will help him conquer in every struggle of day-to-day life, of life itself. And so it often ends up like this, the time of fiesta comes around. One hasn't bought sandals for the children. No one has any clothes. There's nothing. I'm not going to lament the fact that in the state capital there's Sr. Araujo [the owner of a chain of drapery stores] with so many shops while I lack even a small piece of cloth. There's this and that person with an inheritance of so many shops while I've got nothing. Am I going to lament that? No, not at all. I am

going to trust that God is the *dono* of everything. We see something very close to us, right close up, in every corner of the world. Have you ever seen a sparrow with two sets of clothes? No—they've only got one set, all the birds: the parrot, the canary, the ché-ché, the rooster. They might vary in color, but you never saw one with two sets of clothes. The bird eats but he doesn't have a shotgun or a machine gun. He has appropriately nothing. God takes care of him every day. Often we toss sleepless in the early hours with a headache, wondering how we'll manage with so many children in the house and not a bit of coffee to give them. But the sparrow without anything, but with five or six children, you'll find him always singing, so happy. That's how it is with the sparrow who makes himself happy with what the day has to offer—and you've seen how hard he works.

Such statements—in the hearing even more than in the reading infused with the color and cadence of elaborated Gospel parables—tend to confirm the stereotype that lower-class Christian fundamentalists, especially of the Holiness type, are deeply conservative. Indeed, Severino takes stands that would commonly be described as conservative on a number of issues and, always a self-conscious reasoner, appeals to several layers of religious principle to justify the positions he takes. He believes that the poor (who suffer from injustices he describes with vivid passion) should not, in general, take issue and fight for their rights in the political or judicial arena. His reasons for this conservative belief are complex, based on experience as well as religious doctrine, but both experience and doctrine are constantly referred to apocalyptic myth. Everywhere (and especially in Brazil), he thinks, the unjust rich triumph and corrupt governments support them:

God is a long way from these people. However, His eyes aren't shut, His arms aren't folded, His ears record everything. He hears those who petition Him. He is with those who listen to His voice. He is there to attend to whoever holds out his hand for help. Meanwhile the faith of man is that my nation fears yours—you might invade us and take off all our goods. And so all the nations expect war—even when they're not fighting they're on one side or another waiting to fight. That is proof that between men there is no security. Sometimes there are efforts like the United Nations to make union between nation and nation. But within twenty-four hours it all breaks up. You know that problem about Israel, with its frontiers. A treaty is made, but then something goes wrong, and there is conflict again. Here again it's clear: this is not the government of God, it's something set up by men for themselves. But eventually [Severino says *brevemente* (shortly) but later makes it clear that, unlike the Jehovah's Witnesses, he does not believe in the known imminence of the Second Coming] when the Lord destroys these evil qualities, then this Earth will be transformed and, according to Him, we will inhabit it. A just order will come, an end to taking by force. Ultimately, God adjudicates. He told men not to seek revenge for He is the avenger. He is the bringer of justice in the last days.

When I ask him whether the Bible has anything more to say about how we should confront injustice in daily life, particularly injustices in relationships between rich and poor, his response is prompt and didactic.

> Severino: There's a clear line on how to confront this.
> Interviewer: What is that?
> Severino: Knee to the floor. Do you understand?
> Interviewer: No. Knee to the floor?
> Severino: It's to kneel down and ask for grace from the *dono* of all. Because to struggle, to confront wrongdoing [he used the moral term *ímpio* rather than the more political term *injustiça* I had been using], is to row against the tide. So there's one of these Excellencies sitting on something I have a right to — let's say it's Sr. Henrique [Severino is doing his own probing here: *Henrique* is the name I'm known by in Campo Alegre]. I have the right. But you, as a rich man, are opposed to me — you're opposed to the likes of me. You don't want to have any communication with me. You don't want to see me. Well I'm not going to look for another month;[2] nor will I try to harm you; nor will I look for a potion or have witchcraft used against you. It's always [pause] to look for God. For the man who looks for God Heaven has no height: Heaven links itself with the man's head. Because God has said that He hears a man speak from any place he might be. He is the Creator, the Supreme Judge, manager of managers, King of Kings, grandest of the great. And if we pray to God in the spirit of truth, God is completely with man and will help him conquer in every struggle of day-to-day life, of life itself.

Severino's moral code, in conversation with his experience, keeps him out of the political arena. On democracy, he is epigrammatic: "Where others speak of democracy, I speak of laxity." And in his stories of local and state politics, he elaborates the point. Politicians, like the governments they run, operate according to the laws of man, which are, to Severino, the laws of greed. The poor get nowhere in political activity unless they submit to the laws of greed. Hence, rather than striving for more democracy (or for some specific goal through what democracy there is), it is better to support a military president like João Batista, who is able to force the rich to accede to the poor the few rights they have. Political activity invariably comes to grief for the poor, by practical as well as moral criteria.

President João Batista Figueiredo, Brazil's fifth military president since the coup in 1964, might well have been pleased at the support given him by Severino, especially if he knew what an influential person Severino was, in a town mostly for the opposition. He might be surprised and distressed, however, to realize that this support is not inconsistent with a sort of Christian anarchism in Severino.

Interviewer: These great inequalities between the rich man and the poor man, are they going to continue?

Severino: While one man has a fleet of buses and trucks, another lacks even a bicycle. You get to be satisfied with what you've got.

Interviewer: It is the will of God that this situation goes on, that such inequalities continue?

Severino: No, this comes to an end. Because . . . this government, it's not the government of God. It's the government of man. Because man disobeyed God in the Garden of Eden — our first parents — and since then man remains dissolute. God ordered our first parents to leave the Garden and wander far from the gates. And He said to man, "From now on you will have to gain your bread from the sweat of your brow. And you, woman, who listened to the Evil Snake — you know how the story ends — all that you conceive will be against your husband. Increase and multiply and dominate the Earth." Thus mankind increased and multiplied and set up government over us — kings in some parts and constitutions and republics in others. In the appropriation of the fruits of the earth, one improved more than another while yet another desired to increase his possessions and, pushing, buying, and selling, improved himself. And from all this, government begins. The more governments call people to military service and dress the boys up in uniforms with a revolver on one side, the more war and aggression there is. Because the Kingdom of God is peace in the Holy Spirit: there is no disharmony or spilling of blood. God is a long way away from these people.

Severino is no more a simple, unreflecting conservative than he is a stereotyped Puritan or Holiness Protestant. Even in short extracts from several hours of taped interviews, he emerges as politically and religiously complex — an interesting challenge to any stereotypes set up in the attempt to understand him as a political-economic man. His myths of the Creation and Fall render him too cynical to be unquestioningly loyal to any authoritarian government. His *crente* dualistic moralism and eschatological despair feed a radical distrust of democratic politics and politicians. The Holiness aspects of his religion tend to render him apolitical (in a narrow conception of politics): he would trust in the Lord to provide for today and to set things right in the end. But his Puritan's moral eye is acute: he is driven toward a moral critique of political behavior and toward knowledge of the law. His Holiness spontaneity is bounded by Puritan calculations about how to become a more just man and how to achieve a neighborhood more pleasing to a just God — calculations that, again, draw him toward politics. And if he shies away from political activity on his own behalf, his sense of responsibility pushes him forward on behalf of others.

Beyond this static statement of conflicting tendencies, it is possible to follow Severino further in word and action and to present something of the dynamics of religion, politics, and economics in his life. We need to know something of these dynamics if we are to recognize him in context and discern his voice in the present and emerging politics of Campo Alegre. We need to know, for example, how Severino puts together and lives the Holiness and Puritan strands in his thought (strands that I, rather than he, separated out). We need to examine how Severino brings together precepts, images, and myths as he addresses the problems of everyday life in Campo Alegre.

The first of the guiding stereotypes to throw out is probably that of *Puritan.* The very use of the term might suggest that Severino's is a voice for individualistic striving for upward economic mobility in Campo Alegre. But in Severino, the most important element linking Puritan religiosity to proto-capitalistic behavior is missing. Weber's Puritan — anxious about salvation (to the point of "salvation panic") and unable to accept the Catholic church's sacramental mediation — pursues material symbols of salvation. Anxiety about the ultimate goal of salvation, passionately desired, propels the Puritan, taut, wound up, single-minded, in lifelong pursuit of material achievement and success for his soul's sake. Such anxiety and the motivations that pulse it have no part in Severino's religious vision. Central to his vision is certainty about salvation:

[Christ's] death was to achieve one thing, and that achievement, or His death, left us with hopes and expectations. We have hope. If we stand firm until the end, we are saved. This is our conviction. As He promised His disciples, there on a certain occasion when His disciple Philip said to Him, "Lord, show us the Father," and He said to Philip, "Who comes to Me comes to the Father, because I am in the Father and the Father in Me." Everything there was *confiado* [entrusted]. This proves that the Christ who died guaranteed everything. He said, "Everything that you ask in My name I will do for you." On another occasion, feeding His disciples, He said, "I am going to the Father. I am going to prepare a place for you. I will return again and take you with Me so that there where I am you shall be with Me." So He'll come back so that where He is, the people will be. So if this Christ — the son of Joseph and Mary who was born, who lived, and who suffered and was killed by man, who bore everything, and who was raised up into Heaven — if this Christ said He will return, He will return. So we have this complete faith that if we manage to the end we will be completely *rebatada* [recompensed]. When we speak of *rebatados* we don't refer to everybody in the whole world. It's only some — I know you know this — it's only some. He said, "I come to choose; to sort out the sheep from the goats." One will be sorted to the right, another to the left.

To those on the right He will say, "Come with Me to the Father. You may enter into your heritage, the Kingdom is prepared. It has been prepared from the beginning of time." And to those on the left, "Because I do not know you. . . ." And to those who say, "But what about me? I cured, I baptized," He will say, "I have found things against your names, I do not know you apart from the evil ones. Go to eternal fire that was prepared for the Satan and his angels." If you're on the side of life, if you're on the sure side, not seeking those things that those of the left seek, then we have total confidence, a confidence that is nourished, that this Christ will come to gather us to Him. And we wish that Christ who has given us this help will not meet us in an irregular moment in a life of disrepute, but that He will encounter us leading a life full of honesty and love for all.

If Severino seems to feel a powerful anxiety in this, it is that he might not remain impeccably faithful until the end to the true doctrine — to the laws of God, to the very requirement of confidence in God's ultimate beneficence and justice. But this sort of anxiety does not impel a man to seek the sign of salvation in upward mobility. To Severino, the terms of the salvation exchange with his God are perfectly clear and therefore not, in themselves, a source of chronic doubt about the mind of the eternal Judge. God has given clear laws; He has given unambiguous promises about the otherworldly rewards He will dispense to the obedient; and He gives signs that tell a person to his heart that the exchange — salvation for obedience — has taken place.

In accounts of Holiness religion, it is suggested that this lack of Puritan anxiety is associated with a relative lack of concern with an ethical code and ethical issues. That is not the case with Severino. His vision and its attendant anxieties lead to a distinctive profile of effective ethical concerns, not an absence of them. Severino rejects the famous work ethic, or at least important elements of it. But he has well-considered, and indeed well-practised, ethics relating to work. He rejects, very explicitly, any equation of wealth with moral stature, and he denies any empirical correlation between hard labor and wealth. But work, to be meritorious, must be subject to those same exacting moral laws that make self-denial a constant in the life of a *crente*. God-pleasing work requires that the worker should have defined his responsibilities, publicly confirmed them, and fulfilled them to the letter, even when bosses or colleagues fail to fulfil theirs. Virtuous work need not be successful by the standards of men, and material success will often proceed only from sinful activities. Without exception, the successful lawyers, military men, police, landowners, politicians, priests, pastors, and businessmen of Severino's stories are engaged in immoral work. Given radical corruption through competitive greed, almost no occupation that provides great material reward can be expected to be valuable according to the laws of God. Hard labor might be rewarded, but it is not intrinsically good; its merit is contingent on the worker's fulfillment of the laws of God in all areas of life. Even prophecy and other activities that are intrinsically good — because they manifest gifts of God — have merit that is conditional on the moral lawfulness of the worker. God will not bestow His gifts on the morally reprehensible and withdraws them for breaches of His laws. "There are no prophets," says Severino, "there is only prophecy." And to receive that or any other gift of the Spirit, it is necessary to have "a life that is fixed according to the law." Severino's salvation myths and the ethics of exchange with the Savior provide no room for the development of a Protestant work ethic. His dialectic of myth and ethic precludes a mythology of success.

The ethical concerns and moral fervor that Severino brings to the workplace are evident in his critical perceptions of work conditions and relationships. Prior to 1963 Severino worked on the land — as rural laborer on *usinas*, on his father's rented *sítio*, and later, most disastrously, on his own rented plot of unproductive land near Campo Alegre. Many of his friends and neighbors came to him for help and advice when they lost land and livelihood because the owner of the property defining the northern boundary of Campo Alegre expelled, with guile and force, the *sitiantes* (sharecroppers and tenants) on his property. Severino's discussion of his father's, his own, and his neighbors' experiences adds up to a harsh critical analysis — of the working out of greed among landowners and of the corruption that binds government institutions to serve the greedy. In his moral critique, he clearly perceives what is happening to small *agricultores,* and the poor in general, as landowners ignore their responsibilities and operate according only to the dictates of greed. He believes they are not interested in production for the benefit of all but only in private profit. This pursuit of self-interest means that *roça* production (small-scale subsistence and local-market production), of manioc in particular, is disappearing:

> It's disappearing. But people need *farinha* [manioc flour], yams, sweet potatoes, and no one knows who is going to plant these things. Because the rich man wants what? Sugar cane. Or he wants to get the poor off the land to carve it up into expensive lots. It's investment that he's interested in: investment of money to produce interest for himself. And what's the little man, who wants to plant and look after himself while living in town, going to do? Nobody knows. The little man has nothing to eat and nothing to sell now. When he loses his plot, how can he consume? If we had access to that land here where people have just been expelled, we'd produce enough for our own families and to sell to those who work in the aluminum factory. But, as it is, we don't have enough to maintain ourselves or to produce for others. So every-

thing comes through CEASA [the central produce market of Recife]. And, more and more, what's sold there, comes from down south. We don't have an economy. Everyone gets a cut on the way: so we have to pay for transport, taxes, bank interest. And the people have no possibility of resisting. . . . No one takes care of anyone else.

Yet Severino is no more a revolutionary on the basis of these perceptions and analysis than an enthusiast for Brazilian capitalism on the basis of his ascetic ethics. His vision of salvation history and his conviction of the intractability of evil in the man-made world contain his radical diagnoses so that they do not flow into protesting action. When his neighbors ask his advice on how to cope with expulsion from the land, he urges them *não fazer questão* (not to make an issue) with the landowner. Not the least of his reasons is the practical consideration that they will lose in any confrontation. This is argued partly on the basis of local evidence: the landowner is ruthless, prepared to use armed ex-prisoner *pistoleiros* to shoot protesters; he has the local judiciary and police in his pocket; and the people have only hoes and voices for defense. But even behind such practical, local considerations is a general principle: "The world is of the powerful," Severino often says. "If you have, you're worth something; if you don't have, you're worth nothing. That is the way the world has been since the Fall and that is how it will be until Christ comes again." One corollary of this bleak mythology is left unstated by Severino—the absence (notable to ears attuned to middle-class Brazilian political discourse) of any this-worldly utopian vision. Severino's vision provides no images of an alternative world that might motivate active protest against the recognized injustices of this world.

Several related ideas had their own consequences for Severino as political man. One (expressed in my words) is that the field for the application of one's social ethics must be carefully circumscribed, given the inapplicability of those ethics in an unalterably evil wider world. Severino never states this principle as such; but I believe he implies it in our interviews in his firm definitions of topic and concepts. My questions about what can be done about injustice in the world are invariably restated by Severino—as questions about what can be done, in a Campo Alegre neighborhood, to combat greed as it operates between neighbors and what can be done, in charity, to obviate the immediate effects of the greed in neighbors' lives. The just man avoids provoking envy in his neighborhood, refuses to engage in envious and greedy gossip, forgives those who gossip against him or trample on him in their desire to get ahead, helps those who are forgotten because they are beneath envy. When I press for an image of or an agenda for the just man in a wider world, Severino understands what I am after but invariably returns to the basic salvation myth and to first principles, which state that action for justice is possible only in the territory defined by the just man's network of personal relationships.

Correspondingly, he trims the notion of justice itself to its local dimensions. I have already noted Severino's tendency to proceed from my term *injusto* to his more moral, local term *impio*. Usually the shift is less direct, as in this exchange:

> Interviewer: And your faith seems to give you confidence that in the end one will see justice done?
>
> Severino: Yes.
>
> Interviewer: But in the meanwhile, it's clear that in this world we'll find much injustice.
>
> Severino: Injustice. Yes. He told us this. He said that in the world you will have *calábia* [affliction] — ah, you don't know what *calábia* is — it's *disse-me-disse* [gossip], it's *mexe-mexe* [scandal-mongering]. Here there's hostility — the breaking down of relationships, *calábia*, or, more clearly, lying. Someone wants to appear better; someone else wants the pastor's approval and a good place in church to increase something or other. From these things arise the grinding down of people, one by another.

Severino does have images of justice and peace less circumscribed in content and application. But they are apocalyptic in inspiration and temporal location, having no direct force as motivators of political action in the here and now:

> So this Earth will be transformed by God. Some say by fire, others by rains. But God's own word is that it will be fire. When He says it will be done, it will be done according to His words. And He said it will burn. And so all that is evil will disappear. And it is said that those people who have ascended into Heaven will return and set up a Kingdom here. It is said that there will be a new Heaven, the new Jerusalem, and a new City of God. And those who are the children of God will remain children of God for all eternity. It is said that nobody will live in a place that he doesn't own. It is said that when these days arrive, the offspring of the cow will play with the lion, and the child at the breast will play with the wolf cub. It is said that the government of evil will pass away and will end. Between man and animals there will be peace.

The very cadences are those of the Bible, God speaking: God says what He will do; He defines justice and will achieve it at the end of time. In the meantime, the just man does not presume to define and do as God. Rather, under the incessant scrutiny of God, he prepares himself and those for whom he is immediately responsible, family and neighbors, to be considered worthy of Divine justice. There is temporal and spatial discontinuity between the local piety of the man who will be counted just and the cosmic Justice of God. And God does not call on the just man to struggle for the setting up of the New Jerusalem but only to prepare himself to be of the righteous who will inhabit it.

If the vision of hope itself seems to enjoin a certain political passivity, the content of the vision encourages a positive conservatism. "It is said that nobody will live in a place that he does not own." The discontinuity between the here and now and the New Jerusalem lies in the distribution of private property; but this actually highlights the continuity of the institution of private property. Severino's vision of hope does not call him to a Christian communism, nor does it stimulate him to question the very institution around which he sees human greed flourishing.

I had thought that, after his heated denunciation of the local landowner for his unjust treatment of *sitiantes*, Severino might at least have considered that the landowner had lost his right to his land. Severino, like many *crentes*, had often stressed that human beings were only administrators for God who was the owner of all. But Severino was astonished by this lead in my questions. To him, there was no question but that someone who had paid for land and completed the legal formalities of transfer was the owner, with rights that could not be negated by his injustices. God might punish him, and sooner rather than later. But no man had the right to take issue with his ownership and consequent right to dispose of the land as he would. The state might require the landowner to sell part of his property so that more land might be available for much-needed housing in Campo Alegre – and Severino would vote for such a measure. Were title not clearly and legally established (as they were not on the neighboring property), then legal challenge might be mounted – or even ought to be, given that the would-be owner also treated *sitiantes* and workers unjustly. But these modifications aside, ownership in land is inviolable by man. This significantly modulates Severino's political voice. Most of his stories and analyses of injustice have to do with conflicts over property in land. But the dualisms of his religious vision place that institution and its beneficiaries beyond attack, even by those who count themselves marginal and oppressed.

Similarly, focusing on the moral order that is at once so real and so distant, Severino interprets his personal and group status in such a way that he is both critic of the rich and defender of hierarchy and the procedures that establish it. When I tell Severino, four years after my first conversations with him, that several of my students, knowing little about the northeast of Brazil, have wondered how intelligent and energetic a man could be so poor, first he notes that he never wanted to "climb, climb, climb." Then he refers to his decision to look for a secure job with a certain, if small, salary – after years of uncertain income, first as a small farmer and then in a series of jobs after the move to Campo Alegre. Then he reflects more discursively on factors affecting his decisions and moves between material and moral worlds as he interprets job and status. He recognizes his low status in the material world but rejects any association between that status and any moral failure or inherent inferiority. On the contrary, in the light of the moral order the hierarchy of the material order may be inverted: the honest law-abiding poor man is the moral superior of the rich man who has made it through greed or mere inheritance. It is not the hierarchy of the material world that is inherently immoral, only the pretension and unlawful behavior within it.

The Ten Commandments provide the rules; they also consecrate a framework of roles and institutions within which the rules are to be obeyed. They presume the institutions of property, marriage, and the family; and they imply, to Severino, that the differentiations of wealth and status that make the rules necessary are unchallengeable. The man who would be counted just has been provided rules for negotiating hierarchy that are as clear as the rules governing property; and if he follows them, he will be worthy, whatever his position in the material order. The first requirement is to attain certain knowledge: to know one's gifts, qualifications, rights, and duties. On the basis of knowledge, lawful calculation is possible: a man will know where in the material world he stands and what rules he must obey. Knowledge and calculation are high moral values in themselves, because they provide the criteria with which to assess a person's own lawfulness in negotiating the material order. Most work for material reward will be, in itself, morally neutral. Its fit with the worker's qualifications and the ease with which rights and duties may be defined and realized will determine its moral worth. A further criterion is the amount of free time the job allows for engagement in activities that are not morally neutral but morally good and positive in themselves, like counseling or helping one's neighbor — activities in which one directly employs the gifts of the Holy Spirit.

So Severino arrives at a classification of work that disputes the prevailing status hierarchy but affirms hierarchy and the due processes that establish it. In the moral order — which is the Kingdom to come, discontinuous in time and space with the material order — justice will prevail and hierarchies based on greed and false values overturned. That, in the fullness of God's time. In the material order, inherently corrupted by greed, there is hope only in order and right procedure, which provide a framework within which the just man, obeying the Ten Commandments, can prepare himself to inherit the just moral order to be set up by God. As in his political judgments, Severino's essential conservatism with regard to work relations and social hierarchy proceed from a profound moral pessimism about the everyday world.

Critic of politicians and governments, but defender of strong rule and the state; keen analyst of the injustices perpetrated by the propertied, but defender of property and property law; challenger of the pretensions of the rich in the name of the superior dignity of the honest poor, but defender of degree and of due process for its establishment — these contrasting aspects help define the political voice of Severino. Stated baldly they might suggest indecision and even shiftiness. However, placed within the context of his religious vision, Severino's beliefs seem remarkably consistent and unparadoxical. Consistency lies in the dualistic vision of a cosmos divided: a moral order discontinuous in space and time from the material order, presided over by a God who calls men and women to righteousness but not to right a material order that is corrigible only by him.

Without images or myths suggesting that human beings might produce the New Jerusalem in this world, Severino has low expectations of political leaders, and he discounts the efficacy of political activity for any fundamental change — whether in the matter of land or in the hierarchy that favors the unjust. His vision of the New Jerusalem and his myth of its coming help motivate him not only to be a forthright political critic but also to radically distrust anyone entering the political arena with the proclaimed aim of changing the world. As he prepares himself and family to be worthy of citizenship in the City of God, Severino is drawn to energetic and intelligent service to his neighbors in their troubles, and even to the point of becoming a sort of counselor to local politicians. But there is no basis in his vision for grass-roots community-building political activity that would seek economic justice through a politics opposed to authoritarian fiat and populist manipulation. Still less is his intensely individual sense of moral responsibility compatible with a representative politics, in which he would seek a party or another person to do battle for justice on his behalf.

Severino himself likes to draw out the dialectic between his religious vision and convictions, on the one hand, and his political voice and behavior, on the other. His response to my invitation to tell the story of his life draws attention to another element in the dialectic: his own political-economic experience. In his choice of what to tell, in the mode of telling, in the recounted experiences themselves, there is a constant shuttling between religious vision, political-economic experience, and that amalgam of political style, behavior, and discourse that I have been calling Severino's political voice.

Left by himself to decide how to structure the story of his life, Severino seemed to have it all ready. In this he is a true *crente*, prepared to give public testimony to salvation history in his biography. So his is a chronologically ordered set of stories, illustrating cosmic themes in the microcosm of his own life. The gleaning of his life for appropriate stories does not seem to have been difficult. I sensed that the telling of his life was, for Severino, an act of persuasion: an invitation to me to consider through his case that his view of heaven and earth made sense; a reminder to himself of his place in a comprehended cosmos. He is communicating not his raw experience but, like anyone speaking autobiographically, his myth of experience, and, like any *crente*, the Christian myths of Creation, Fall, and Redemption. There were pauses in the lengthy and effortless telling, when Severino would extend me the courtesy of "Perhaps it's different in your country." But he seemed to expect the return courtesy "No, not very much, actually." Myths of experience and myths defining the cosmos have shaped, though not simply determined, one another.

Severino's childhood and adolescence are told in stories of the vicissitudes of family fortunes, of his struggle to learn to read and write, and of his teenage conversion to the Assembly of God. Having told me his date of birth, 19 November 1931, Severino observes, "I didn't have a good start." His father was a *bagaceiro* on a sugar farm. The word *bagaceiro* means, strictly, a workman who feeds sugar-cane husks into the furnace, but it also signifies a person of low status. He moved from place to place during Severino's childhood, moving on when it became clear that "the situation there wasn't good." At one time he became a cutter of hay. Just before World War II, things were starting to get better: his father, paying a small rent, produced fruit and vegetables from a small plot of land for the family and a local market. Then, with the coming of the war, the Army wanted the land for training purposes. The family moved on and found another plot with a house, which his father was able to rent from the textile factory that owned much of the land in the area. By this time, Severino was working like an adult on the family plot. "I was brought up working," he observes.

Being brought up working meant to be like father and grandfather, to work on the land and never receive an education. Severino is proud that he battled against the stream on the matter of education. The story of his struggle for literacy was the most important chapter in his preadult years. When he was twelve years old and at the local market, he saw a man, blind in one eye, reading a story book. "Here was a man with only one eye who had managed to learn to read . . . and I, with two good eyes, remained ignorant." That very day he resolved to learn to read and write and bought a reading primer, a pencil, and an exercise book. His father objected. Nobody in the family had ever learned to read and write before, and they were none the worse farmers for that. Education was difficult to arrange and took time away from farm work. If Severino persisted in this mad endeavor and took classes at night, he would find the door shut on his return and would have to sleep with the animals or in the manioc shed. Severino persisted, working during the day for his father or for the landowner, attending school at night and sleeping outside on his return. After a couple of years the struggle became too much. But Severino was so intent on finishing his primary education that he left his family for about three years, took jobs in the town, and supported himself while he finished school. "It was a matter of willpower. It's so much easier today."

Severino draws an intense contrast between his story of life on the farm, on the one hand, and his story of education and the life that education made possible, on the other. After completing his education, Severino returned to the farm, and the story is much the same as in his childhood. Things would go well for a while, and then nature would set them back — family members, or their animals, would get sick — or nature might exercise benevolence, but landowners would dispose of them malevolently. On one occasion, when the farm was doing well, a lawyer told Severino's father that he was entitled, under a new law, to a large sum of money — an indemnity from the company he had worked for and whose land he was renting. He persuaded Severino's father to press his claim. The result was protracted negotiations, in which the entitlement offered by the company diminished progressively. Finally, an accountant of the company came and told him he was going to get thrown off the land because he had made an issue of his right to an indemnity. The family left the land immediately, with goats and other belongings, and found a plot that the family could work in exchange for a set number of days' work for the owner. Nature and the owner combined to terminate that arrangement — after a month, Severino's father became ill, the owner accused him of laziness, and the family was on the move again.

The theme of the land stories is always clear, and pointed out by Severino. A small farmer without his own land lives at the mercy of nature and the landowners, and this is particularly true for the unlettered farmer, who lacks not only resources but also the understanding and skills necessary to hold onto what he has when the landowners set lawyers and officials onto him:

> The poor man can't do a thing without the rich man soon getting a lawyer onto him. The lawyer is prepared to catch the layman, the man who has learnt nothing. With two or three words he can beat the layman down and have him condemned. The poor man might get another lawyer, but he will say "you've not got enough money to fight a case." When the two lawyers get together, they debate, and the thing finishes in a lecture. Through all this the rich man gains everything, and the poor man who has nothing to offer can't enter into the land because he has nothing to promise. And so it is: the poor

man always poor, the rich man ever richer, taking by force, ordering the poor man around with the police at the door. Where I used to live there was a case of this . . . on a sugar farm . . . a woman, three days after giving birth. The rich man sent for the police. They knocked down the door of the house and did what they liked inside. The woman didn't die, but she went mad. There she was, lying down inside the house, recovering from childbirth. So she went mad. What happened? Nothing, nothing, nothing. Who has, has. Who has little can only have less. There are all sorts of proof. . . .

Layer upon layer of story deepens the point: the unlettered poor man is forced into a miserable life over which he has no control. Material welfare has no relation to personal effort; rights may be counted as offenses; death or madness is the only escape. Or there is learning, which provides the tools for survival, for some control over destiny, and for the acquirement of doctrine that, against all odds, sustains confidence in law-abiding, self-controlled action.

For Severino, the struggle for literacy yielded three things. The first was some degree of independence from the uncontrollable destiny of defeat that is the theme of his stories about his father and neighbors. The second was the means for acquiring and developing a vision of hope and purpose that has, he believes, given him inner strength to resist the pressures of everyday life leading toward despair and the resultant immoralities of greed, animal lust, and envy. The third was the ability to negotiate independently the requirements of bureaucratic Brazil, so that he is equipped for moral and material survival. Severino concludes the story of his education with an account of how difficult life would be if he were illiterate. Again only Biblical cadences seem adequate to catalogue the doom avoided. *Aí de mim* (woe is me) is the phrase he uses repetitively to give moral depth to each of the material disasters he describes befalling a person of his background who cannot sign his name or read the documents that chart the paths and pitfalls of modern life.

In his conversion story, Severino links his conversion with his literacy. He was converted in town when he had left home to complete his schooling. His teacher was a *crente*, and a *crente* congregation met in the house on the evenings when he had lessons. Above all, conversion was "reading, reading, reading, and thinking, thinking, thinking." Severino wanted me to know that it took time, reading time, before he was ready to experience the feeling of salvation and to formally declare his conversion. Conversion took place away from home, through the use of those skills that made him different from father, family, and neighbors, and conversion finally confirmed him as self-consciously independent of his father's moral world and destiny. Severino moved back to his family and never escaped its material deprivations. But he considers that his struggle for literacy and his use of it in conversion have allowed him a freedom and a fullness of life and purpose that his father's moral world of *ignorância* could never have afforded. Severino's biographical stories contain the double message: life teaches what faith enjoins; and faith, in the life of the convert, can transform the experience of life itself.

In his adult life this two-way relationship has continued. Political experience (or rather his experience of politicians) is intertwined with the place of politics in Severino's moral world. In a time of great material need, patronage politics failed him. His last attempt at tenant farming was a failure: he didn't have enough land, the soil was too sandy, the crops failed, and his wife became ill because he did not have the money to fix the roof of their little wattle-and-daub hut in the rainy season. Severino decided that his destiny lay in the town of Campo Alegre rather than on the land. But jobs were not easy to come by. He tried casual laboring jobs, fishing. But, for a man with a family, those activities were as precarious a means of survival as farming. He knew that the big political patron of the area had provided jobs for a number of people: in the nearby prison he had established or in the post office where he controlled appointments. So, in 1963 when the great man was vice-governor of the state, Severino went to the city, to the governor's palace, to ask for a secure job. He did it boldly. Asserting his right to talk to the highest authorities, he gained admission, first, to the office of the governor. The governor listened to Severino's request and said that he could not help, explaining that he had been cutting his own staff drastically as an economy measure. He referred him to the vice-governor. Severino went to the vice-governor who listened but said he could do nothing because he was in conflict with the governor and, therefore, had no funds at his disposal. Severino's ambitious attempt to get something out of top politicians had failed. Severino says that he had always believed that governments of what he calls the *paisano* type ("a government that is not military, that is not of force or of the sword") were of no use to him: "They pass laws that they don't respect and cannot enforce." Now he concluded that they were not even any good for occasional patronage, however open to the needy they might appear. Experience, again, fits the expectation that arises from religious vision: both lead to the conclusion that the least, but also the highest, criterion for a good government is that it should be able to enforce laws defining and guaranteeing the rights of the poor.

In 1968, after working for more than a year carrying loaded sacks at a caustic soda factory, Severino was back to odd laboring jobs and fishing. Five of his children had measles; two of them were desperately ill; and he was unable to provide milk and medicines for them. This crisis, he said, forced him to decide on municipal employment, a move he had been thinking of making for some time but that he had been leaving until a job was definitely available. He went to the mayor and explained his problem. The mayor told him he was right to seek secure, if low-paid, employment with so large a family, in which only the breadwinner seemed spared ill-health. Within three weeks he started work and has worked as a street cleaner and a laborer for the municipality ever since. This is the job that Severino values so highly because it gives him a fixed return for fulfillment of clearly defined responsibilities. Severino's work experience has taught him that there are four major statuses: fortuitous wealth, wealth that is inherited or comes to one by luck; corrupt wealth that is usually gained as a person "rises on the sweat of the poor"; insecure poverty of the kind available in governmental bureaucracies; and the only honorable status (for Severino), secure poverty.

Judgments like this match propositions that Severino draws from his religious vision. The political voice that articulates experience and the political voice that enunciates religious vision inform one another. In pithy phrases, Severino sums up what experience has taught him; and he repeats these phrases in both his interpretations of current events and in discussions of his religion. Experience teaches political pessimism and caution: "This Brazil belongs to the powerful; the poor man will lose when he makes an issue." Experience evokes criticism of the rich and powerful, and cynicism about their ideologies: "The rich and powerful want only more for themselves and are not interested in production and development for all." Experience denies the big people's myth of continuing development: "When one of these projects or inventions comes along to improve things, something else gets worse. The machine that cuts cane cuts down the breadwinners of families." Experience denies myths of mobility in the material world: "The poor man can't get ahead except by becoming greedy or by luck." Although experience challenges the pretensions and propaganda of the rich and powerful, it also teaches the poor man to know his place and not to hope for change from the political arena: "Governments are good only when they are strong and can guarantee obedience to the laws we have; the opening up of politics, the return to *paisano* government is an open sack for us all to fall into." Experience shows that the poor man can gain freedom and dignity only by overcoming his own *ignorância* and by coming to know what God has done for us, what He requires of us, and what He will do to right wrongs when the moral world is fully realized in the material world: "Only with doctrine and *confiança* [trust] in God can a man be free and happy and know his destiny."

The resonance between these dicta of experience and moral vision does not lead to quiescence. In the limited area where Severino considers himself not only able but called upon to seek justice and challenge the powers-that-be, he does so — with the courage of a visionary and the skill of one whose business it is to know how the world works. His brother, who turned up during the 1982 interview, encouraged him to tell the story of his protracted struggle, some years ago, to bring a local police chief to justice for having shot the son of a neighbor, whom he did not like. In some danger to his own life, Severino gathered the facts of the case, lined up witnesses, and took the matter to the headquarters of the Department of Public Security in the capital, and to local politicians as well. In the end, the policeman was fired and forbidden to return to the town — a most unusual outcome to such an affair. On grounds of faith and experience, Severino does not expect justice to come from human institutions; he distrusts even his own church's ability to resist the laws of greed and envy. And just as no one can represent him before his God, so no one can represent his moral stand for justice in the material world. The consequences in Severino's political voice are obvious: in the territory defined by faith and experience for effective exercise of personal responsibility, Severino speaks and acts loudly and clearly, as an individual, for justice and peace. Outside that territory he is quiet, not only resistant to recruitment to class or party movements for change but critical of any person or organization that would try to mobilize him or his neighbors. From experience he knows such mobilization is doomed to defeat and corruption; morally he knows it is pointless.

Severino criticizes and separates himself from the Catholic radicals along just these lines. But even in this, his stance is characteristically complex. He is deeply committed to discussion — to proclaiming and refining his beliefs and perceptions in conversation with some young Franciscan seminarians, themselves committed to dialogue, who live in the street next to his. The political morality that Severino practices and preaches and that is so firmly rooted in vision and experience is also, as a matter of principle, negotiable. That commitment to negotiation is itself an important element in Severino's political voice.

We may conceive of negotiation in Campo Alegre not only in terms of the substantive issues of the day (the land problem, the next elections) but also in terms of political voice (the enunciations, however implicit or incoherent, of cultural paradigms). The cultural mélange of Campo Alegre emerges in daily exchanges of gestures and stories, in arguments about the mundane quotidian rather than in abstract declarations of allegiance. Severino has a special talent for constructing ideal types and labeling them (the *paisano* government, for example), but even he expresses his own, clearly discernible cultural paradigm discursively, in anecdote and symbol.

In developing the image of political voice, I found it helpful to think of types of such discursive expression as dialects, and the individual variations within these dialects as accents. These metaphors help me appreciate the distinctiveness, strangeness, and even the threat, of any one paradigm in confrontation with another; but they also remind me that confrontations occur daily, between ordinary people in the negotiation of their daily lives. For each of the paradigms I described earlier — *coronelismo, populismo,* bureaucratic authoritarianism, and the priest's communalism — I think of a dialect with the same label. Severino's voice places him in the mélange of political dialects and accents heard in Campo Alegre. In his conversations and arguments we can see how he establishes his dialect and accent, and how he hears other voices selectively — thereby, within his network of influence, increasing or diminishing the social purchase of those voices.

Severino's receptivity and use of the authoritarian dialect is selective. He neither registers nor employs much of the authoritarian vocabulary of legitimacy. Appeals to legitimacy — based on a claim of superior ability to usher in a new era of progress and prosperity for all in Brazil — make no sense to him. His myth of the Fall, his doctrine of the irremediable perversity of the rich and powerful, and his own experiences of landowners and politicians, all define progress as an illusion, and hence a meaningless justification for the exercise of power. Just as senseless to him are the equations of worth with wealth or power that may be found in authoritarian discourse. Again, neither his interpreted experience nor his myths of the origins and course of evil and suffering in the world — his theodicy myths — allow meaning to any such equations.

But the same myths and experiences open his views to the *ascetics* of authoritarianism. Since all, through the taint of the Fall, have a tendency to destroy themselves and society through greed and envy, it makes sense that a strong, central authority is needed to extract obedience to laws that enforce the minimum of order and cooperation necessary for individual and social survival. Doctrine and experience teach that the just man needs both law and well-policed space to realize his own lawfulness. In this mode, the authoritarian dialect, to Severino's ears, is infinitely more attuned to reality than the populist or the communitarian dialects, which are dominated by utopian reference. (Severino, in 1982, approves the military president, João Batista Figueiredo, when he looks and sounds like his former self as head of Brazil's security apparatus, but Severino is simply puzzled when, as champion of *abertura* [the opening up of the regime], Figueiredo begins to sound like ex-president Jánio Quadros — the image, for Severino, of vacuity and anarchism in populist politics.) Severino understands the populist dialect. But he studiously refrains from speaking it; and he does not care to hear too much of it.

Severino is not familiar with the communitarian dialect and tends to misunderstand those who speak it — (in my view) confusing it with a form of populist dialect. Curiously, though, his own voice is heavily accented with communitarian. He understands and broadcasts the communitarian call to be like Jesus, or even the young David, and to do personal battle for justice among one's neighbors. His radical critique of specific events and institutions sounds communitarian. Simple sentences of the new dialect are understood and voiced, but not its complex propositions about a new Brazil and liberation for the poor here on earth. To Severino, that all sounds like populism with a new but all-too-clerical accent.

Severino's political voice, then, is a blend of political dialects and accents. Understood through an analysis of its matrix of religious myth, doctrine, and experience, it is certainly no ad hoc mix designed for just the current issue or listener. It is coherent and consistent. But it is not derived simply from *crente* doctrine and myth — even if analysis of it does help map a fairly distinctive *crente* range in the relationships between political voice, religious vision, and experience. All *crentes* of the Assembly of God in Campo Alegre share Severino's myths of Creation, the Fall, and salvation, and his theodicy and stories defining relationships between the human and the Divine in the present world. But the myths are variously emphasized; ambiguities are evident in contrasting doctrinal interpretations; and myth and doctrine meet under different experiential circumstances.

From these differences arise marked divergences in political voice. Some Assembly *crentes* emphasize the myth of the Fall and deemphasize the salvation stories of heroes in this world. Telling their own stories of corruption or suffering in the political arena, some *crentes* eschew all political dialects as best they can, talk the quiet tongue of religious tribe, and try to venture as little as possible from the unambiguous world of the temple.

At the other extreme, a very few *crentes* emphasize even more than Severino the doctrine that worthiness includes striving to anticipate the just moral order in one's own personal world. From experience in local collective action — in challenging local power-holders believed to be acting immorally — they have come to speak the communitarian dialect more clearly and more self-consciously than Severino does. With this range, some further introductions are needed, before we can weigh the issue of a distinctive *crente* contribution to the shaping of political voice and the definition of political ethos in Campo Alegre.

TERESA AND ZÉ

Like Severino, Teresa first impresses one with her energy. She is herself conscious of possessing *força* (drive), and she considers it a gift from God that she has cultivated. She is forthright and vivid on the wide range of topics she addresses: the uncontrolled rapacity of the rich Goliaths who have pushed her off the land; the uneducated rudeness of some of the teachers at her children's school; the economics of running a household of eight on one minimum salary of $75 a month; the evils of drunkenness and devil-worship in the lives of her neighbors. Her very mode of speaking exudes energy. She speaks rapidly, her whole body moves with her words, her eyes open wide with alternating laughter and indignation. She is constantly on the move — out gathering wood, shopping for cheap stale bread at the bakeries, helping to nurse sick friends or her own children, coordinating the errant energies of her brood in the family's struggle for survival; or in talk. But there is control and religious focus in all the motion. She and her husband, Zé, claim that while doing other things they also "do the Lord's work through the day, singing hymns silently, praying, thinking."[3] The energy that impresses is not only physical but reflective.

This energy of a whole personality is the more impressive perhaps, because, to an outsider reading her circumstances from her prematurely aged frame, her ragged clothing, her unrendered mud hut, lassitude and the dullness of resignation is to be expected. Much of the detail of her life-story enhances that expectation. She was born into an agricultural laborer's family, and schooling was never considered a possibility. From childhood she was an agricultural laborer too. Like Severino, before and after marriage, she had to move from place to place as the heads of her families would lose a *sítio* and have to find another. When my wife traced out where she had moved on a map of the state, Teresa observed, "My life has made a snake." The loss of a small plot on the large estate on the northern boundary of the town in 1976 was a disaster. The family had been pushed right to the edge of the sea and, it seemed, there was no more land available. Now they would have to rely on Zé's salary as a cleaner in a nearby factory — but even that was in doubt because Zé was going blind in one eye as a result of an accident at work. Illness was a constant problem in the family: the eldest daughter had to receive treatment for epileptic fits; Teresa herself has twice been near death in recent years, the last time with kidney failure. And then there are the problems of daily life in a neighborhood where petty squabbles and real violence are rife.

In counterpoint to these details of poverty and impoverishment, however, are Teresa's mode of telling her story and the themes she sees in it.

The stories are never told with pathos but always with vigor and a certain pride that, with God's help, a life of inner peace and fidelity has been constructed in the midst of harsh trials. As storyteller, Teresa is no less persuasive than Severino; but she is less inclined to link her story to a cosmic theme, through statement of doctrine, and more inclined simply to locate her experience as episodes in the larger story of salvation history. The great myths not only lend meaning to autobiography but also provide *força* for confronting the disasters of her life. As a corollary, it is necessary to turn to autobiography to reconstruct Teresa's religious vision. Extracts from her telling of her own problems on the land illustrate this point and lead into a comparison of her version of *crente* mythology with Severino's version.

> The Kingdom of God will take all the land at one stroke. In my case it has already happened. God ordained that the land had to have owners. I am here because the land was owned. . . . It is as the Word of God says. . . . You can see that up to now no one was interested in taking land and now everyone has to have his piece of it. Why? Because it is desired by God that it should be that way. It's the will of God. Jesus said that Heaven and Earth may pass away but My word will not pass away. . . . Now I'm telling you what I know in faith, which is pure and a gift from God. Now God didn't leave the land to sell to anybody. But now this man looks after this bit and another looks after another bit. That's how it is. The world is compressing, compressing, compressing [*apertando*]. And we came from the interior and arrived here and that's how it is here. Thus everything is trampled. The poor are below and the rich are on top. The old beat their breasts, the people of the backlands are silenced. Because only God is God, so nobody has any place to run. For what has happened is the fulfillment of the word of God and no one can run away from it . . . just as Jesus said. So now all the land has a name on it — of this person and that. God left the land for all the inhabitants of the earth. But there are many who have taken it all for themselves. So here we are. And just as light and darkness are opposed, and as the night doesn't mix with the day, and as the moon is splendid in the night and nothing in the day — so it is with rich and poor. They collide and repel one another. The rich man won't control himself, and the poor, with nothing, have to conform. That's how it is, even if God is the owner of the earth. That's how it was with Dives and Lazarus [she tells the story]. . . . That's why it's more difficult for a rich man to enter into the Kingdom of Heaven than for a camel to pass through the eye of a needle. And the rich are like Dives, the poor like Lazarus, and justice will come only after Christ comes.

Here Teresa's Creation myth differs from Severino's on a point of detail. God himself institutes ownership. Even unequal ownership and exclusion of the poor from ownership, in a world that is *apertando*, are a part of God's mysterious plan. I asked Teresa and Zé about the origin of the difference between rich and poor. Their responses made clear their belief that the hierarchy of material riches was created by God. To be rich is to have received a gift from God, even though the gift entails temptations few of the rich are able to resist. Even though there is a distinction between God's absolute law and the law that is flexible in the hands of rich people's lawyers, the latter is also part of the order created by God.

The difference in detail, in concert with other myths and beliefs, entails an acceptance more total than Severino's in the face of recognized injustice. The world's inequalities and attendant injustices are not only intractable, they are also a part of God's Creation, part of what the *crente* must conform to as a test of obedience and patience if he is to be faithful to the Creator. Teresa's Creation myth leaves no territory wherein recognized injustice must be righted by the just person. In the struggle for salvation, the field of battle must be the self. The battle is between the spirit, which tends to rise to God, and the flesh, "which pulls toward the ground." The material world is presented by God to humans as a sort of obstacle course in which the spirit triumphs or is defeated according to success or failure in the practice of the supreme virtues taught by God and revealed in the person of Jesus: obedience, patience, and control. Severino's myth, stressing the human creation of unjust institutions, allowed at least a local territory in which the individual was called upon to defeat injustice. Teresa's myth enjoins withdrawal, though not silence or a limp waiting for the Lord. She is passive only from the perspective of the political activist.

The link between Creation myth and selective emphasis within the range of *crente* beliefs emerges in the reasons Teresa gave for not making an issue of her most recent expulsion from the land. One reason derives directly from her myth of God as Creator and Planner. To lose land, whatever the precise circumstances, is to experience the *apertando* that is part of God's plan. That process, in which less and less land is available to the poor, is essentially irresistible, and even though the poor *crente* must proclaim any wrongdoing on the part of the landowner or the authorities, the major moral task is to confront the consequences of expulsion with patience, self-control, and obedience to God's law. A second reason is that to make an issue, especially with a landowner who has shown that he is violent and ruthless, is to risk losing self-control, to risk turning to animal violence oneself. Teresa explained that had she tried to stay, the landowner would have bulldozed her crop (as he did to others). She could not bear to see the fruit of her work be destroyed like that; she would have lost control. And thus she would have failed the God-given trial. A third reason is related. To make an issue is not only to risk compromising a key virtue but also to turn aside from the mission that should be all-absorbing, which is to subjugate the flesh and fill one's life with the hymns, the prayers, the duties, the works of love, the experiences of the Lord that free the spirit for its ascent to God. In the economy of a person's time, social protest or action in the political sphere, even against an unjust landowner, is time taken from godly activity.

By comparison, Severino's religious vision allows that a greater proportion of this-worldly, local activity should be counted as godly. Teresa is more unequivocally in the Holiness stream of the Assembly of God. Like Severino, Teresa religiously identifies the injustices she and her neighbors have suffered. Her religious myths inform her critical identifications: the landowner is Goliath, the landowners as a group are Philistines, she is the young David. But her construction of myth and doctrine, together with her assessment of her lack of resources for engaging in conflict, convince her not to make an issue. The only course of action that makes practical as well as moral sense is construction of a world apart within oneself and around one's church.

Remembering and recounting their conversion stories is more important to Teresa and Zé than it is to Severino. They like to recall "that commotion in the heart" before receiving baptism of the Holy Spirit. They dwell on "that happiness that is the reward of praying in church," and they lament that I am ineligible for the experience. Both rejoice in the knowledge that comes from the Holy Spirit directly when praying with others in church, and they make a point of devaluing mere human knowledge, the knowledge that comes from books. Valuing these experiences of inner and church worlds apart, they construct their social relationships and measure their time to maximize their apartness, their chances of contact with God's love and power and their avoidance of worldly corruption. Through visiting, mutual help, and assistance at church services, they construct a fairly exclusive confessional network of social relationships. They impress their children with the dangers of socializing with non-*crentes* and guide them appropriately. They self-consciously fill time, even working time, with hymns, to tune out the distractions of the world, the anxieties it provokes, its temptations. Through one of her favorite hymns, which she wanted me to record, Teresa defines for herself that other world for which she prepares:

> In the beautiful sky one day I saw my Lord.
> I heard the holy melody that they sing in His praise.
> Thus will I be happy among the redeemed,
> And to Him I will speak my joy unendingly.
> Because there in Heaven there will be no lamentations,
> And Heaven will be a place of glory for me.
> There I will intone a holy hymn
> Of exaltation to the name of Jesus.

Because in Heaven my name is written,
And Heaven will be a place of glory for me.
In beautiful Heaven I will have my friends,
And I will be with my brothers and sisters also.
Without any more fear, sadness, and danger,
I will be happy in the world beyond.
Then I will be a shining angel,
And I will live there forever.
For in Heaven joy is permanent,
And Heaven will be a place of glory for me.

Teresa — continually forced to move on, clothed in rags, unable to write her name in any book, living in the midst of fear, sadness, and danger — prepares and moves toward her alternative world with energy and will. She works hard in this world that she might anticipate and thus merit that better world.

Just as her exacting God makes colossal demands on her, so she makes the demand of strict obedience on her children, whom God has entrusted to her care. She believes that she is called to show the love and joy that comes to those who accept salvation, and she is happy when people ask her why she is smiling and untroubled. But love and joy, she says, come only to the obedient. And love itself demands obedience. The chronic disobedience of Teresa's eldest daughter led Teresa and Zé to decide that she had opted for the world. Zé, with Teresa's backing, refused to put forward his daughter for baptism into the Assembly. Both parents believe, with deep grief, that their decision has been proved correct by her subsequent experiences. She ran away from home with a man who abandoned her pregnant; then she nearly died after a backyard abortion. Such are the wages of disobedience and opting for the world as Teresa and Zé see it.

Talking of God and family, Teresa and Zé seem to speak the authoritarian dialect even more fluently and forcefully than Severino does. It seems they might be easily mobilized in support of authoritarian politics, by anyone using the appropriate images (the father of the state like the father of the family like God the Father). But that is only a guess. Neither Teresa nor Zé could be drawn into explicit political discussion. By conviction and interest they are resolutely apolitical.

It would be difficult for any party or movement acting in the political arena to mobilize Teresa for participation or support. She is not to be seduced by calls to worldly success any more than is Severino; but she is also less committed to central order. Like Severino, she energetically identifies injustice among other immoralities; but myth, doctrine, and experience lead her to deploy that energy away from even the local communal involvements of Severino. Her immense energies are directed to constructing a small world different and necessarily apart from the mess that she calls the world of flesh. She works to turn herself, her family, and her neighboring co-religionists to the themes of the hymns of the Assembly of God. In that work, she excludes herself from the wider engagements of Severino: she is further than he is from communication with the communitarian stream among local Catholics. Yet within the tight boundaries she draws around her alternative world, she fulfills the communitarian ideals: she shares her meager resources generously, inspires her chosen friends with her cheer and informed indignation, and communicates hope through her own success in surviving with dignity and decency against crushing odds.

VALDO AND MADALENA

Severino, Teresa, and Zé do not complete the array of *crente* types in Campo Alegre. Another couple, Valdo and Madalena, are briefly introduced here because they are much more churchy than the other three; and this in two senses. Compared to Severino, they are at the opposite end of a range: from noninvolvement in the organized church to near-professional absorption. Compared to Teresa, they (especially Valdo) express themselves more through their church dogma than through elaborated myths and images of Pentecostal belief. Through them we may see something of the transformation of the Assembly of God itself: from a sect (a small group without a pastor gathering in a tiny house) to a church (with its temple and quite elaborate organizational structure).

Valdo and Madalena are also much further than Severino, Teresa, and Zé from absolute poverty. Valdo is a young, skilled factory worker, on a low wage but able to provide regular and adequate food, housing, and clothing for his family. He was able to buy his wife an electric sewing machine, so she can take in sewing for extra money. However, he and his extended family are not without problems in what they refer to as "the material life"; and Valdo's address to these problems recalls much of Teresa and Zé's response to their loss of land.

Valdo is frequently ill. He suffered a terrible injury in a factory accident three years before my first conversations with him in 1977, and he has never fully recovered. He did not receive compensation from the factory, though his friends and relatives thought him legally entitled to it. He decided not to *fazer questão* of the matter, and he stresses the importance of his regular wage. When I first met him, he was more worried about the problems of members of his extended family: his brother-in-law, expecting a child and chronically unemployed, his aging parents facing expulsion from the house and land just outside the town where they had lived and worked for a lifetime.

It was difficult to draw him out on these problems. He conceived of them as private troubles, certainly not worth talking about as public issues. Like many *crentes*, he refers frequently to life as *a vida passageira* (the passing life of trial) in which we are, above all else, bound to remain faithful in our acceptance of the salvation won for us by Christ against the powers of darkness. Only within the context of that vision — of Christ offering and requiring and Satan tempting and undoing — will Valdo refer to his troubles. Troubles take on importance only as trials in the cosmic struggle, with their meaning to be found in doctrine and Biblical text.[4]

Like Teresa and Zé, Valdo contrasts the community of the church with the evils and corruptions of the everyday world. Unlike them, he is fond of court and classroom images to express the contrast. God watches us; and all is recorded in the Book of Life, from which we are judged, with Christ acting as our defense lawyer. God expects discipline from us, like a good teacher; for without disciplined obedience we fail to understand what He wants of us. Doctrine and experience in the world point to life in the church as the only way to lead a defensible and disciplined life. That means for Valdo and his family (to a degree much greater than for Teresa and Zé), deep involvement in the organized life of the church. (Figure 1 provides some measure of how fully Valdo and Madalena block out their lives with organized religious activities, though the hymn singing between times is not recorded.)

Valdo's work, including travel time, keeps him away from church activities for twelve hours a day from Monday to Friday and for six hours on Saturdays. But even in his leisure time, which he spends almost invariably with the extended family, the church is never far away. All members of the family (except Valdo's father, who remains a taciturn non-practising Catholic) are active members of the Assembly. Valdo's mother, who dates change in Campo Alegre to the days when she saw the bridge being built, became a Baptist in her twenties and then, as a mother with six children, switched to the Assembly, taking her children with her. It is not only God who watches with a judging eye over her now adult children. They gather around her as often as possible, talking frequently about church matters and singing favorite hymns.

Extended family leading to church and the church itself constitute Valdo and Madalena's social life. Doctrine and Biblical cosmology require that the boundaries around that life be preserved and strengthened. Only within those boundaries might life's trials be coped with and passed through. To make an issue (or, more senselessly, a political issue) is to breach the

	Morning	Afternoon	Evening
Sunday	10.30–12.30 Sunday school	Two Sundays a month: youth group prayers or visits to the sick	Main public service 7.00–9.30 PM
Monday	Youth group prayer in temple 8.00–10.00 AM (Madalena only)	House visit to the sick (Madalena only)	Closed-door prayer meeting in temple 7.00–9.00 PM
Tuesday		Bible teaching for women (Madalena only) 2.00–4.00 PM	Choir practice 7.00–9.00 PM
Wednesday		Closed-door prayer meeting (this goes on all day but Madalena usually chooses 2.00–4.00 PM)	Congregation meeting in private home 7.00–9.00 PM
Thursday	8.00–10.00 AM Campaign of Adoration (testimonies, prayers, hymns)	Visits to the sick 2.00–4.00 PM	Instruction and, once a month, Holy Supper 7.00–9.00 PM
Friday			Preparation for Sunday-school teachers
Saturday		Sometimes, Adoration with group for children	

Figure 1. Valdo and Madalena's organized religious activities

boundaries and enter the world where Satan holds sway. Valdo, unlike Severino, does not feel drawn to take action against even local injustice.

He does, however, feel able to criticize the folly and moral danger of his father's attachment to the old politics of the days of the patrons and the old religion of the brotherhood. He criticizes his father's preferences and links the Catholic fiestas with moral aberrations and idolatry, saying what a waste of time it is to find and court patrons and what a fruitless thing to lament for town life as it was. So he has no time for his father's religion of place and the politics of *coronelismo* that went with the place. His attention is fixed on the end of time, his own and the world's, and the maneuvers and blandishments of politicians in his own day are unworthy of attention. Unlike Severino, Valdo offers no positive (even if qualified) endorsement of the military regime; but he does see much to criticize in participatory democracy. We may be sure that Valdo would approve of any authoritarian regime that, embarking on a moral crusade, was willing to crack down on brothels, dance halls, and the sale of alcoholic liquor. But he left me only with an informed guess that, in general, he preferred the military regime to any alternative.

A number of themes about God and the world recurred throughout our long interviews. Valdo's God is stern, exigent, even punitive. The Bible stories he emphasizes, when I try to explore injustice and suffering in the world, are the stories of human infidelity and disobedience followed by God's punishment. My examples of injustice and suffering are located easily in the familiar vista of the stories. The sufferings of a group or even of a whole people are preceded, as in the case of the Israelites, by the group's abandonment of God and his laws. Injustice, domination by enemies, and slavery are the wages of a disobedient people. Valdo returns constantly to the Flood and the subsequent vicissitudes of the Israelites as images of God's retribution. Injustice is God's punishment and proceeds from the moral corruption that is disobedience to God's law. The individual suffering injustice must regard it as a test to be passed—a test of obedience and fidelity to God, and one among the tests of temptation that come constantly from the world controlled by Satan. The correct response to injustice and suffering is obvious to Valdo. For individuals, it is to deny the world, to live in faith and obedience, and to prepare for the better life that is the reward for obedience. For groups and whole nations, moral reform is necessary, but that is achieved only when individuals are obedient to God's moral precepts as defined in the Ten Commandments.

For individuals who do not reform, the punishment may be in this life but also most certainly in the next, in "the lake of fire." For disobedient societies, war is the likely and ultimate punishment, as it was for the Israelites. God is an "exacting Father" as well as a stern Teacher. Valdo considers His severity necessary, not only because of human weakness but because of the state of war between "the dominion of the Prince of Darkness" and "Jesus, the light of the world." Satan puts the desire for things that destroy—drugs, prostitution—into the minds of men. God, to save us, shows us how to reject "all impurities, which is to say, the world." But that requires of us the loyalty and obedience we give to the Father who protects and the Teacher who shows the way.

God is Father and Teacher. In the person of the Son, says Valdo, he is also Lawyer, our advocate before the Father, who will argue on the basis of what is recorded in the Book of Life that our obedience and fidelity have exceeded our transgressions and failures. These images of God as traditional father, teacher, and lawyer, in Valdo's own use of them, not only identify the God that he reveres but allow God to bestow His blessings upon traditional family roles and a social order based on professional expertise. Valdo, much more easily than Severino, allows God's approval of earthly social arrangements, reflecting this in his metaphors and similes for illumination of the sacred realm.

Valdo is also far from Severino, and nearer to Zé and Teresa, in his conception of the hierarchy of riches as created and blessed by God. Just as God chose not to create each of our fingers of equal length, so He chose to distribute the gift of riches unequally. "Rich people must thank God for being rich. So also the poor man thanks God because everything conforms to the will of God." Valdo makes a distinction that Severino raises but rejects as invalid: on the one hand, there are the hierarchies of the worldly order ordained by God to which we must conform; on the other, there is Satan's world of individual immorality. It is Satan's world from which the sufferings of the poor arise and that is the world the *crente* is concerned to resist. Inequalities of color and wealth neither are themselves a source of suffering nor, as ordained by God, can they be a source of concern to *crentes*.

Valdo's variations on *crente* images and myths attune his ear to the claims of bureaucratic and authoritarian Brazil. God (through Valdo's images of Him as professional expert) canonizes the claims of professional expertise. The sacred panorama of God and Satan, locked in battle in a world at war, seems to inform respect for claims to wage military war against worldly corruption, including the corruptions of civilian politics. God's authorship of inequality and His requirement of acceptance of the tests of place prepare Valdo for compliant, patient citizenship in an authoritarian regime. But his compliance is passive: if his images of God and salvation history lend plausibility to the claims of authoritarian expertise, they also rank the concerns of governments and leaders of the state as second order.

Liberation, security, peace — all the concerns that any government might seek legitimacy in serving — are won or lost in the battle against sin. The Israelites lost these things when they worshiped false Gods and broke other Commandments. Jesus won these things for us in rejecting the world, as He did when tempted by Satan, and when He allowed Himself to be crucified. We attain what He won by following His rules and prescriptions for rejection of the world. In the face of our troubles and sufferings we must be *manso* (tame, gentle); in the cause of morality we are called to heroism, like Jesus. The heroic turning aside from the world is achieved in our life in the church. It is in church life that liberation, security, peace, and salvation are won — not in political activity, which turns us back into the world. And so, for Valdo and other more-church-centered *crentes*, citizenship as an individual is, in effect, less important than citizenship through membership of the church. This (as we shall see) has important implications for the politics of the more churchy members of the Assembly of God.

Before we set out from the cases presented in this chapter toward a more complete identification of the political voices of *crentes*, we must examine the life of the church itself. Valdo and Madalena, and other *crentes* who are not so church centered, can be appreciated as citizens only if we examine the reality constituted by Assembly church rituals and the politics enacted in the structures of Assembly.

CHAPTER FOUR

The Assembly of God

RITUALS OF CHURCH AND SECT

EVERY SUNDAY EVENING at eight o'clock, the Assembly of God in Campo Alegre is on display for its members. It is also on display for outsiders who might be attracted in. The door and windows of the temple are open, and external loudspeakers broadcast hymns, testimonies, and announcements to the square outside and the streets beyond. This is not the only ritual gathering of the Assembly of God. There are *congregações* (house-meetings), Sunday-school meetings, monthly Holy Suppers, and closed-door prayer sessions for full members of the church. These other gatherings contain their own messages about the *crentes'* cultural paradigms, and there are tensions within the Assembly of God community that are expressed in contrasting themes in the different rituals. The public Sunday *culto* (worship) displays some of these tensions, but at the same time it expresses themes that run through all the rituals.

By eight o'clock about two hundred *crentes* and a few visitors come from the darkness into the bright blue light of the temple. Some visitors remain outside, looking in through the windows and the main door. All who come inside know where to place themselves. Ten or so men, most of them in suits, move to benches close to the *tribuno* (podium), where some will be called to take a place with the pastor or deacon in charge of the *culto*. In all, there are about sixty adult men. Most of them are in a group on benches in the back half of the temple, neatly dressed, but few of them in suits. About seventy children, some as young as eight and the oldest perhaps twelve, occupy the benches in front of the podium; about twenty of them are grouped as the children's choir, many of them groomed and dressed for this special occasion. The one hundred twenty women go to various places—a few to the instrumental group and its choir, its thirty-five members located on benches arranged out from the wall to the left of the *tribuno;* more to the main choir, its fifty members facing in toward the instrumentalists from the wall to the right of the *tribuno;* other women, without a place in these groups, sit together in a central block of benches in the back half of the temple, separated from the men by aisles. The women are variously but conservatively dressed: a simple full cotton dress, white or of some sober color, is the favored mode.

It is an ordered and organized congregation that faces the *tribuno,* the electric clock, and (above a side entrance) the idyllic river scene in the mural behind the *tribuno.* The temple is indeed a *sala* (a grand room for public exchanges), of the size and with the furnishings of other *salas* like the courtroom, the mayor's chamber, or the office of the factory director. And like those other *salas,* it has its chief officer. Time and place have been measured out (various activities are timed by the clock and space is carefully allocated to various statuses — men, women, children, deacons, elders, choirs) as the evangelizer of Campo Alegre or a deacon takes up his role as master of ceremonies for the evening and names a hymn, often the old favorite "Come, Come, Come, Come, to the Assembly of God." The singing is harsh and strong. But as soon as the many verses are completed, there is so much talk that the leader has to call for attention, with the aid of a handbell on the lectern. Some Sundays — when he has not ordered the program well, there is nothing special on, or the testimonies are dull — he must use the bell often. More usually even the children quieten down as the whole congregation becomes involved in a fine performance from the choir or a moving testimony to God's power and concern. Then members of the congregation cry out "Praised be the Lord . . . thanks be to God," and this noise tells the leader that, thank the Lord, the Spirit is moving His people tonight.

Hoping in the Spirit, the leader nevertheless has a routine structure to follow. After initial hymns and a welcome to visitors, he or a deacon will read from sacred scripture. Then, having offered a short prayer on the scripture theme, the leader will either lead the congregation in collective prayer or call on another senior member, perhaps a visitor from another Assembly, to do so. Standing, with raised right arm, each and every member of the congregation prays aloud as the Spirit moves, for four or five minutes. One protests sorrow and hope to Our Lord; another repeats mantras of praise. An avalanche of prayer seems to carry everyone.

There follow six to ten individual testimonies interspersed with performances of the choirs. Often there will be an anniversary to celebrate — the foundation of the youth group, for example — marked with a special performance of individuals or groups singing or a series of special testimonies related to the occasion. At the end of the *culto,* the leader will

9. At a Sunday evening *culto* of the Assembly of God. A uniformed band is visiting from another town.

preach a sort of résumé sermon, picking up a theme from a scripture reading or a testimony and finishing up with an appeal for converts of the evening to come forward. Should someone approach the *tribuno*, the evangelizer will ask all to pray with him as he or a deacon places his hands on the head of the one who has come to acknowledge salvation in the Lord. Quite often there is nobody, and the *culto* ends rapidly with a final hymn. The *crentes* disperse in small groups to their homes, scattered throughout the town.

In content, as in form, there is much routine and repetition in the *culto*. Most testimonies are impersonal and formulaic: there was a time before, a life of sin with the unhappy wages of sin for self and family; there has been an acceptance of God's saving invitation; and now, confident in God's mercy and His power and watchfulness over me as demonstrated in my life, I am happier and better able to cope with life's problems. You too, by resisting the world and answering God's call, might have your obedience recorded in the Book of Life, and you will be protected on your course through life by the all-powerful King of Kings. Most of the nearly two hundred testimonies I have heard follow the sequence and content of this synthesis. Sometimes there is more elaboration of the before or the after; or there is less salvation story and more exhortation. But these are minor variations on constant themes.

Longer sermons by the evangelizer or visiting preachers are often extended testimonies. But they display a fuller range of *crente* beliefs and the images connecting them. Power is an insistent theme in sermons; the constant focus is God, omnipotent but merciful, who works miracles for those who accept His Word. In all the *cultos* I attended in Campo Alegre in 1977, the text that drew the most enthusiastic response was Psalm 103. The sermon following merely filled out with local stories its images of God's power reversing human adversity.

> Bless Yahweh, my soul,
> and remember all His kindnesses:
> in forgiving your offenses,
> in curing all your diseases,
> in redeeming your life from the pit,
> in crowning you with love and tenderness,
> in filling your years with prosperity,
> in renewing your youth like an eagle's,
> Yahweh, who does what is right,
> is always on the side of the oppressed;
> He revealed his intentions to Moses,
> His prowess to the sons of Israel. . . .
> He never treats us, never punishes us,
> as our guilt and our sins deserve.

And then the verse repeats again and again throughout the evening: "No less than the height of Heaven over earth / is the greatness of His love for those who fear Him."

The corollary of the all-powerful, merciful God in sermon, testimony, and hymn is the weak human individual, unable to control animal passions within or the assailing temptations of the world without, unless through the strength and protection offered by God. If most sermons emphasize how beautiful life can be in the security of faith, the counterpoint ground bass is never far from hearing: *precipitação* (rashness), pride, blindness to God's marvels, backsliding, and despair are endemic to the human condition, so constant vigilance is necessary.

That conclusion joins another great theme of the *culto:* that life in the church is the guarantee of vigilance. Life in the church reminds us constantly of what is expected of us and shows us what God will achieve for His people who remain vigilant in the church. The *culto,* together with the Sunday school, emphasizes this theme more than other Assembly of God rituals. It is a theme expressed as much in the action and sound of the *culto* itself as in explicit verbal message.

Indeed all the themes are enacted, expressed choreographically in the *culto*. And it is through dramatic enactment that the potential dullness of a reiterated message and a set program can be avoided. The *culto* must be described not only in terms of its verbalized messages but also in the terms that *crentes* themselves use to evaluate *cultos* in general and any particular *culto*: as experience of God's power, of human salvation, and (most especially) of God's church.

The special *culto*, at which a young Brazilian missionary from Venezuela is going to speak, goes well from the beginning. The temple is filled to overflowing early. Six cars are parked in the square outside, and the men who came in them have taken seats on the *tribuno*. One of them, a tall handsome man in a beautifully tailored suit, is pointed out as the missionary, seated next to Pastor Moisés, the senior pastor for the whole region. The missionary's wife (who, they say, speaks only Spanish) is on a bench in front with her children. She is very beautiful and dressed in a style and colors that *crente* women over thirty in Campo Alegre would disapprove of, were their visitor not a foreigner and clearly such a good *crente* wife. The children are dressed in expensive clothes and are well behaved. All this has been noted and discussed by the time the first hymn begins.

Perhaps because there are more voices or because this is a special occasion, the opening hymn is louder and unusually punctuated with "Amen" and "Praise be the Lord." Pastor Moisés takes over as leader (his old mother was converted from Presbyterianism to the new Assembly by one of the founders, back in the twenties in Belém). He starts out with the customary welcomes and calls on a young woman from his church who has written a book of prayers and meditations to give testimony. She speaks of her conversion through an introduction to the Bible and of the changes the Bible has worked in her life. Her voice rises as she thanks God for the gift of the Bible. She chokes with emotion as she repeats that the Bible has brought her to Jesus and Jesus has brought her happiness in the knowledge of her salvation. There are shouts of praise as she finishes giving thanks.

The young missionary translates as his wife speaks briefly about the growth of the Assembly in Venezuela. There is silence before this beauty from another world. Then he speaks. Now he is a racy raconteur outlining the adventures of his mission from the time when he was instructed in a dream to turn down a lucrative executive position to become a missionary. He tells of the miracles needed to negotiate financial and bureaucratic hurdles on the way to Venezuela. His anecdotes illustrate the eventual material and spiritual success that God bestowed upon him in response to his living with faith.

10. The evangelizer, at the microphone, leads a moment of enthusiastic prayer from the *tribuno*.

Now he changes voice and gesture to the confessional mode as he communicates how his own faith grew as God's blessings showered on him — good food, clothes from the start, then, on the occasion of his marriage, the president of the republic provides a lavish reception and honeymoon and sends a silver tea pot. He takes off his glasses to wipe his eyes as he relives the emotion of his gratitude to the Lord. Tears run down the battered face of Alfonso, one of Campo Alegre's three most senior deacons. Two weeks ago the back of his mud hut collapsed after the rain, injuring his pregnant wife. The family do not survive well on his pension and her sewing. "But in the Lord's time the Lord blesses,"[1] perhaps with the abundance bestowed upon the missionary from Venezuela.

Now the missionary turns to exhortation. There need not be hunger and suffering. God provides for those who have the courage to accept him as Savior. Believe in the Bible and follow its messages. Don't be cowardly . . . (the word *covardia* [cowardice] is repeated; the exhortation is delivered with great emotion and received emotionally). . . . Might not even our local evangelizer be cowardly in not proclaiming the message of the Bible? We are all tempted to *covardia* . . . (the missionary emphasizes the word with a loud slap on the lectern and there are many groans of agreement) . . . but God will fill us with His *força* if we allow Him entrance into our hearts.

The high emotional pitch is maintained for over an hour of sermon. Then Pastor Moisés takes over and maintains the sorrow and hope as he offers thanks for the love and strength that God is bringing us. He leads the congregation into prayer. The *força* of each becomes the church's roar of praise and supplication. Pastor Moisés himself emerges from prayer to exhort those who have heard and seen to declare for Jesus Christ. The congregation shouts support for his pleas. Two women near the back of the *templo* signal, a little hesitantly, their conversion. Moisés urges them forward and, with microphone in hand, comes down from the *tribuno* to pray over those who are prepared to set out on their journey into the church. The area beneath the *tribuno* becomes a dramatic tableau. The two women are kneeling. Each is embraced by women who have come forward as sponsors. Pastor Moisés stands in front of them, one hand raised high, his body angled as though he were suspended by the hand, as he prays over the women. The roar of prayer gathers again. A teenage girl and then a teenage boy come forward.

And then a real miracle happens. Another young man comes up from the back of the *templo*. The young man is the prodigal son of Campo Alegre's evangelizer, who has come back this very night to his family and his church. His father comes down from the *tribuno,* his mother comes over from her place in the choir and embraces him. The sobbing of the family is echoed throughout the congregation. The Lord who is so plainly with us is praised and His name glorified. The meeting ends quite suddenly with a prayer of thanks from Pastor Moisés. I walk back with neighbors who are happily exhausted and grateful for what they have been part of.

Pastor Moisés is even more central, and the Assembly of God as organized church even more triumphantly enacted, in the second special *culto* of 1977. It takes place in the large central temple of the region, in a town midway between Campo Alegre and Recife. The special *culto* is to celebrate the end of a week of study in which pastors, evangelists, deacons, and senior members of congregations from all over the region have taken part. The temple can only just hold the six hundred faithful who crowd in. Officials of the church are seated together in a large elevated area around the *tribuno;* they are joined by about twenty dignitaries—town councillors, a couple of military brass, the manager of a large new local factory, a visiting sociologist from Australia (the author). About a third of the congregation has some role in the service—a choir of sixty from one town; a blue-uniformed male band from another; a female band from the home church, each of the thirty members in a white dress and a white jacket over a golden blouse.

Pastor Moisés calls on the pastors or evangelizers of each temple in the region to give testimony. Then he preaches, modulating his voice from whispered assurance to shouts of exhortation and triumph. The church-triumphant theme dominates. Pastor Moisés takes off from a hymn, sung by a special choir, about the founding of the Assembly in Belém in 1919. He points to his mother, seated with the dignitaries, as the link with the beginning. And he recounts the story of the church's growth in the region. Groans of anguish accompany his stories and images of the trials of early days — crentes dismissed from jobs because they owned up to being crentes; politicians listening to priests and preventing the establishment of temples. But then the times to be greeted with Alleluias — over twelve thousand members of the Assembly, baptized and with certificates; a regional Assembly school; temples where the Catholics now have nothing — "Alleluia! Alleluia!" The congregation seems hardly to need telling at the end that triumph is confirmed when a young woman and two children answer the call.

Not all the cultos are as triumphal, dramatic, inspiring, or rewarding as these two examples clearly were. Sometimes the routine program and the reiteration of message seems to leave a congregation flat. But — on the evidence of responses of the moment and recollection days later — many Sunday evening cultos in Campo Alegre do indeed move and motivate and confirm. What is received is not by any means the one crente packet of messages that synthetic description might lead us to expect.

For regularly attending crentes, and especially for the church-centered crentes like Valdo and Madalena, the culto signifies, achieves, and legitimates that church-world-apart, where the crente knows and feels a taking over by God's power and purpose. Valdo, at least, attends every culto he can, not just dutifully but out of a clear sense that in the culto he is what he wants to be. Like Severino, Zé, and Teresa, he views human nature as frail and the world as threatening destruction; and he wishes to be of that otherworld of the all-powerful God and His promised Kingdom. Like Severino, he understands that to be of that otherworld he and his fellow crentes must be homens separados (people apart). Unlike Severino — and rather more than Zé and Teresa — he considers the culto the guarantee and the acme of separateness.

In fact, for Valdo the culto constitutes the reality of separateness. His experience of cultos like the two described confirms his choice of a church-centered way of life. The church triumphant and the testimonies to God's miracles of salvation demonstrate the power of God. Valdo's reaction to the culto in the central regional church shows him engaged by the church-centered symbolism of all open-door Sunday *cultos.* In conversations in 1977, he compared other *cultos* to that great *culto* of the year, noting its demonstration of God leading His people (organized in a secure and respected church) to individual victory over "the forces of darkness and chaos."[2] (Four years after my first interviews with him, Valdo became the evangelizer of the temple on the island connected by bridge to Campo Alegre. He moved, that is, to the very center of life of the organized church.)

The reactions of other *crentes* point to other motifs in the *culto,* as well as to a tension between the *culto* and other rituals of the Assembly of God. For some *crentes,* the high point of the *culto* celebrating the visit of the missionary from Venezuela was that moment when the missionary suggested even the evangelizer of Campo Alegre might be guilty of *covardia.* Other *crentes* dislike the noise and hype of the special *cultos.* And these discussions suggest that although all the *crentes* who attend are attached to the *cultos,* as providing effective signs of the world-of-God-apart, these may include different modes of apartness.

In the two special *cultos* just described, Valdo is engaged by various features: the church's links with and the respectability among elites; God's material rewards for those who devote themselves to His church; the eloquence of star professional churchmen; the organized noise of conviction and triumph. These features of the *cultos* are, for him, signs that the apartness necessary for individual peace and salvation in a dangerous world is achieved in a strong, well-organized church world that confronts and can defend the poor and the weak against the strong and well-organized world of Satan.

But there is another mode of apartness to be engaged in and valued in *cultos.* The *culto* is an assembly of ordinary poor, who, in their testimonies to one another, show God's special concern for them. In the *culto,* one sees how God chooses the illiterate and the marginal to bring His word and manifest His power. In the *culto* one learns from one's inspired peers, not by being shouted at by superiors. The *culto* can be, and is, read by many *crentes* as an achievement of apartness by inversion of the worldly everyday, rather than as a sort of purified duplication of it. As I interpret it, they are engaged by and place value on the *culto* as a set of effective symbols of the Assembly of God as a sect rather than a church. Insofar as they control the *culto* and control the interpretation of it, these *crentes* constitute, in the *culto,* a reality apart from and radically rejecting the non-*crente* experience. In Campo Alegre, however, the extent of control by such *crentes* is problematic, and other rituals become more central.

Zé and Teresa go to *cultos* whenever they can and are at pains to draw attention to the miraculous inversions there to be seen and experienced.

But they are not overly impressed, or entirely comfortable, with the church-triumphant themes that are so important to Valdo. The size and formality of the temple bother them too. They value two other *crente* rituals much more highly than the *culto* — the closed-door prayer meeting and the *congregação*. In the closed-door prayer meeting, the world is literally shut out: the windows of the temples are closed, the main door locked. A smaller number of baptized *crentes* in good standing gather together to pray as the Spirit moves them. The meeting starts and finishes at an appointed time and though, from outside, the sounds of inspired prayer may appear the antithesis of the schooled harmonies of the *culto* choirs, there is a framework of decorum. As now one, now another voice dominates in the flow of prayer, the group produces harmonies more intricate than the choir's.

The *tribuno* is empty and the faithful kneel, resting on the benches with their backs to it. No pastor or evangelizer leads. Decorum and harmony are achieved by the group. As many *crentes* love to tell me (the incorrigibly High Church doctor from the foreign university), the Spirit chooses to speak most frequently and most eloquently through the humblest members of the group. And leadership passes to eloquence. Where, over a year, the same stars are called on to give testimony at the Sunday *culto*, at the closed-door meeting, the prayer of Zé or of Teresa will lead the group to the heights of fervor. In a rising and falling, high-pitched, powerful falsetto, Zé, speaking in tongues, might declare the love and *força* of the Holy Spirit with scarcely a comprehensible word of Portuguese.

Zé and Teresa, and other rank-and-file *crentes* like them, might also lead in the house meeting or *congregação*. On most nights of the week in one or other neighborhood of Campo Alegre, a small group of *crentes* gather in a private house to sing hymns, read passages of the Bible, and give testimony to one another. In many ways the *congregação* meetings are like the Sunday *cultos* writ small: they are often led by a besuited deacon sitting at a table with Bible and clock; the hymns are the old favorites heard on Sundays; the doors are open, and passersby can hear the familiar themes and teaching of the Assembly rather than the exotic sounds of inspired prayer.

But they are small meetings of neighbors in a neighborhood house. Before the *templo* was built this was how the *crentes* assembled; and this was the public form of the Assembly where Severino, Zé, and Teresa joined years ago and in a more rural world. An ordinary *crente* can feel at home and be in control here. Here, Zé reminds me again, one can be confident in the message of Matthew 11:25, "At that time Jesus exclaimed, I bless you, Father, Lord of heaven and of earth, for hiding these things from the learned and the clever and revealing them to mere children."

11. A *congregação* meeting of the Assembly of God is run to the clock but not by the time-keepers of the secular world.

In the *congregação*, and in even greater measure in the closed-door prayer meeting, teaching is inspirational in form and content rather than propositional: leadership passes to inspired Spirit-chosen prophet of the moment rather than to the institutionally designated pastor; the spontaneity of the Spirit rather than the organized church is manifest and glorified; signs of charisma distinguish a brother or a sister rather than a functionary in the organized church. In all these ways, the *congregação* and the prayer meeting allow the Assembly of God to be experienced more as a sect than as a church. It is the experience of sectarian apartness that engages and assures Zé and Teresa. Even Severino, distrustful of the Assembly as a church, remembers with affection the Assembly as a sect.

The Sunday school, as it is now conducted in Campo Alegre, stands in stark contrast to the prayer meeting, as the enactment of the Assembly as church. (It also contrasts with Severino's account of his education in the Assembly nearly forty years ago.) Written on a small blackboard at the *tribuno* end of the *templo* are the vital statistics of the Sunday school for the previous week:

>313 enrolled
>198 present
>24 unenrolled visitors
>116 Bibles brought

Those present are divided up into groups, the children separated from the adults. Each group is assigned a teacher — the evangelizer, one of the deacons, Valdo, the stars of the Sunday culto. Each teacher takes texts, questions, and answers from a primer *Lições biblicas*, issued as a quarterly from the Department of Sunday School from the publishing house of the Assemblies of God in Brazil.

The teachers often have trouble getting the correct answers, and most of them abandon questions and answers for minisermons. At the end, the pastor sums up the theme of the day with a sermon. In the last three months of 1977, when the book of Joshua was being studied, the themes included: (1) The all-powerful God fed six hundred thousand Israelites for forty years as they wandered in the desert; so He can do anything for us, despite what seems to us to be immense problems. (2) The *crente*, faithful and humble, is raised up by God to do His work — as was Joshua after the death of Moses. (3) God wishes to lead us to a life more profound and abundant in the "heavenly places" in Jesus Christ — this is based on the "golden text" of the day, "Joshua said to the people, 'Sanctify yourselves for tomorrow, because tomorrow Yahweh will work wonders among you.'"[3]

Themes celebrated in the Assembly as sect and as church unfold week after week in the Sunday school, but they emerge very much under the auspices of the church. Church officials teach the printed word with the authority designated by church; they dispense the fruits of church organization; they are the teachers, the leaders, the interpreters of the church's formulated doctrine, placed above and correcting the merely inspired. Many *crentes* extol the worth of Sunday school precisely because of its authority; the numbers on the blackboard become part of the data of the church triumphant and a consolation amid the problems of life. Others are cowed by its schoollike features. Teresa, who has never been to school, remains firm in her faith but, legitimately enough, finds she is too busy to attend Sunday school. Severino is not cowed but (as the limiting case sectarian) perceives and distrusts the human apparatus required by the Sunday school. He expects his children to attend but then to grow out of it.

As yet, *crentes* in Campo Alegre do not have to go as far away from church as Severino has done to remain firm in sect engagements and preferences. But the church/sect differences are clear enough and deep enough to entail a sort of multivalence in the relationship between Assembly of God religiosity and politics.

THE POLITICS OF PENTECOSTALISM IN CAMPO ALEGRE

Church-centered Crentes

The religion of church-centered *crentes* in Campo Alegre has what Max Weber called an "elective affinity" with conservative and authoritarian politics in two ways. The first is the institutional. The fortunes of the church triumphant and the social triumph of prominent churchmen become, for Valdo and Madalena, focal guarantees of that *crente* apartness necessary for salvation in Satan's world. Ritual enactments in the *culto* of the Assembly-as-church help establish those guarantees. The ritual celebrates actual relationships with political and economic elites that are established by church leaders like Pastor Moisés and the evangelizer in Campo Alegre. Valdo, Madalena, and other church-centered *crentes* are incorporated into networks of influence and exchange through some (by them) unintended consequences of their ritual-nurtured religious culture.

The extent of the evangelizer's involvement in the government party became clear to me in 1982. Campaigning for the multilevel national elections — especially for the municipal level — was well underway, and the evangelizer was deeply involved. Support for the government party (PDS) was weak in Campo Alegre. Campo Alegrenses supported the opposition party (PMDB) because, among other reasons, the PDS dominated in the municipal seat, and Campo Alegre traditionally asserted its independence by challenging power based in the rival town. But the PDS — which included a faction led by the new landowner, who had expelled farmers from land bordering the town — was anxious to find a mayoral candidate with a chance of winning in Campo Alegre. The evangelizer himself was considered but was ruled out because he was registered as a voter in another town. The local powerbrokers of the PDS thought the ideal candidate would be the owner of one of Campo Alegre's two largest haberdashery and hardware stores (the Assembly of God evangelizer was the owner of the other), Antônio Dos Santos. He had been associated with opposition causes and had been an opposition councillor, but he was disenchanted with the populist wheeling-and-dealing style of the PMDB candidate. He was a close associate of the priest and yet was known and respected in his own right for his political wisdom and as a just businessman of twenty-five years' standing in the town. It was often said of him that he could have been much richer or a really successful politician if he had not been such a good man.

This ideal candidate, however, would need much persuasion to stand. The PDS was not his natural home, and he was disinclined to reenter party politics. So a delegation was formed to approach him. And one of its members was the evangelizer of the Assembly of God. He and Pastor Moisés had become important "influentials" in the PDS, not just in the town but on a regional basis. The delegation failed in its mission — not least because Antônio Dos Santos had been told (by some of the Catholic farmers involved in the struggle with the landowner) that the evangelizer was part of the landowner's network and had advised *crente* farmers who had consulted him not to struggle but to accept nominal compensation for lost crops and livelihood.

From the *tribuno*, the evangelizer never preached directly his conservative politics; nor did he reveal the connections that the triumph of his church required. Some of the guest speakers at the *culto* were not so circumspect. One, a government party councillor from Recife who was also a deacon of the Assembly of God, launched into an attack on the Catholic church for aiding subversion in the name of social justice for farmers and workers. He had undoubtedly been briefed on the situation in Campo Alegre because, as he spoke, he pointed dramatically in the exact position of the Catholic church. "Those in other churches, under the false flag of social justice are trying to rally public opinion behind them . . . they are substituting social justice for the word of the Bible. But social justice is to be found only in accepting the word of God, accepting salvation in Jesus Christ." "*É verdade*" (it's true), shouted one of the senior members of the Campo Alegre church as the councillor leveled his charge.

Unlike the councillor, Valdo is not interested in taking on the Catholic church. But he preaches the same understanding of social justice. And that, it seems to me, predisposes him to accept without question the political orientation of his church as dramatized by the councillor. His panorama of salvation history and his location of his church triumphant – as the necessary means for attaining that apartness from the world that salvation requires – entail that his citizenship be defined by the church. It is in this sense that Valdo's religion has an elective affinity with conservative and authoritarian politics, actually through the mediation of the institutional church that he desires. In this, Valdo is very different from Severino, who will not allow the church to mediate anything on his behalf and who proclaims his type of citizenship clearly and directly.

Valdo's mediating church is indeed the church that he desires, on the basis of his religious vision. And his own understandings of God and Satan, and of the world as a battlefield, make congenial to him the political stance defined for him by his church leaders and through their alliances. In this sense, his church-oriented *crente* religiosity directly elects him to citizenship – albeit a politically passive and inarticulate citizenship – among the bureaucratic authoritarians.

I have tried to summarize some of the different elective tendencies that distinguish Valdo's church version of *crente* faith from Severino's (and even Zé's and Teresa's) more sectarian versions. Teresa, in particular, would caution us about the limitations of all such typologies. The church *crente* returns home from the *culto* reminded of human weakness and the moral perils of everyday life in Satan's world. But the *culto* has also offered consolation: it has demonstrated that, though God tests, he also loves and saves and allows triumph to those who brave the tests and assemble regularly in the safety of the church. So the church *crente* resolves to accept the tests of sickness, or of inadequate return from long hours of hard work, or of loss of land – sure in the hope that God not only records the faithful struggle in the Book of Life but allows victory over sin (and the suffering that arises from sin) in the victories of the church. God – Himself authoritarian Teacher, Lawyer, Father, Doctor, and King – works through the division of labor that is based on the division of His gifts. His church, as it triumphs, purifies and incorporates the structures of unequal wealth, power, and expertise.

So the church *crente* is disposed to accept the idea that social change for the benefit of the poor may be achieved from the top down, through elites sanctioned by the church as free from the corruptions of the world. And just as the church itself manifests and dispenses the *força* – the energy of God necessary to overcome the power of darkness – so the legitimacy of elites is demonstrated by the display of *força* in the elimination of corruption, the enforcement of law, and the completion of development projects. Although the ordinary church *crente* of Campo Alegre will not feel competent or called upon to engage in legitimate politics, she or he will be confident that leading *crentes*, as they contribute to the triumph of the church, are entering into alliances with legitimate power.

Sectarian Crentes

The sectarian *crente* seen in extreme form in Severino, and in a milder form in Zé and Teresa, acknowledges the dangers of the world and the need for a world apart, just as much as the church *crente*. But that world apart is not located in and equated with the organized church. In some ways, the sectarian *crente* is even more confident than the church *crente* of the miracles that God's *força* can achieve in individual believers. To the sectarian, all human organizations and structures are liable to corruption, even a church that assumes a hierarchy of set functions rather than a hierarchy of inspiration. The *crente* might receive inspiration and *força* in Assembly, especially in closed prayer or congregation meetings, but she or he is ultimately alone with life's problems sent to test or to tempt. No organization, not even the church, can mediate the defeat of temptation or the negotiation of the test: the individual, armed with God-given *força* and knowledge of right and wrong, must decide and act for herself or himself. Action may include the challenging of those who are seen to be acting immorally, whatever their position or power. The claims of office, expertise, or wealth are suspect, given the inherent corruptibility of human structures; just authority must be respected but no person in a position of authority should claim obedience or legitimacy except on the basis of moral uprightness; no citizen should accept any authority except on the basis of personal moral scrutiny. When that scrutiny reveals another's wrongdoing as cause of one's own or one's neighbor's troubles, then action may be taken, and others who share both problem and motivation may be enlisted as allies. But action should not be taken for the sake of making an issue, or against the dictates of prudence, or, as Teresa reminds us, at the risk of dropping defenses against Satan and jeopardizing salvation.

Despite these provisos, the sectarian *crente* is clearly not as compliant a citizen in bureaucratic authoritarian Brazil as the church *crente*. The sectarian's distrust of human institutions serves as a barrier against metaphors for the apprehension of God and of His dealings with human beings, which stops the flow of images for interpreting the prevailing social order. Not even the church provides a model that can sanctify structures of expertise or wealth. If the generals or their experts may expect, at best, a cool reception for their claims to hegemony and legitimacy, then populists and paternalistic *coronéis* receive even harsher rejection. Curiously (as Severino's case suggests), it may be the Catholic communalists who come closest to sharing political dialect with the sectarian *crentes.*

(At risk of caricature, some of the differences between sect and church political culture are summarized in Figure 2.)

THE POLITICS OF PENTECOSTALISM IN BRAZIL

This distinction between the politics of church and sect *crentes,* related to basic religious differences, fits in with and helps make sense of interesting ambiguities and conflicts in the literature on Pentecostalism in Brazil. After slow growth from 1910, the Pentecostal movement took off in the fifties. Not all of this occurred in one Pentecostal church, but the Assembly of God is easily the largest of several. By 1980 the Assembly had about three and a half million members; the next largest (according to Rolim), *Brazil para o Cristo* (Brazil for Christ), had about one million; and a variety of smaller groups account for over a million more.[4] By 1990 membership in the Assemblies of God was estimated at eight million; followed by the Christian Congregation with two million;

Elements of political culture	Church	Sect
definition of problems (private troubles or public issues)	private tests from God; not actionable by the individual even at local level	private but actionable against immoral perpetrators of injustice
acceptance of hegemonic ideas	acceptance of inequalities of hierarchy and accredited expert authority	acceptance of moral hierarchy and regard for just authority. But suspicion of the claims of expertise and wealth
responses to claims of legitimacy	criterion of *força* as institutionally manifested	criterion of righteousness as personally witnessed
congenial alliances	with respectable representatives of legitimate institutions as indicated by church	with others struggling against immoral perpetrators of injustice – whether respectable or not

Figure 2. Elements of political culture emerging from the Assembly of God – church and sect tendencies

Brazil para o Cristo with one million; and there was a host of burgeoning newcomers in addition to two older groups with over a quarter million members each. It has been estimated that at the present rate of growth,
there will be over thirty million Pentecostal *crentes* by the turn of the
century.[5]

This spectacular growth provoked speculation and investigation concerning the political consequences of Pentecostalism. One line of interpretation was developed by Emílio Willems, who argues that:

> The organizational pattern of the Pentecostal sects seems to express a protest
> against the Catholic church and its ally, the ruling class. It does so by point-
> edly stressing egalitarianism within the sect and by opposing the Catholic prin-
> ciple of an ecclesiastical hierarchy and a highly specialized priesthood with
> the principles of the privacy of the laity, the priesthood of all believers and
> a self-made charismatic leadership sanctioned by the Holy Spirit. Pentecostal-
> ism thus turns out to be a symbolic subversion of the traditional social order.

Willems argues that the rural migrants who have poured into Brazilian
cities since World War II express their freedom from the constraints of
rural life in Pentecostalism as they form new communities in an anomic
society. As they subvert the old order symbolically and construct their
new communities, Willems suggests they contribute to the growth of a
new, less authoritarian, more democratic, and therefore less upper-class-
dominated Brazil.[6] In their Pentecostal groups, the poor learn to question
hegemonic values, to organize themselves, and to acquire both the skills
of democracy and the confidence to require a more egalitarian order. Political challenge spills over as an unintended consequence from Pentecostal
religious life.

More recently, David Martin, in his review of studies of the Protestant Pentecostal "explosion" in Latin America, has powerfully endorsed
Willems's arguments. In Martin's view, though Pentecostals may appear
apolitical or may vote conservatively, they rehearse, behind sect walls,
values and forms of association that are subversive of an old, centralized,
authoritarian, patron-client order. Hermetically sealed from the corruptions of politics and violent, macho, popular culture, the Pentecostals are
"on strike *from* society."[7] In their world apart they acquire and build a
surrogate family where family has been destroyed and a sense of worth
and achievement otherwise unavailable through peaceable means in the
world outside. Within this obviously attractive free space, millions of Brazilians are acquiring the values, expectations, aspirations, energies, and
disciplines that make them latent carriers of liberal-democratic transformations. Just as Arminian Protestantism in the U.S.A. first anticipated
liberty and deep democracy in the religious sphere, and later protest "moved

from a cultural to a structural expression," so, in Brazil and indeed the whole of Latin America, we may expect from the Pentecostals a move from symbolic challenge to structural challenge of the prevailing order.[8]

Francisco Cartaxo Rolim, who must be regarded as the outstanding Marxist interpreter of Brazilian Pentecostalism over the last decade, disagrees with Willems's interpretation and, it must be expected, with Martin's conclusions.[9] He notes that there are, indeed, symbolic inversions of *crentes'* social experience in Pentecostal ritual and ongoing action. He makes the point in Marxist categories. Each Pentecostal *crente,* of whatever official status in the church, has direct access to the means of religious production. All members are direct producers of their religious goods: regardless of status they are co-producers of their religious world. In a survey of Pentecostals that he conducted in the area of Greater Rio de Janeiro, he found that over 80 percent of *crentes* were, in his terms, "of the lower levels of the petite bourgeoisie" — employed at low levels in a variety of service industries, commerce, and transport. Though preoccupied with security and upward mobility, they are peculiarly dependent and remote from the direct production of goods (compare the proletariat) and from control over the means of production (compare the bourgeoisie). In this sense their control and direct production of religious goods is an inversion of class-structured experience.

But, argues Rolim, in this same sense the religious world of the Pentecostals emerges from the class system and relationships of subordination based on class. And Pentecostals, as they construct their religious world in the social space provided them, cut themselves off from movements for social transformation because they enclose themselves in an exclusively religious world. They become not the independent constructors of an alternative Brazil as conceived by Willems but dependent reproducers of the status quo. They are doubly dependent: their religious consciousness is formed in submission to the established social order, and they are then tied to the interior authority of their sect and congregation. Instead of the spilling over of symbolic inversions into social transformation, as imagined by Willems and later by Martin, Rolim sees a religiously imposed containment of challenge to the prevailing system of class relations.

Rolim is not only our best source on the variety of Pentecostal groups and their genesis, but, dedicated scholar that he is, he assembles much of the evidence that might be used to challenge his conclusions.[10] He remains firm, however, that his conclusions apply to Pentecostalism as a movement, despite cases of individual Pentecostals challenging injustice and oppression. Reviewing the history of Pentecostalism, he concludes that the Brazilian stream — growing out of the white and purely sacral wing of the U.S. Pentecostal movement — has always been a refuge from and an alternative to savagely repressed movements of class struggle. Pentecostalism appealed first to Italian workers in São Paulo who were defeated in their attempts to wage a European-style class struggle in the early years of the century. Now it appeals to the petite bourgeoisie, thwarted in attempts to move upward and discouraged by the repression of working-class movements. Always it diverts its members away from direct political action.

Considering cases, largely from the north and northeast of Brazil, where Pentecostals in rural areas have been engaged in opposition to landowners, Rolim offers two lines of argument. In some cases he believes Pentecostal religiosity (though not the churches) has been involved in protest but has dampened and contained this protest within the confines of a narrow legalism. Along these lines he comments on a case studied by Regina C. Reyes Novaes, in which members of the Assembly of God became engaged in a struggle between rural unions and landowners.[11] In Rolim's view, the *crentes* involved seemed constrained to act only within the very narrow framework allowed them by the law, limited their demands strictly to immediate economic issues, and appeared unable or unwilling to conceive of their actions as class action.

In other cases, he implies that *crentes* have been drawn out of their hermetic religious world by being caught up in social struggle: that *crentes* have indeed become involved or have even assumed leadership in transformative class action, but this *despite* their Pentecostal religiosity. Quite implausibly, in my view, he so interprets the autobiography of the *crente* agitator and political outlaw of Maranhão, Manuel da Conceição.[12] In his own simple account of his struggles, Manuel clearly reveals the sort of dialectic between experience, interpreted experience, and religious culture that we have seen in the case of Severino. Manuel's sense and perception of injustice and his rejection of claims of legality and legitimacy on the parts of the powers-that-be (*coronéis* and more modern authoritarians) emerge very obviously from a Pentecostal cosmos (though part of his story is that he was expelled from the Assembly of God by anxious officials of the church). But to Rolim, Manuel's political actions "are a living testament as to how social involvements, even the most general, generate consciousness of the social and broaden the horizon of religiosity." Rolim accounts for the high proportion of *crente* leaders in the pre-1964 *Ligas Camponeses* (Peasant Leagues) with the same argument.[13] *Crente* religiosity is damned, when it enters the political arena only to tame *crente* activists, and it is dismissed as an operative factor, when untamed *crentes* like Manuel da Conceição are indisputably radical.

Support is lent to Rolim's contention that Brazilian Pentecostalism is essentially conservative by a non-Marxist analyst, Judith Hoffnagel. In her doctoral thesis on the Assembly of God in Recife, Hoffnagel finds that, though members of the church value the inversions of everyday life in the Assembly, there is no spillover effect such that new norms and values developed in the church might promote action against the status quo. On the contrary, Hoffnagel finds that the Assembly in Recife has become an established church. Its leaders are concerned to be respectable, have adopted bureaucratic modes of organization, and operate (self-consciously) as a successful business concern. They urge members to support conservative authoritarian political leaders. And the values of the members themselves, taken together with their compliance, suggest that the leaders' orientations are accepted. The changes that individual members experience through living as good *crentes* incorporate them closely into existing social and political structures.[14]

But there are dissenters who, while not adopting Willems's arguments, nonetheless point to another face of Pentecostalism. Regina C. Reyes Novaes complains of analyses that seem to assume a simple opposition between alienated *crente* religion, on the one hand, and class consciousness issuing in radical action, on the other. She criticizes studies that fail to distinguish between different Pentecostal movements, that analyze explicit formal doctrine rather than belief-as-lived, and that fail to examine the details of relationships between *crentes* and others involved in actual situations of conflict. Careful historical analysis, she argues, will show *crentes* less closed and less homogeneous than sometimes assumed. She suggests that it might be particularly important to note differences between nonautonomous new congregations and more settled churchlike groups; and, related to that difference, she observes political differences between more homogeneous groups of *crente* farmers and more heterogeneous urban groups.[15]

This distinction between at least two types of Pentecostalism, in terms of internal structure, effective belief, and linkage to structures of class, is a key theme in a study by Carlos Rodrigues Brandão.[16] This is a study of popular religions in the town of Itapira. Brandão applies an extraordinarily creative Marxist perspective to his sensitive fieldwork data and analyzes relationships between the "erudite" and the popular streams in Catholicism, spiritism, and Protestantism. Within each tradition he shows how the complex history of class relationships in the area is bound up with the development of the various religious traditions. Acknowledging important differences between the religions, he nonetheless sees common themes in the streaming that has occurred in all three traditions; and he focuses on common features of the popular stream in each. Unlike Rolim, he does not conclude that the popular stream in Pentecostalism effectively withdraws devotees from active, autonomous contributions to the making of local, or even national, history.

On the contrary, as the very poor in Itapira form their sects and cults and engage in their separate rituals, they are acting very politically — and often, on Brandão's evidence, with considerable consciousness that they are resisting domination and manipulation by the upper classes. These groups of the poor are well aware that the order of erudite religion — the traditional priest's church, the established Protestant churches (including now the Assembly of God), or the "white table" of middle-class spiritualist organizations — is a religious ordering of political dominance.[17] They conceive of their own groups as a religious defense of the lowest class and its communities against manipulation from on high. Class battles are fought out in the religious sphere — but not, as some Marxists have argued, in such a way that political and economic realities are altogether mystified and the poor successfully diverted from action in the real world. Religion, for Brandão's interviewees, is to use, more than to serve and follow; and one self-conscious use, in each of the religious traditions, is to resist the attempts at incorporation, pacification, and mystification of class relationships made through the erudite streams. In Itapira, lower-class autonomy and resistance is inconceivable — except through its enactment in the sects and cults — just as, historically, class dominance has been exercised through the erudite streams of religion.

There is a suggestion in Brandão's work that, though all the nonerudite streams in each of the religious traditions share this theme of resistance, the *crente* resisters are less likely than others to become locked into group-controlled magical procedures for dealing with the problems of daily life. *Crentes* expect miracles of healing and other forms of divine intervention from their all-powerful God. But their messianic beliefs — their sensitivity to the social signs of apocalypse — may turn attention from the daily troubles and miraculous or magical solutions to historical trends and drastic social upheaval.[18]

CAMPO ALEGRE *CRENTES* AND THE INTERPRETERS OF PENTECOSTALISM

The interpreters of Brazilian Pentecostalism and the Assembly of God *crentes* of Campo Alegre have much to say to one another. In their diversity and individual richness of thought and imagery, Severino, Teresa, and Valdo vindicate Regina Novaes's pleas that Pentecostals should not be stereotyped. On the other hand, Campo Alegre's

Assembly of God undermines Willems's vision of grass-roots democracy emerging from the Pentecostal sects. Judith Hoffnagel's Assembly of God seems to prefigure what Pentecostalism in Campo Alegre will become, and indeed the Campo Alegre Assembly has become steadily more incorporated in the metropolitan church she has described. While Severino, the house *congregação* meetings, and closed-door services all proclaim the same restless sectarian creativity as Brandão's *crentes* of Itapira, Campo Alegre's evangelizer and the noise of the Sunday *culto* announce a much more settled and conservative church.

Indeed, Campo Alegre's Pentecostals, especially when assembled in their church, seem to call "Amen" to some of the broader aspects of Rolim's interpretation. When the majority of regularly attending, tithe-paying *crentes* accompany Valdo and find their world apart in full immersion in the life and structures of the church, they construct something like Rolim's double dependence for themselves. Located across the wide variety of Campo Alegre's exchange networks, they are almost all subordinate and dependent in these networks, and consciously so. Their response to that dependence, expressed in their testimonies to one another, at very least risks a second dependence on the church, in which and through which they would challenge the humiliations of worldly dependence.

The past, recounted in the testimonies of the Sunday *culto*, is described as a time of drifting, when one could easily fall prey to the temptations of Satan. As fisherman, or factory worker, or washerwoman, one's hold on material necessities and livelihood was precarious. Employers' whims, political machinations, uncontrollable economic catastrophes (that have made Campo Alegre a town of the displaced, as we have seen) — these are the coordinates of the *vida materia* as it was once experienced. Submission to Satan, in the past, deepened one's dependence on the forces of corruption inherent in the material life. A downward spiral into degradation and darkness was the result.

Then with conversion came a new future, into a new journey, through time, into the light, which makes possible a different experience of the present. The converted *crente* lives now out of the future (much as a culture-bound Søren Kierkegaard thought all humans do). The sense of the precariousness of material life, of worldly dependence, of the reality of the Valley of Darkness remains. But, in the church and in submission to its disciplines, including its demands on time, one lives an alternative present in transit to eternal life with God. When that church itself becomes a sort of icon symbolizing and mapping the eternity-ridden present, dependence on it becomes a fact of life. The church *crente* — eschewing the creative autonomy that Severino shows to be a possibility in Pentecostalism — suspends inspired judgment on the world and allows church leaders effectively to define his citizenship. Attempting to deal with his first dependence, the church *crente* embraces a second.

In this sense, what might be called a weak version of Rolim's double-dependence thesis helps us portray the dialectics of economic experience, religion, and politics among the church *crentes* of Campo Alegre. That notion helps us avoid the danger of overgeneralizing from a single star like Severino. On the other hand, Severino and the more sectarian members of the Assembly of God in Campo Alegre help us question overgeneralization in Rolim and draw to our attention those dialectics of experience, religion, and politics that tend to disappear in Rolim's Marxist systems analysis.

The first challenge to the strong version of Rolim's interpretations arises from a consideration of the worldly experience of the Campo Alegre *crentes*. In Rolim's strong version, Pentecostalism is a, perhaps even the, religion of the petite bourgeoisie in Brazil. The great majority of his surveyed Pentecostals, he claims, are of that class. Their worldly experience can be characterized in terms of their nonproductive labor, their economic dependence, and their blocked upward mobility. It is the inversion of this experience that Pentecostals seek in their religious world, where they become productive, autonomous, and mobile.

The *crentes* of Campo Alegre are certainly dependent in their worldly order and conscious of their dependence. But they are not easily classified across their participation in various exchange networks in and beyond the town, as members of a petite bourgeoisie. Still less does it seem possible to reduce the major features of church Pentecostalism, let alone of sect Pentecostalism, in Campo Alegre to origins in the distinguishing characteristics of the petit-bourgeois experience. It would be possible to orchestrate too much protest to the strong version of Rolim's interpretation. Heads of *crente* households, small farmers, and fishermen who are not themselves petit bourgeois by work experience often have what might be called petit-bourgeois aspirations for their children. Examining the backgrounds of those who occupy the *tribuno* on Sundays, it could be noted that at least one deacon and the evangelizer himself were from snug niches in what I think Rolim means by the petit-bourgeois class. And visiting groups and individuals from Recife display the dress and manners of that class, or perhaps of the bourgeoisie itself, when they sing and sermonize in the Campo Alegre temple. A case could be made for domination by the petite bourgeoisie over a membership that is not predominantly of that class.

It is a long way from concessions like these, however, to vindication of Rolim's strong version. Campo Alegre's Pentecostals suggest that Rolim's structural Marxism has led him to impose on Pentecostals not only too narrow a class base but a religiosity too tightly defined and a politics too easily predicted. Against Rolim's programmed Pentecostals we have in individual *crentes* like Severino, and, even in certain rituals of the Assembly itself, evidence for a sect dialectic of Pentecostalism. In that dialectic the conditions of dependence, precariousness, and injustice are interpreted into experience, by *crentes*, with the myths and images not only of trial and submission and ascetic withdrawal from the world, but also of moral outrage against injustice and righteous action against oppression, just as Willems and Martin would have us suspect. Emerging from that dialectic there are traces in Campo Alegre, as in the case of Manuel da Conceição and some of Regina Novaes's stories, of a *crente* political culture of critique and limited resistance.

The Campo Alegre *crentes* certainly do not allow any radical rejection of Rolim's arguments about their religiosity and its political consequences. In the limiting case of the church *crente*, like Valdo, there is much of what we could call a mystification of social, political and economic relations; and from that mystification a political culture emerges. God, conceived of as absolute Lord of history, only leaves room for human action that fits into an inscrutable divine plan. There is no motivation to engage in critical social analysis: all evils, the social undifferentiated from the individual, are to be addressed through submission to the disciplines and projects of the church — that is, to church elites. They, in turn (and at least in part as actors pursuing religious meanings), are dedicated to the inclusion of their church in the matrix of institutions linking political power and influence to prestige in civil society. In effect, in Campo Alegre, a *crente* religious option for apartness from the uncontrollable evils of the world at the local level becomes a mode of inclusion into modern bureaucratic-authoritarian Brazil.

As we have seen, however, there are options within *crente* religiosity that are less mystificatory, in the sense that they allow for much more human agency in the making of history and even include a sort of class analysis of experienced injustice — the rich versus the poor as Goliath versus David, for example, where David struggles and triumphs with God's justice on his side. Further, even among *crentes* of the more churchy type, the myths and symbols that nurture distrust of all human institutions remain vivid so that aggregate inclusion in bureaucratic authoritarian Brazil is not automatically rooted in fervent, uncritical acceptance of a regime by individuals. At very least, among Campo Alegre *crentes*, and even within individual believers, there is an active tension between passive acquiescence in a regime and critical address to local wrongs.

In this active tension, the Campo Alegre *crentes* question another aspect of Rolim's more radical thesis — the picture of Pentecostal communities hermetically sealed off from the rest of Brazilian society. The tension between engagement and detachment arises, in part, out of the several modes of achieving the apartness that all *crentes* value. Severino's mode is of the head, one might say. He stands apart from his everyday social world through a constantly maintained, Bible-inspired reflectiveness on the world. Zé and Teresa construct their world apart with inner music (silent hymn singing) and visitations almost exclusively with other *crentes.* Others seek apartness through immersion in the life of the church. Rolim seems to have these last principally in mind, but theirs is not the only *crente* mode of apartness.

Moreover, even church *crentes* are neighbors of non-*crentes* and members of religiously mixed families. In their church life, too, they must negotiate their faith with *crentes* who are more of the sectarian type. The negotiations with neighbors, with family, and with fellow *crentes* constitute a politics of culture that, I am arguing, is part of general political history in the making and not just the religious politics of a separate Pentecostal world. Brandão's account of class struggle waged in the religious sphere is nearer Campo Alegre reality than Rolim's account of an ersatz religious politics engaged in as a refuge from the pain of class conflict.

The reply of Rolim might be simply to urge that by the eighties, there is little of religious politics in Brazilian Pentecostalism. The church of the erudite stream has triumphed. Severino keeps his distance; Manuel da Conceição is expelled; the sectarians of Itapira are left behind, hoping for more miracles to help them survive. I have probably provided grounds for this sort of reply by my setting up the sect *crente*/church *crente* dichotomy. The question must surely be asked: are there enough sect *crentes* around to sustain the sort of religious politics I describe?

At one stage in my research, persuaded by the intuition that there were two types, I estimated, on the basis of nonrandom interviews and conversations with *crentes* of the Assembly of God in Campo Alegre, that about 20 percent were of the sectarian type. I began to suspect a pattern: that sectarians were more likely to reside in more peripheral areas of the town, to be poorer and of more recent rural origin than church *crentes.* I did not do the careful, formal, random survey of *crentes* that I thought, at one point, might have established the validity of these impressions.

My later, and I believe more informed and thoughtful, opinion is that earlier impressions would not be sustained by such a survey. The church/sect distinction is my distinction between ideal types. It has been drawn out of my exploration of the religiosity of Severino and Valdo and other *crentes*, and it has, in turn, helped make communicable sense out of the raw data from those explorations. But the distinction is an analytical one and does not correspond to real subgroups within the *crente* population of Campo Alegre. There may be examples, like Severino and Valdo, of sectarian and church tendencies. But almost all *crentes* draw (and not with the consistency of the exemplars or of theologians or sociologists) from a *crente* repertoire that includes sect and church options. The sense that either a Severino or a Valdo has arrived at does not constitute a common sense for distinct types of *crentes*.

What is distinctive about *crentes* in the cultural mélange of Campo Alegre, then, is not one settled political ideology, or even an unambiguous and uniform religiosity. It is the repertoire of myth, symbol, doctrine, and practice that is distinctive. The *crentes* are a cultural and political presence in Campo Alegre as they debate their repertoire within themselves, between themselves, and with non-*crente* neighbors.

Politically it is quite clear that the repertoire sets boundaries for *crentes*. The *crente* repertoire does not include myths and symbols that might rally the faithful for social transformation in the name of this-worldly utopia. I have argued against Rolim that Campo Alegre Pentecostalism, at least, is not essentially or distinctively mystificatory, though selection from its repertoire might well involve mystifications of injustice and exploitation. But I also argue that even Severino's moral critique of injustice is a long way from, say, the messianic enthusiasm for the cause of liberty of the eighteenth-century New England clergy. Severino's religious interpretation of the world has no place for a city upon a hill, which God's faithful must construct and defend through political struggle. There seems to be no basis in the Pentecostal religious imagination, as mapped for us by Severino, for the pursuit of civil liberty and social justice as a sacred cause. Nor is there a basis upon which the battle for religious liberty, as celebrated by Pastor Moisés, might be extended into a struggle for a new social order along the lines of the priest's communitarian dreams. In neither sect nor church components of the Pentecostal repertoire in Campo Alegre is there a clear notion of a covenant through which God alerts good citizens to the limit of their compliance to an unjust order and, further, to their responsibility to achieve a just order as part of the pursuit of salvation. Not even in the rich range of possibilities suggested by Severino is there an open gate on to the tortuous path from a Cotton Mather to a Jonathan Mayhew.

At most, in the dialectic of everyday experience and the *crente* repertoire, a politics of local resistance emerges. Final solutions to worldly suffering may be in the hands of God and made available to individuals only in the next life. But a fervent moralism, a conviction that God punishes the unjust in this world as well as in the next, and Old Testament images of a people struggling against injustice may motivate *crentes* to denounce and resist the unjust patron or the compromised bureaucrat. Manuel da

Conceição may be exceptional in his resistance to landed patrons and the public power backing them in Maranhão. But he is a *crente* all the way as he resists, and has not simply been jolted out of his Pentecostal religion by experience as Rolim would have us believe. In Severino, Teresa, Zé, and in indignant testimonies in the Assembly of God *congregações*, we see something of the socially critical moralism of Pentecostalism and the religious *força* that impels it into the political arena. That energy may be diverted and diffused by a local evangelizer, intent on the politics of church; but in Campo Alegre at any rate, that diversion is still not a foregone conclusion.

At very least, Pentecostal images of God's power and the corruptibility of human institutions seem to prompt *crentes* as individual citizens to reject the hegemonic claims of bureaucratic-authoritarian Brazil. The same images arm them against the blandishments of populist politicians. Rolim (with his rather narrow Marxist structuralist view of what constitutes a political act) notes only that Pentecostals in their hermetic religious world are unavailable for mobilization in the class struggle. The *crentes* of Campo Alegre (like Brandão's *crentes* of Itapira) bid us, on the one hand, to widen our conceptions of what constitutes a political act and, on the other, to consider that Pentecostal life is incompatible with mobilization for any national cause in the arena of formal politics. Pentecostal *crentes* set limits to mobilization, not only for the class struggle but for the causes of the state and elites of both populist and bureaucratic-authoritarian kinds.

In Campo Alegre, the absence of the *crentes* from the fiesta defines a feature of the town's cultural mélange. Their absence also suggests a resistance to the restoration of either *coronelismo* or *populismo* and a serious challenge to both the priest's communitarian vision and the hegemonic claims of bureaucratic-authoritarian Brazil. Their absence from an important local event helps us chart the chances of political cultures in Campo Alegre. I am now suggesting that the absence of *crentes*, better understood, may have something to say about limitations to all claimants for power in Brazil, including those elites that construct and promote the bureaucratic-authoritarian elements in the Brazilian state.

CHAPTER FIVE

The Afro-Brazilian Spiritists: Against the Stream

THE SPIRITISTS are not as easily placed as the *crentes* of the Assembly of God in the cultural mélange of Campo Alegre. They do not establish presence and identity, as the *crentes* did, in staying away from the fiesta of the patron saint: most will attend, telling themselves (as they will tell the census taker) that they are Catholics. There is no central temple in which spiritists might gather, but fourteen different *centros* (centers), *salões* (salons), or *terreiros* (place for cult rituals) maintained by cult leaders, many of whom have an acute sense of difference from and rivalry with other leaders. There is no one spiritist quite like the *crente* Severino, who is able to display, even in eccentricity, the central motifs and potential ambiguities that define a distinctive religious world.

Nevertheless, comparing case with case, it is possible to detect a sort of spiritist hue (or, as I think some of the older priests thought of it, stain) in the mélange. It is difficult to find anything as simple as the church-sect difference among *crentes* that might allow us to appreciate both variation and theme characterizing spiritists. But in this and the next chapter, four of the fourteen groups will be compared and contrasted, so we may appreciate the variety they engender in forms of association and predispositions in dealing with the problems of everyday life. In this chapter I shall describe two groups with very different pantheons; but I shall begin an argument that they are dissenting groups, against the stream in two senses. They encourage the construction of a citizenship that is markedly different from that encouraged in most of Campo Alegre's spiritist groups; and in doing so they challenge conventional academic wisdom about the politics of Brazilian spiritism.

PAI FULÓ'S GROUP

Fuló is the nickname given by townspeople to the *pai de santo* (father of the saint) who leads Campo Alegre's only Xangô cult. He was an old man, seventy-six years old in 1977. Having established various centers in the suburbs of Recife and in Goiana, a large town north of Recife, he came to Campo Alegre in 1972. All his centers have been exclusively of the family of cults known in Recife by the name of Xangô — the powerful African spirit of thunder and lightning and mythic King of Dahomey who was brought to Brazil, Cuba, and other places in the Americas by West African slaves. Xangô is also Fuló's personal spirit, his *santo de cabeça* (spirit of his head).

Fuló's home is the *centro* for the cult, and fixed to the rendered-mud outer wall is a sign telling passersby that this is a

> *terreiro dos cultos*
> *africanos anagó*
> *são joão*
> *batista*

(the place of the African Nagô cults, Saint John the Baptist). The naming encapsulates a great deal about Fuló and his cult. Fuló is insistent on the Africanness of his cult. He is himself clearly of African ancestry, as are many, though by no means all, of his cult members. The Nagô cults are Yoruba in origin, and he stresses the point: the ritual chants of his house are in Nagô rather than in Portuguese, because Nagô is the language to which the great African spirits respond. As a guardian and communicator of myth and ritual — the role that he considers central and most important — Fuló passes on to his followers, preferably while they are very young, enough Nagô language and lore for them to be able to bear their spirits into the world.

But note that this is the place of the African cults called Saint John the Baptist. Fuló celebrates and recreates Africanness but uses the nomenclature of his Christianity. In my first conversations with him, he identifies himself as a member of the Holy Roman Catholic Apostolic Church — each adjective carefully enunciated as though the correct formula might banish doubt. He points out to me that each of the spirits whose image resides in the *pejí* (repository) room of his house has both an African and a Catholic saint's name — Iemanjá, the spirit of the sea and mother of many of the other great spirits, is Our Lady, Mary, the mother of Jesus. Xangô, whose name is popularly given to the whole cult, is represented by symbols of lightning and kingship but also by a picture of Saint John the Baptist, Xangô's Catholic identity.

12. Pai Fuló's house, the Xangô "family" home and ritual center.

In the naming of the house, as in the naming and representation of the spirits, Fuló's Xangô adopts outward forms and labels from appropriated aspects of the dominant religious culture. But the character of the spirits and the concerns of the extended household in relationship to them remain, in the eyes of the group, essentially African. Fuló explains that he is not of the *cultura alta* (high culture), even when, in my first conversations with him, he protests his good standing within it. He and his *filhos e filhas de santo* (sons and daughters in the saint) identify themselves with *Brasil selvagem* (savage Brazil), and they do not accept the valuation placed on it by the *cultura alta*.

They are continuing an old tradition, investigated by Roger Bastide, in which the Catholic saints become masks for the *orixás* (African spirits), so that the *orixás* and the ways of life integrated around them may avoid suppression.[1] But it is the *orixás* who rule and to whose required mode of living Fuló and at least some of his group respond. Reinterpretation of the Christian saints and of the *cultura alta* in general has been accomplished in terms of the values, cognitions, and modes of relationship (between man and nature and between man and man) that are distinctive of *Brasil selvagem*.

If not in word then in ritual action and symbol, Fuló and his "family" construct alternatives to much of the *cultura alta*. Their lives bear the stamp of poverty, but, though they do not politically attack the system head on, they reject its judgments of them and assert alternative identity for the poor. Even the Portuguese language is denied its superiority in the Nagô chants. It is noteworthy that Nagô is used and taught by Fuló, not as a priestly language for mystery and for the arcane controlled by him, but for the acquirement by all members of a counterculture: Fuló's Nagô does not mirror, but exactly negates, the function of the traditional priest's Latin. The group's blood sacrifices ignore modern urban Brazil's rules of hygiene and separation from raw nature — and for this alone, members of other Afro-Brazilian cults label followers of Xangô ignorant and uneducated. But sacrifice, Fuló explains, is one of the things the spirits demand, if they are to infuse their followers with their diverse strengths and protect them from harm.

Fuló and the inner members of his family are even more profoundly countercultural in their social relations. In a society where, even at the local level, authority claims legitimation through formal qualifications and expertise, Fuló exercises traditional authority — authority based on wisdom passed on through the generations in deep personal relationships. Fuló neither intends, nor is expected, to hoard his wisdom as an expert for specific functions; rather, his standing relies on his transposing his wisdom from his life to as many other lives as he can. His proudest boast to me is that he has left communities of *filhos* and *filhas de santo* all over Brazil — that means he has fulfilled his roles as ambassador of the spirits and *zelador* (watchman) of the wisdom of Africa and *Brasil selvagem*.[2]

Fuló's aims and intentions are reflected in the form and content of the rituals of his house. The disposition and use of ritual space provide clues for a reading of the cult rituals. In Figure 3 the first thing to note is that the ritual space, the *salão*, is located in a home: to receive the wisdom and strength of the spirits one has to become a member of a household. In the *salão* itself everything is moveable: it is a space for learning through community-in-motion rather than through the raised expert, commanding or pouring specific chunks of knowledge into empty vessels. The *peji* is a place apart, but not for individual therapy: when a member of the group is performing his obligation to his spirit — which is also an obligation to the group, involving provision of a high-protein meal for all participants — the member is secluded for a time in the special place of the spirits. But the obligation is fulfilled only when the member emerges from the *peji*, bearing the spirit in trance out into the group to move among and inspire the others.

Fuló's is a poor house. His sons and daughters in the saint find it difficult to save or borrow the money necessary to pay their obligations to their spirits. Each of the spirits calls for a *toque* — a ritual in which that

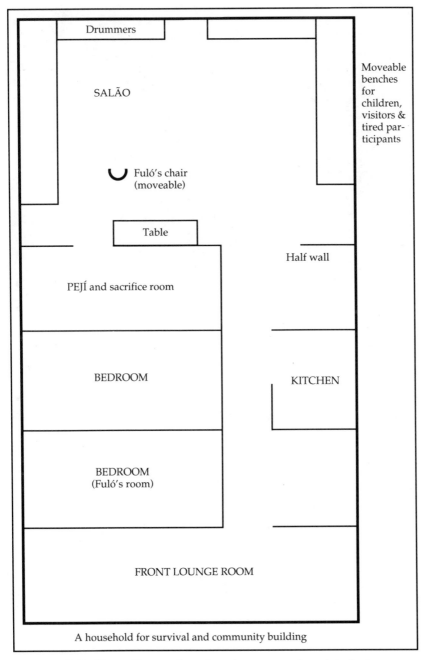

Drummers

SALÃO

Moveable benches for children, visitors & tired participants

Fuló's chair
(moveable)

Table

Half wall

PEJÍ and sacrifice room

BEDROOM

KITCHEN

BEDROOM
(Fuló's room)

FRONT LOUNGE ROOM

A household for survival and community building

Figure 3. Fuló's House: Terreiro dos cultos africanos anagô são joão batista

13. The food prepared from sacrificed animals is set out for the *orixá* — to be eaten later by members of Pai Fuló's "family" and their guests.

spirit (and each of the major African spirits of the Xangô cult), when called by chant and drum and dance, descends on the sons and daughters who have learned how to receive them. Each spirit has its own requirements for sacrifices: chickens, pigeons, goats, calves, and foods to be offered and shared with the family. If the mother or father of the group has wealthy clients and patrons who come to ask for counsel, protection, or strength from the spirits, and if the sons and daughters are well-off, then there will be many *toques* in which obligations are paid. But when, as in the case of Fuló's group, the sons and daughters are poor fishermen, shellfish gatherers, and domestic servants — with only a few better-off members of the group from outside Campo Alegre — then there will be few such *toques* in any year.

But ordinary *toques*, in which the group as a whole pays an obligation and shares the costs, are held on the feasts of each of the spirits. Many of these have a special feature. On the feast of Iemanjá, the spirit of the sea, a basket of flowers and offerings is taken to the beach and placed in the water. On the feast of Oxum, spirit of fresh water, a similar basket is taken to a river. But there is a basic form to all the *toques*.

When Fuló feels that the time is right — the key drummer has rushed in late from work in the cement factory, a dispute between two of the daughters (about who should wear which long skirt) has been resolved, a would-be (drunk) participant has been turned away, and the children seem under reasonable control—he orders that the *toque* begin. He is dressed in white shirt and trousers and wears a white cap on his head. His wife, a fully fledged mother in the saint, and a few other senior women who can afford it are dressed in long full dresses of the color of their spirit or of the spirit whose feast is being celebrated. Around their necks are the beads that tell of their progress in the cult—a necklace received on initiation, others marking advancement in knowledge, seniority, and performance in the rites of the cult. About twenty other women (with fewer necklaces and wearing only tattered reminders of the full finery celebrated by the government tourist agency in selected *terreiros* in Recife) stand in a circle. They are joined by only five men, three of whom are dressed in well-worn street clothes and sandals.

Fuló stops the three drummers before the chanting can begin, because he wants to make a short statement. He welcomes all who have come to his house, which is open to all—even *crentes* who do not understand what he does. This house is open to all, members of Congress, military officers, the poorest of the poor. And tonight on the feast of Ogun the warrior spirit, Saint George, we ask the warrior saints, including the spirit Iansã, the beloved of Xangô, who is Joan of Arc, to intervene to prevent war coming. May they prevent a world war developing from the conflict between Argentina and England in the Islas Malvinas. We ask the *orixás* to give *força* to world leaders to avoid a war.

Then the *toque* proceeds normally. Exú, the messenger between this world and the world of spirits, is first summoned, and praised, and then dispatched out the open door of the *salão*. As an intermediary between the two worlds, Exú is a trickster and must be removed lest he disrupt the dignified celebration of the other spirits. Then the drumbeat starts the call to the first of the spirits, who is asked to descend. The long chants and hymns are led by a middle-aged farmer who started training with Fuló twelve years ago, before Fuló came to Campo Alegre. He is obviously competent, but Fuló the teacher watches the dancers, listens to the complex rhythms of the drums, and monitors the exchange between the leader and the circling chorus. No incorrect line or sloppy rhythm is allowed to pass—Fuló corrects all errors, singing the corrected chant himself, if necessary, until the sons and daughters get it right.

The first spirit descends on one of the daughters. As she goes into trance her dancing falters, but she is helped by one of the senior ladies in the circle. Her beads and pins from her hair are removed to avoid her being injured while entranced. She glides into the center of the ring, already moving as the spirit moves. Soon she goes to Fuló and embraces him, and

14. Pai Fuló with some of his spiritual sons and daughters.

from time to time she embraces other senior members of the group, in order according to their status in the cult. As the chanting, drumming, and dancing tell of the spirit's story and character, the spirit descends on other dancers who then enact his or her presence, with variations on prescribed movement and gesture.

Occasionally Fuló assists when one of the *manifestadas* (those manifesting the spirit), at the end of the time for a particular spirit, seems to be experiencing a difficult and painful return from trance state to normal consciousness. Sometimes, again as critical but caring teacher, he will suggest that the difficulty has arisen because in trance the son or daughter was expressing something within so that the *orixá* was not allowed to appear: the pain is an expression of the spirit's frustration. An untrained medium would experience similar pain, arising again from the spirit's frustration.

But usually the spirit leaves, and the recipient is able to return to the circle, perhaps a little tired but happy to have borne the spirit and the spirit's *força* into the world. Then the other spirits descend as they are called. Daughters, receiving Ogun, strut like macho soldiers and call for swords as they enact male aggressiveness. Luíz, a tall beach fisherman, joins some of the daughters manifesting Iemanjá: the whole group moves with the restless grace of a gentle sea and Iemanjá-Luíz, arms stretched out in Iemanjá's statuesque protectiveness, reminds brothers and sisters of the nurture and care the spirits provide in a dangerous world.

15. The first spirit descends on one of the daughters.

Fuló and Luíz and other trained members of the group read the *toque* and the central purpose of the cult group in this way. The group's knowledge of ritual and of the spirits enables the spirits to descend and remind humans of the various strengths they can bring into the world—the male strength of Xangô and Ogun, the female aggressiveness and persistence of Iansã, the fortitude of the aged Oxalufã. The diverse energies of the great African spirits and their Christian co-identities are available to those prepared to devote the time and resources necessary to keep a family (and a whole genealogy of families stretching back into the African past) alive and functioning. In one sense, Fuló concedes, the African spirits are distant figures from an African past. In other ways they are close to the unchanging human condition: they are jealous (Iemanjá, Xangô's wife, is jealous of Iansã, her rival for his affection); they are demanding and occasionally petulant. When their needs and desires are discovered and met by humans incorporated in the genealogy that is their destiny, then they enter fully into human life again—helping individual family members develop their special strengths and protecting the family so that it might protect its members.

Some people come only as paying clients. They regard the African spirits as powerful, and Fuló is reputed to be a knowledgeable and successful mediator with the spirits. So they come to hear him read their destiny from a casting of cowrie shells or to seek his advice in matters of health or family problems. The police will occasionally bring him someone who has gone berserk and is believed to have been acted upon by one of the African spirits. Though he will help clients, especially for a fee, Fuló does not consider them members of his family, nor does he consider his work with them worthy of his calling. He is quite frank, though, about his need for his clients' money.

So some of the participants in the *toques* and the life of the family continue with a rather clientelistic view of Fuló and their own participation. One lady, whom I met as a participant in 1977, had abandoned the group by 1982, when it was in any case extremely fragile, due to the advanced age and ill-health of Fuló and to conflicts within the family that he was no longer able to control. Her account, in 1982, of her involvement in 1977 may serve as a caution to any romantic interpretation that would assume identity of vision between the leader and the followers in a cult. Her husband had died in 1975, and she had tried to get a widow's pension, without success. She was born a Baptist but had long since left practice of that faith. She wasn't accustomed to making *promessas* (vows to do something for a Catholic saint in exchange for a favor) but thought that there might be some help available in spiritism. So she went from one spiritist group to another. I happened to meet her when she was providing sacrificial animals for Fuló and participating in various other ways in the hope that his spirits might be able to help her. But she came no nearer to getting her pension and was disturbed at the outlay necessary to please Fuló and other cult leaders. So she abandoned the spiritists and returned to her "basic Baptist convictions" (her words). God is the lawyer of the lawyers and he has the power — so she would make a *voto* with God (the *voto* is the *crente* equivalent of the Catholic *promessa*, but concluded with God rather than with a saint or the Virgin Mary). And the *voto* worked. Little over a month after making her *voto*, Naícia Sebastiana de Medeiros obtained her pension. She has not been near Fuló, or any other spiritist leader, since then.[3]

Fuló would be as worried by some of the variations on his religious vision in some members closer than Naícia ever was to the center of his group. Elsa went to Fuló for help on the advice of a friend when her daughter appeared to be suffering some form of nervous breakdown.[4] Fuló helped and she and her many children (various fathers) have been attached to the cult group ever since. Elsa has come to regard Fuló as her "own father." She considers her religion to be Catholic, and she continues to make *promessas* to Our Lady, especially in the month of May, paying with candles. But her most valued religious relationship is with Iemanjá-Mary whom Fuló has divined as the spirit of her head. And it is the spirits whom she thanks for giving her strength (when they are properly treated). None of this would disturb Fuló.

What would disturb him is the conclusion and emphases Elsa draws from his initial successful diagnosis of her daughter's problems. They were, she recalls him telling her, due to the fact that her daughter was a daughter of Oxum, and the spirit was "feeling hungry" because of a lack of response to the spirit of her head. Oxum, in frustration, was causing the girl to become disoriented. When the girl recovered — after various offerings to Oxum, participation in *toques* and classes of instruction offered by Fuló (and small payments and gifts gratefully received by him) — Elsa seems to have generalized the diagnosis. She emphasizes the jealousy and the demands of the spirits, and she accounts for all manner of health problems, crises in personal relationships, financial failures, as the outcome of battles between spirits and unrequited relationships between humans and spirits. Fuló's diagnosis for a pathological condition has become the key to an interpretation of life's vicissitudes. He rejects both the view of the spirits and the theodicy that Elsa has drawn, at least in part, from his diagnosis.

There are other Elsas, in Fuló's group and in other spiritist groups in Campo Alegre. But interviews and life histories of other members of Fuló's group show that, although there are various ways of being a member of the group and various modes in which the rich symbolism of Xangô myth and ritual may be assembled into or included in a paradigm for living, a core of about a dozen members do seem to share much of what Fuló himself considers important in his vision.

In that vision, the poor man of *Brasil selvagem* actively seeks identity and strength for dealing with life's problems in religious community. That community, while ideally on good terms with the authorities and the *cultura alta*, is not to be subservient. Its members are to co-opt things of value from the wider society but are to resist evaluation in the terms of the dominant groups. They will evaluate one another in terms of their fidelity to the *orixás;* and the *orixás* will reward them with the gifts of character — imagination, resilience, controlled aggression, loving tenderness — rather than solutions to specific problems.

The fragility of that group-carried vision was clear on my visit in 1982. Fuló was ill and no longer able to control tensions within his family. His wife, a senior member of the Xangô cult, was a prickly lady and had fallen out with several other members of the group — including the second-most-senior female, who had been Fuló's daughter in the saint in another town where hers was a wealthy family. The most promising of the young daughters in the saint had run off with a young man, who was in and out of trouble with the law while she was in and out of pregnancy. Numbers taking part in and attending the *toques* and paying their obligations to their spirits had fallen. Of those who did remain none had sufficient resources to help maintain the group, and three or four were reputed to be in trouble with the police or to have severe drinking problems. Fuló's reputation in town was sinking because he was no longer able to discipline his family. The group seemed unlikely to survive him; and indeed when I returned briefly in 1988, after he had died, I found that the house had been sold and the group dispersed.

On the other hand, by 1982, the son of the most revered mother of the saint in the region (she had died in 1977) had become a very evangelistic *zelador* of the *orixás* in Campo Alegre. Fuló's Xangô family might die with him but not the tradition of a family united around the cult of the *orixás*. Gregório, very stout for a man in his mid-thirties and very black, had grown up in a "household of the spirits," as he put it. His mother had trained many of the practising mediums of the area, even those who had later abandoned the *orixás* for more modern spirits. His sister continued the family tradition in her house in Campo Alegre where she had two altars — one for the spirits of the Jurema cult and the other for the *orixás* of Xangô. Gregório's sense of family, however, extended far beyond the bloodline, as did Fuló's.

I interviewed him as he prepared to play the drum at a *toque* for the

16. Flowers for Mother Oxum are taken to the water by the *mãe de santo*, Gregório's sister.

feast of the spirit Oxum (the spirit of freshwater streams and lakes) held in his sister's *salão*.[5] He moved very quickly from an account of his role as a sort of co-producer of the *toque* to an outline of his hopes and ambitions for the family of Xangô (he used the word *Candomblé* that is more usually employed to designate the cult of the *orixás* in Bahia). He listed the lineage of fathers and mothers in the saint from which he had emerged and asserted not only his solidarity with the generations of that extended family but his feeling of responsibility for regeneration. That meant a lot of hard work for him in the small amount of time available after his hours of work as a public servant. He had not only to keep on learning himself but to train others in the Nagô language chants, the stories of the *orixás*, the appropriate drum patterns for each of the spirits, and the required offerings and sacrifices when a son or daughter in the saint was paying an obligation. The *orixás* themselves would help, providing strength and wisdom. But Gregório stressed the difficulties confronting a *zelador* in the modern world, the attraction of the Umbanda cult where only Portuguese was used, the discipline required to maintain a family and meet the stern requirements of the *orixás*, his own need to earn a living. Despite all these things and attendant anxieties, despite the sorrows and tensions of family life itself in *Candomblé*, the effort was worth it, and success was possible. Gregório felt that he was part of a family, more dispersed and fragile than his mother's or even than his sister's, but a family none the less, "in which the strength and character of the *orixás* continued through the generations."

MARIA PRETINHA'S GROUP

Among the spiritist groups of Campo Alegre, it is by no means clear that it is the African pantheon of spirits that encourages group autonomy and individual skepticism toward the claims of modern authority and that it is the more modern pantheons that encourage compliance to modernity. Maria Pretinha (Little Black Mary, a nickname) as a medium operates with spirits from the intertwined Umbanda and Jurema families of spirits, and she has been greatly influenced by her own reading of Alain Kardec and the "white-table" form of ritual associated with white middle-class spiritism in Brazil.

At this point I beg the indulgence of the reader who is unfamiliar with the names of the various spiritist streams. It is not possible to define the different families of spiritism neatly. By accumulation of detail, the reader might better be able to define differences by the end of the next chapter. For now it suffices to say that Umbanda emerged from attempts in Rio de Janeiro, from the twenties to the forties, to create and codify in print

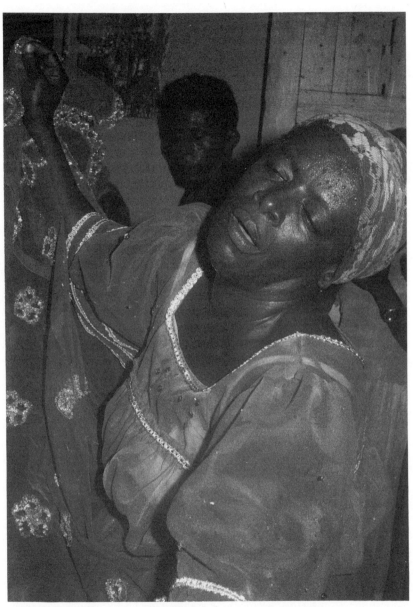

17. Oxum comes to Campo Alegre.

a syncretism of middle-class European style spiritualism, a variety of Afro cults of the spirits and a reconstruction of Amerindian spirit cults. The Jurema family consists of *caboclo* Amerindian spirits and spirit masters, who seem to be shared with Umbanda. Alain Kardec was a Belgian whose spiritualism, celebrated around tables in middle-class drawing rooms (hence the name "white table"), inspired some of Brazil's enthusiastic modernizers and founders of public charities in late nineteenth-century Brazil.

Maria Pretinha respects Fuló and has occasionally attended *toques* at his place, but she is not at all interested in working with the African *orixás* and does not think *toques* of the Xangô or Umbanda variety worthwhile. The African *orixás*, she says, are inarticulate and unable to communicate wisdom in the grunts and groans they produce through their mediums. The *toques* are noisy and their chants are in a language no one understands — so they are unsuitable occasions for the learning exchanges that, for Maria, are the glory of spiritism and central to the spiritist way of life.

Those exchanges, to her, are rich and complex. Maria Pretinha conceives of a hierarchy of spirits — from the least developed (the spirits of Indian children, for example) through the articulate, wise, but rather rough-diamond, spirits whom she works with as a medium, to the more developed spirits who include the Catholic saints and the popular priest-hero Padre Cícero (1844–1934). The hierarchy is not settled, nor is it the job of the medium to serve merely as a conduit for the wisdom and skills of the very highest spirits. (In these respects Maria contrasts with most other mediums in Campo Alegre, as we shall see.) The spirits continue to struggle toward higher spiritual development in the spirit world — the inarticulate strive to become articulate, the violent to become gentle, the drunk to attain sobriety, the ignorant to attain knowledge, especially that knowledge that leads toward wisdom and understanding in dealing with life's problems.

The role of the medium is to work on exchanges that cater to the ordinary people, the mediums, and the spirits themselves as they all struggle for spiritual development. Maria as medium and counselor works mainly with the wily old city-slicker spirit known throughout Brazil as Zé Pelintra. To her, Pelintra in his earthly life was not entirely successful in achieving the spiritual development that God expects us to achieve. He tried, but he was vain, drank too much, chased after women, got into too many fights. When he died, his spirit was not pure and developed enough to be with God, and he was required by God to return as a spirit to earth to mature through service to the living. That is what he has been doing. And though in his manifestations he still displays his imperfections — in rough language, flirtation, calling for beer and *cachaça* (rum), and playing the trickster — he also listens to the problems people bring to

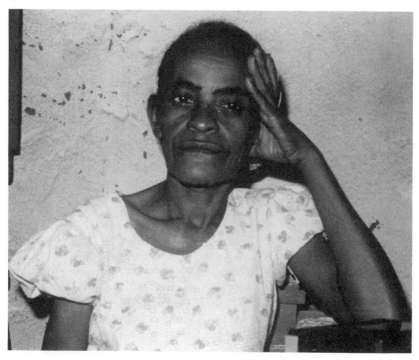

18. Maria Pretinha.

him and draws on the wisdom he has acquired in his material and spiritual lives to help resolve those problems. He has become a master spirit for the quality of the services he renders to the living. But in order to develop further through service he requires the understanding and goodwill of mediums like Maria Pretinha. "I live helping him, don't I, in this mission, because, Seu Henrique, the spirit is like an unemployed person. The spirit comes to look for the people so they will help him accomplish his mission—until the time when he has achieved his evolution and development and when he no longer has any need of this world."[6] Zé Pelintra (and other spirits like him) is also like a student whom mediums have to teach. When mediums fail to help the spirits in their quest to learn and to serve, they become frustrated and can cause great harm as they turn in anger against the living. Frustrated spirits can turn mediums mad and cause all manner of misfortune for those in some way implicated in their frustration. Spirits less developed than Zé, once *revoltados* (outraged) in their failure to be taught and used for good by mediums, can become agents for black magic, harnessed to do evil. Maria worries that this too easily happens in the case of the African *orixás*, since "none of those who watch over them *(que zeladô deles)* is interested in teaching them how to develop themselves."

The breakdown in the exchange between spirits and mediums, has, in its consequences, an exact parallel in the breakdown of exchanges in the modern urban world:

> So often a person goes to the house of someone she knows looking for money — because the person needs it, you understand. But when she gets there, her suffering isn't understood. There's no attempt to understand. When the person asks for money, and the reply is "I don't have any, my dear," the person is *revoltado*, knowing that his neighbor has it. And many a person in this way turns into a robber. . . . I believe that these days, the world is completely full of robbers. And often it's because of this sort of thing.

The good citizen must be alive to the needs of neighbors and to her own capacity to provide what is needed, if a new round of individual degradation and social breakdown is to be avoided. The good medium, likewise, trains herself to respond to the needs of the spirits. And as she mediates between the world of the spirits and the material, visible, everyday world, she helps open up the possibility of exchanges between the spirits and the living. Through the medium the parallel material and spiritual worlds are linked. For the living, the benefits of these exchanges are both individual and social. With the help of spirits like Zé Pelintra, a person can gain control over the animal passions that produce human misery and the strength to "pass the trials of the material life." When you have a number of strong, controlled people in a town like Campo Alegre then you have the basis for community. When you have community created out of spiritual strength, then the problems of material life (including the problem of unjust exclusion from farming land) can be tackled with some hope of success. Without community based on spiritual development, in which poor people have liberated themselves from "ill will, rancor, iniquity, hate, and revenge," then communal action is bound to fail. Without community, Maria proclaimed on a number of occasions, "the strike is death in Brazil." The chain of exchanges, between spirit and medium, between spirit and ordinary citizen, between neighbor and neighbor, must be intact if efforts to make a better material life are not to be "a mad pursuit of illusions." Unless mediums respond to the spirits — and the wisdom and strength of the spirit pass to developing human beings so they respond to one another's needs — then political struggle is a matter of "snake swallowing snake."

A moral self-discipline — as stern, as dualistic, and as otherworldly as that of the *crentes* — underlies Maria's vision of social exchange and a better world. The basic source of evil and suffering in the world is the weakness of the flesh. The necessary, but not quite sufficient, remedy to the world's ills is that men and women should banish from their lives the "illusions and mystifications" that divert them from the disciplines necessary for the conquest of the flesh and the development of the spirit through success in the trials of this *vida passageira* (life of passage).

These have been the lessons of her own life, she urges, as well as the lessons she has learned from spiritism and the spirits. "Spiritism is a school in which people who aren't understanding — the spirit comes and explains how it is and they reach understanding." But life itself has taught her much: "one's life is a book and the world is a teacher." She considers her life to have been a life of suffering, but her practice of spiritism has brought her understanding, and understanding has been the basis of a limited happiness.

She remembers childhood as a time of "much sickness, sores, hunger, and fatigue." Her father was a landless rural laborer on a property close to the municipal seat. That was fifty years ago. There was never enough money, even for food, so everyone in the family of eight fell ill from time to time. Maria wanted to go to school but there was no money for that, and she had to work in the fields while still a child. Her father, like Severino's, saw no point in education and thought it positively harmful for girls, who would use literacy for writing love letters and reading things that were better left unread. At one stage — again a little like Severino — she arranged to do extra work and attend some evening classes run by nuns in the town. In a few weeks she had learned a lot, and when she was later able to read the *Prayers* of Alain Kardec, she thought it as much a miracle as due to the lessons. But she could stand the strain of combined work and study for only a short time.

At the age of fifteen, she went to Recife as a domestic servant, desperate to escape the outdoor labor she was too frail to bear. There she fell ill and experienced a number of minor but inexplicable domestic accidents. A sympathetic *patroa* (employer) took her to a doctor who was also a spiritist. His explanation of her problems made sense to her. She had the gift of mediumship, and spirits were trying to tell her to develop her gift so she could serve them. She returned home still ill, and, while she was recuperating, a relative gave her Alain Kardec's *Prayers* to read. With initial difficulty but eventual ease, Maria read the prayers and, helped and inspired by them, went on to read other works by Kardec. Her father had no sympathy for this dabbling in the things of Satan. But Maria, even while living and working at home, managed to go on developing her gift.

Her suffering continued. In the early fifties, the family moved to the large property bordering Campo Alegre. Maria was expected to marry, but her *namorados* (suitors) were either disapproved of by her parents or did not suit her. One man whom she did marry turned out to be a "savage beast"—she gave me no further details. A second husband gave her children but nothing to live on, and he, in time, took up with another woman. Ill health continued to be a problem. Through all her suffering, as she now sees it, the fact that she was in contact with the spirits and working as a medium with clients allowed her a certain happiness for the first time in her life (now in the early sixties). She understood better the peculiar combination of spiritual underdevelopment and material poverty that lay at the root of her problems. And her increased understanding, together with a small income from clients who paid for their consultations with the spirits, gave her greater liberty in life.

For a time in the late sixties and early seventies she worked with Lauro, Campo Alegre's most financially successful spirit medium. With Lauro she learned the rituals of the form of spiritism most common in Campo Alegre: a mixture of the Jurema cult with elements from Umbanda (Zé Pelintra has been borrowed from Umbanda and incorporated as a master spirit of Jurema) and from Kardecian prayer books. Skilled in ritual, and with the consulting rooms of Lauro's large modern center available to her, Maria could probably have attained financial security had she stayed on. But she left, and her several reasons for disassociating herself from Lauro tell something of her own dialectic of experience and spiritist belief.

In her critique of Lauro's group, and of several others in Campo Alegre, Maria uses a set of key concepts and dualities. She disapproves of leaders and groups who promote mystification and illusion. She criticizes these groups for offering instant remedies that require no fundamental changes in the way of life that causes spiritual derangement and its physical consequences, rather than helping members in the arduous work of spiritual development and preparation for the next life. There are groups that undermine the concentration necessary for spiritual progress with noisy or merely spectacular ritual. There are mediums who conduct businesses: selling only short-term physical remedies and claiming illusory miracles rather than focusing on the real responsibility of mediumship, which is the development of the gift and through it the refinement of a community of spirits. As she became more aware of her own responsibilities and saw the consequences of irresponsible mediumship, so she became more unhappy with her participation in Lauro's center. It had become, in her eyes, a commercial concern, a dispensary of instant remedies, and a place of mystification where the mediums themselves were regressing rather than advancing in awareness. The belief on which ritual and consultations were based had become, as she put it, "belief with lips and not with spirit and heart." Where the work of mediumship should be essentially a work of charity, Lauro's work had become an exhausting round of attending to short-term, paying clients; and as a consequence there was no time to develop the person-to-person and medium-to-spirit relationships necessary in "the vocation of charity."

Mediumship in Campo Alegre is a competitive business, and competition entails criticism, often vindictive, among the mediums. When Maria explains her departure from Lauro's group in terms of its commercialization and encouragement of mystification, we must wonder about an untold story of envy, rivalry, incompatibility. My own friendship and regard for Maria cause me to hedge my skepticism. But participation in the variety of rituals and consultations in Maria's home (as we shall see in the following extracts from my field notes taken in 1977 and 1982) also suggests to me that her own practice is well described with the positive categories implied in her negative critique of Lauro and his group. These field notes, of some of the rituals I attended, get as close as I can to a presentation of self and worldview as performed by Maria herself. (By this I mean simply that the field notes from 1977 and 1982 are edited only slightly for grammar and sense, and, although they are not naive records of all there was to see and hear, they are less heavily filtered through my own developing theses than the synthesized accounts I may write in 1988.)

4 May 1977, Afternoon.
I passed by Maria Pretinha's house to see whether there was to be a *reunião* [group meeting] this evening. Maria was in, talking with two teenage girls. She was not sure whether there will be a *reunião*. The people of Campo Alegre are so lacking in religion and faith and are so full of *vaidade* [vain frivolity] that they'd rather watch television than come along. Sometimes they've come in such numbers that the house can't fit them in. But at the moment the combination of rains and television keeps them away. People think that television can do something for the spirit. But it can't. They're mistaken. Such vanity. What sort of people don't have sufficient faith in Jesus Christ to want to learn more? They won't accept that learning is always a discipline, and the teacher has always to make certain demands on their time. The problem is that a medium can't make rules about television and other things like a parent can. It's so different in Aguas Belas (in the high *sertão* [interior] of Pernambuco where, according to Maria, most of the people are pure Indian). There, in fifteen days I hardly rested, there were so many people seeking to deepen their faith.

Evening
I went back to Maria's. This time there was a *reunião*. When I entered the front room, Maria was seated at her table facing three women who had turned up (later, three more women came in). The table was spread with a white cloth.

Maria, in a white dress, looked very small but very much the focal point through the candles and the six water-filled glasses. Also on the table were a bottle of cologne, two of Alain Kardec's books, a push-button bell, and one large artificial flower in a vase. The room, as usual, was sparsely tidy, softened a little by the kerosene and candle lighting. Maria looked preoccupied and buried her head in her hands frequently. The start of the *reunião* was delayed because of carousing from the little bar that had recently been opened by her next-door neighbor. But he was summoned, came in, and promised to quieten his friends down immediately. After some time he succeeded, and the rather fine *sertanejo* [backlands] singing and drumming stopped interfering with Maria's concentration.

Then Maria hits the bell three times to announce the beginning of the meeting. First she recites a series of Christian prayers, asking for the blessing of Jesus Christ on the proceedings. Her head is bowed, supported by steepled fingers. There is much movement of fingers and legs. She sings two rather dirgelike and highly repetitive hymns, in which the blessings of Jesus and the spirits of Jurema are sought. She calls on blessings for all—that we should all come to understand that our task is to prepare our spirits for eternal life; that we should gain the right perspective on this passing life, this life without hope (in the sense that decay and death of the flesh is inevitable, I think); that we should recognize that the realities of the spirit are the only realities.

After the preparatory hymns and prayers (most to be found in various publications from Editora Eco) the first manifestations occur. Each time a spirit arrives, Maria grunts, as we might on experiencing a stab of pain. Then her voice rises, and her speech becomes more rapid as she repeats the same short prayer to each of the spirits. Some of the spirits deliver exhortations, on themes prefigured in the blessings sought earlier. Others sing a hymn in praise of the Jurema cult or alluding to part of its syncretic mythology. One spirit (Joanna, I think—one of the spirits with whom Maria works) asked me questions. How was I? What did I want? I replied that I wanted to learn, and the spirit seemed satisfied.

More grunts and shudders preceded the arrival of another spirit—a *cabocla* spirit given to clicking of fingers and babbling in *"cabocla* language." Despite the problem of language, it made known its demands for a drinking bowl, a ritual bow and arrow, and, later, a pipe (this could not be found but a cigarette was acceptable). The bow and its set arrow were held above the head and clicked several times while the spirit repeated unintelligible phrases. To my great confusion the spirit addressed me; but neither I nor anyone else could understand what was being asked. Two of the ladies replied softly, "He doesn't understand your speech, sister." The spirit then summoned Xavier, a prison warden who lived opposite and who had often attended the *reunião* but whose wife (recently cured of an eye disease by a spirit eye-surgeon arranged by correspondence with a spiritist center in São Paulo) was presently estranged from Maria. He arrived promptly, neatly dressed and with hair combed, as though the summons were not unexpected. He went over to the table, and the spirit spoke, trying to get him to understand. He concentrated, looked puzzled, occasionally laughed a little nervously, turning to Maria Pretinha's brother who, from time to time, offered suggestions about what the spirit might mean. Meanwhile, the sounds of a "bang-bang" on a neighbor's television kept drifting in. Xavier, however, stayed until the end of the meeting, looking frequently over toward his house, very much as though he'd rather have been watching television.

The *cabocla* spirit left and Joanna arrived (or returned?). She called each of us in turn for a blessing and a purification in which the cologne was used. After my name was asked I was called to the table, and while one of my hands was held, I was given quite a long instruction. The instruction was in some of the essentials of spiritism, delivered in the form of aphorisms.

Always act so that the left hand knows what the right is doing.

Act not only openly but in harmony with the teachings of Jesus Christ.

Always act to prepare the spirit rather than follow the illusions of the flesh.

There was much repetition and each aphorism was punctuated with "*Entende?*" [understand?].

Some received just the blessing and the *limpeza* [the cleaning] in which the hands are splashed with cologne, then rubbed together, and the perfume inhaled three times. The lady next to me didn't get off as lightly as I with a general instruction but, by way of continuation of a previous consultation, was called disobedient. A teenage girl didn't want to go up. The next lady, another neighbor, went up and asked for advice about a young relative who had come to her house complaining of an excessive punishment she'd received in her home. How should she respond? Joanna replied that the girl needed a lot of understanding and sympathy.

Joanna led some more prayers (one addressed Oxum, Ogun, and other *orixás*). Some of the prayers were in litany form, and those who knew the replies responded. Then, with a few grunts, Joanna departed and Maria brought the meeting to an end with a ring of the bell.

A neighbor and I stayed for a while, the others leaving straight away. When asked what I thought of the meeting I said I'd been rather thrown by not being able to understand the *cabocla* spirit. "Oh her," said Maria, "no one can understand her, she hasn't learnt to communicate with us yet." She then invited me to another meeting, next week, a meeting not for the *caboclos,* communicative and otherwise, but for the *spiritos mestres* [master spirits]. Some of these spirits, like Zé Pelintra with whom she worked, were still developing so that, in the meantime, their whims for *cachaça* and smoking had to be met. Then Maria, sounding very much as Joanna had earlier, launched into another mini-sermon about spiritual reality as the only reality and life as a *vida passageira*.

14 May 1977

Maria had invited me to the one *toque* she has each year on the nearest possible day to May 13, the day commemorating the abolition of slavery in Brazil. That is the day on which the master spirit with whom she works, Zé Pelintra, likes to have a *toque*. Maria, when extending the invitation to me, reiterated her lack of enthusiasm for *toques* and the cult of the *orixás* but explained that it was an important part of her relationship with Zé that she should organize it for him.

I arrived at Maria's house just before the start of the *toque* at 9.15 PM. There was standing room only available — about forty people, mostly women and including from twelve to twenty women who danced in the *gira* [circle] while the *orixás* were celebrated. Altogether about fourteen men stayed on, including the alcohol-addled incompetent whom Maria had asked to lead the *toque;* young Moisés who ran his own center as a medium and who *did* know the chants; some of his young friends; the prison warden Xavier; and the old coconut harvester whom I've seen at other *toques.* Maria had managed to have the electricity connected, so the light was much harsher. The floors of the front room and the tiny alcove were strewn with eucalyptus leaves. The women waiting to take part in the *gira* were not as well dressed as at Fuló's (though his group too is clearly much poorer than most Recife groups I've seen). On the other hand, some of the ladies clearly move from group to group — at least three of the ladies here had participated at Fuló's. Some of them were able to help when Maria's chosen leader (through incompetence) or Moisés (because he slipped away) were not able to keep the *toque* going.

Maria started with a disclaimer about her ability to lead the *gira*. And the opening was indeed chaotic, halting, dramatically disastrous. The ladies in the *gira* seemed restless and anxious as the chant and drumming faltered a number of times. Maria's prayer for the blessing of Jesus Christ and the dispatching of Exú went well enough, but nobody who was willing to lead could think of how to start the next chants. Eventually, a very black lady (whom I have since encountered as a sort of teacher and adviser in other groups) led the chants so that they were able to proceed, even though leadership was never clear. Dona Marina, who had once had her own *salão*, also helped at a number of points, after much cajoling. But she complained a number of times that no one would respond to the chants that she led.

Somehow, though, the *toque* did take off. The *cabocla* spirits were called first. Maria became the center of dramatic attention when she was visited by a *cabocla* spirit. Her hair loose and wild-looking, she prowled with her bow and arrow, and we all tried in vain to make out what she was saying. After the *caboclos* had been farewelled, the *orixás* were called, one by one. However, this was more an Umbanda calling than Nagô. There was much more Portuguese in the chants, with more popular melodic line, and black slave spirits were included with the *orixás*. Maria was briefly *manifestada,* but she did not become the center of dramatic attention; nor were the African spirits awarded the same time and attention as the *caboclos* and the *mestres*.

When the African spirits had departed, Maria left the front room for a moment to change into a pair of white slacks, ready for her own *mestre,* Zé Pelintra. She was quickly *manifestada,* and Zé dominated the rest of the *toque* though some other *mestres* were manifested as well. Their hosts hitched up their dresses to look like pants and the *mestres* showed their mettle by embracing, in a macho fashion, the ladies of the *gira*. But Zé defined himself more extravagantly. His deep rough voice, his mode of speaking, his body movements, especially his dance steps, are all very masculine, in the way of the Northeast. He tells us about himself — he's a *cachaceiro* [an overindulging drinker of *cachaça*]; he's unable yet to go to heaven so he must wander around; he is a friend of all. He talks about Maria as very different from himself: a nondrinker, averse to swearing and his other bad habits. He is very patronizing. Then he talks to some of us, to straighten out a few things, it seems. The old coconut gatherer is reproved for being a standoffish onlooker who comes along for spectacle but not to learn. He gets angry with a couple for feigning manifestation (the man had been sitting next to me and did seem to go into trance, but in a wild, uncontrolled way). Having very much established presence, character, authority, Zé moved around giving counsel — listening to domestic, health, and financial problems and giving advice. But there was time off, too, for drinking what seemed to me to be large amounts of *cachaça*, though some of this was shared. I had to take a couple of swigs from the bottle while being told to loosen up and wished good luck with my researches.

After a very long manifestation (I didn't time it — two hours?) Zé announced he would soon leave us. The *toque* was brought to a fairly rapid, if slightly ragged, end. Participants and the house were cleansed of the presence of any of the troublesome Exú spirits; but one of them remained stubbornly in a tall, dark lady. Eventually the problem was solved. Blessing us all individually with passes in which a bottle of *cachaça* was used like a wand, Zé Pelintra left us. After staggering a little, Maria was back with us, apparently none the worse for the *cachaça*. It was 3 AM, but Maria still had time to laugh with us as we told her what Zé had said and done.

21 September 1977
When I arrived there were only two others present, two women neighbors. Maria was sitting at her table, two candles already lit. She said we would have just prayers if no one else came. But three teenage girls arrived with a well-dressed woman in her late twenties from the city. One of the girls is an apprentice medium and was invited by Maria to the table. Later on two men arrived. One, I think, is the father of the apprentice.

The meeting started late. Before it started, the apprentice gave Maria a book of prayers for mediums for examination. Maria went through the book indicating which prayers she should say and which not. She was to leave aside prayers that were only for *reuniões*. Other prayers, for various illnesses, were only to be said in cases of genuine need. But others were to be read — the prayer of Ishmael and others — regularly.

Apprenticeship was the theme of the meeting. Maria read the opening prayers this time — rather haltingly because of the weak candlelight and her weak eyes. Then she recited a long prayer at the end of which the manifestations started. The longest and most didactic was Joanna de Barros who spoke about the requirements for good mediumship. An essential requirement was concentration. The medium is like a radio. She must be fully in tune to receive and transmit the messages passed to her. So she must train her powers of concentration and purify herself so that the spirit can communicate. The medium should also understand that what is important in the meetings is not the *manobras* [manipulations] that the spirits perform on the bodies of the mediums but the wisdom that they communicate.

When the manifestations had finished, Maria continued with further instructions on baths to be taken on days other than Monday and Friday, as part of the preparation for mediumship.

In 1982, Maria's Zé Pelintra told me that there was much I still did not understand about *espiritismo*. But I think it is possible to note some fairly obvious features of the world being performed in these rituals. Maria's Campo Alegre is populated by spirit visitors who can act on and with the physically present population so that the course of private, individual lives and the quality of communal life may be altered. But the spirit visitors do not cause the private ills and the public deficiencies of life in Campo Alegre. Even relatively developed spirits like Joanna de Barros and Zé Pelintra are approached cautiously by Maria Pretinha, as they might cause misfortune through their clumsy reactions to frustration. Less developed spirits perform even more clumsily or heavy-handedly, and Maria says that unscrupulous mediums might manipulate these spirits to do harm to the living. But the performed relationships between the living and the spirits are always bonds manifesting, effecting, discovering, or enhancing responsible action by the living. Maria's *reuniões* are exercises in concentration against the noise (the bar next door and the two or three television sets in the street) and the drift of everyday life. Head in hands, drawing us into stretches of Quaker silence or softly reciting preparatory prayers, Maria, in her *caboclo* meetings, leads us in focusing on questions that the more articulate spirits take up in discussion and counseling. What is happening to me in everyday life? What is the relationship between what is happening to me and what I am doing, especially in my relationships with others? How do I communicate what I know about these things with others, seen and unseen, whose lives impinge on mine? The whole performance, then, shifts the boundaries between that which happens to me or which I cause to happen inadvertently and that over which I have control and exercise responsibility: the area of the former diminishes, the area of the latter increases, provided that, as Maria and Joanna de Barros insist, participation in the ritual has meant movement of the heart and not just movement of the lips. The gestures of concentration, the rituals of communication with the inarticulate, and question and answer with the more developed spirits are, quite self-consciously for Maria at any rate, achievements of responsibility over normal everyday drift and manipulated or manipulative behavior.

When the *mestres* like Zé Pelintra descend, they perform a world in which responsibility involves something other than the perfect act from out-of-the-world actors or paragons. Zé drinks and swears and then reproves us for not attending to the questions of responsibility. Zé is still a public reprobate, but he draws Maria and those who consult him to responsible action as he grows in responsibility himself. Maria's own harsh dualist rhetoric, dividing spirit from flesh, is belied, or at least softened, as Zé sends up priggishness, drinks too much *cachaça,* and points out to a coconut gatherer that he is too much the mere spectator of life. In Maria's meetings, the models of responsible action and those who counsel and push us toward greater responsibility are not other than us — they are not distant European saints, or the one God of the Bible, or the learned priest, or the Assembly of God ascetic who has created a monastic world apart — but a diverse, even polyglot, band of triers. Joanna de Barros, most articulate of *caboclas,* puffs on her cigars and instructs young mediums in how they might enter into controlled relationships with the spirits and mediate the chain of responsibility from ordinary citizen through to highest spirits. Zé Pelintra uses the roughest language to jolt us all out of drift or pathos.

Maria gives plenty of guidance to anyone attempting to discern political concomitants of this religious ethic of responsibility. In her comments on local politicians as they campaigned for the elections of November 1982, in her assessments of the land problem as it had taken shape in Campo Alegre by that year, and in her advice to clients, firm lines of political assessment and judgment emerge. First, she construes most of the problems of poverty or injustice that she observes or that are brought to her as not being amenable to political remedy. As we have seen, this is partly because, in Maria's view, there is no political remedy available to individuals in the absence of a greater degree of communal responsibility than she finds in Campo Alegre. In the absence of a developing communal responsibility, political activity degenerates (or has degenerated, she avers) into destructive individual competitiveness. But at the individual level too, spiritual development (including, above all, the perception of one's own responsibility for private troubles) is at once a necessary prerequisite for seeking any political remedy and likely to be sufficient for attaining greater happiness and satisfaction. Maria's moral economy of responsibility does not exactly deny political economic structures as causes of private troubles; but, in her descriptions and analyses of the problems of everyday life in Campo Alegre, moral categories have salience and priority over the social-structural.

Second, Maria's application of her ethic of responsibility to the politicians and political systems known to her finds them all wanting. She is

19. Seu Boiadeiro visits Campo Alegre, much as Zé Pelintra does, drinks *cachaça* and gives good counsel.

as skeptical as Severino of the claims of populist and military politicians because none of them measures up to her standards of responsibility. She chides Campo Alegrenses who still seek the good patron, proclaiming the moral failure of her own father's patron on the land bordering the town when he neglected to secure continuity of tenure for his tenants at the time of selling to the current, more ruthlessly businesslike owner.

Third, and as a consequence of both the low priority she accords to political activity and her skepticism toward the claims of all politicians, Maria eschews all political alliances. As a neighborhood influential she has been approached for support by a variety of local political hopefuls but has turned them away. While considering herself a Catholic, she judges the priest a failure as a religious leader and as an administrator of the church patrimony, so his experiments in communal politics hold no attraction for her.

In any narrow conception of politics in Campo Alegre, Maria Pretinha's must be counted a weak voice. Determinedly without political allies, focusing on long-term moral renewal, scornful of short-term political solutions, and with a very small group of participating followers, Maria counts for nothing much either in electoral politics or in the ongoing struggles for justice waged in the local political arena. Nonetheless, in the sense of politics developed in this book, Maria does have a distinctive voice. It is a voice for political skepticism, resistant to the various claims for hegemony heard in Campo Alegre and constantly warning Campo Alegrenses to beware of the illusions spun by those who would manipulate them politically. It is a voice urging the formation of moral community as a prerequisite for a politics of justice and redress. As a weak voice, should it have been registered at such length here? In part the response to this question is the reason for the inclusion of Severino's eccentric voice at even greater length: variation within the religious group (in this case the greater range of variation within spiritism) can the better be appreciated by way of contrast with the rich, fluent, if lonely, voice of a virtuoso.

In any case, she is not quite alone. I would suggest that she and Fuló, together with their small groups of core participants and as they live their religious visions, are co-constructors of a common politics. Perhaps their mutual respect derives from their realizing that this is so, despite the different spirits they work with. (And after consideration of the cases outlined in the next chapter, even their different spirits might seem to have more in common than they recognize.) Unlike the spirits of most of the other *centros* of Campo Alegre, neither Zé Pelintra nor Fuló's *orixás* accept the lowly place assigned to them by the *cultura alta*. They are spirits of the inferior races and classes who refuse to accept inferiority, and who invite the living to do likewise. And though they act upon the living they are scornful of what we might call magic and pathos. They demand that the living relate to them in cumulative and community-fostered exchanges rather than in discontinuous, episodic encounters arranged by a medium as the remedy for an individual's immediate troubles (these latter encounters involving magical relationships between spirits, mediums, and clients). They will not allow the living to blame their episodic misfortunes on the spirits (the response of pathos) but insist that the only appropriate response to the problems of everyday life is the search for pattern and meaning and the sources of communal strength.

These characteristics of the spirits with whom Fuló and Maria work have religious corollaries of at least potential political consequence. As mediators of such spirits, both Fuló and Maria see themselves and act as *zeladores* — guardians and teachers of religious heritage and experience — rather than as controllers of power. As *zeladores*, both consider that consultations with clients to deal with immediate problems form the lesser part of their work as mediums. Though both receive money from clients who are not participating members, or who value specific solutions to specific problems received in consultation over the religious life of the group, neither encourages or approves of the episodic medium-client relationship. More important is the building of a small community of those who will study with the *zelador* to banish mystification from their lives and to develop spiritually, even as they help and please the spirits through exchanges with them. Both call on mere clients to work hard over the years to overcome ignorance about identity and purpose in life.

Associated with this religious praxis, and not just in the leaders but in a small band of core participants, are the lineaments of a political culture. Members of Fuló's and Maria's groups are not inclined to construe all the problems of everyday life as private punishments or trials or visitations of malign spirits. Many instances of suffering in their own lives and in the lives of neighbors are recognized as connected with public issues of injustice and foul play perpetrated by the strong, if spiritually immature, against the weak. But direct, protracted, political struggle is not predicated by this stream of spiritism. The sense of what a real community might be, capable of withstanding the evident rigors and corruptions of political action, is so strong as to guarantee extreme skepticism about any actual, viable, political base for political action in Campo Alegre. On the other hand, if the necessary communal base for political action cannot be found at least in the short run, it may conceivably be found in the long run, through the religious community building that produces political activity of a kind more advanced than snake swallowing snake. In the meantime, none of the power structures that be — or leaders that would be — is congenial within the religious visions of these groups. Patron-clientage of the old or newer populist forms is corrupt and spiritually corrupting, especially for those who might be wooed as clients; and not one of the would-be patrons (in Maria's explicit views at any rate) has the moral stature to merit respect. The bureaucratic-authoritarian claims to legitimacy also ring hollow within these groups: the power of duly accredited experts is denied, and alternative histories of legitimate power and achievement are told and enacted.

This political culture of skepticism and indirect resistance, of slow and uncertain creation of bases for an alternative politics at the grass roots, may well be distant from the political culture nurtured by more mainstream forms of Afro-Brazilian spiritism.

CHAPTER SIX

The Afro-Brazilian Spiritists: The Mainstream?

POLITICAL SKEPTICISM; disengagement from the structures and sentiments of paternalism, populism, and modern authoritarian bureaucracy; sustained attempts to construct alternative community, the recent literature, by and large, would not lead us to expect these things from Afro-Brazilian spiritist groups. Fuló, Maria Pretinha, and the groups they try to hold together seem very aberrant indeed in the context of that literature. Are they curious, but insignificant, departures from the mainstream of Afro-Brazilian religion in Campo Alegre and elsewhere in Brazil? Or do they represent a minority but at the same time an important development in the tortuous history of Afro-Brazilian syncretism, not only in Campo Alegre but in Brazil as a whole?

The modern literature is adamant for the former rather than the latter possibility. Renato Ortiz — justly one of the most influential scholars of the cults — argues that the family of Umbanda cults possesses an ideology, formulated largely by whites, that functions to extend the hegemony of white elites. Umbanda is the largest, regionally most extensive, and fastest-growing of the cults. Ortiz argues that in ritual, organization, and mythology, Umbanda achieves "the white death of the black shaman."[1] In terms of the categories I have been using, Umbanda groups are not autonomous but manipulable and dependent, ultimately, on the resources and direction of dominant elites. Umbanda ideology does not encourage the articulation of critical awareness and values among the lower classes but — through its scientism and its placing of African spirits and practices at the bottom of an evolutionary scale — expresses white, upper-class hegemony. As it expresses, so does it socialize: its members enter modern society, not as members of a grass-roots community but as individuals competing for often illusory upward mobility. At the end of his book, Ortiz speculates further that the state, no longer finding Catholicism congenial as a legitimating power, might turn to Umbanda.

The state would be able to choose . . . in the religious market a religion which would suit it better in the implantation of a given socioeconomic order. In proportion as the present orientation of the Church (the National Council of Bishops, CNBB) enters into conflict with the dominant ideology, the Umbanda religion becomes an important reserve weapon, well able to inculcate values of submission to the established order.[2]

Other case studies suggest ways in which Afro-Brazilian cults (and especially Umbanda), short of becoming an official legitimating religion, may yet serve either or both the patronal-representative and bureaucratic-authoritarian political economies rather than provide a grass-roots base for an alternative politics. Diana Brown has shown in her case studies how Umbanda may restore broken lines of patronage in urban areas, helping to incorporate submissive lower-class members in systems of economic and political exchange that maintain domination by elites. Patrícia Birman, in a brief analysis of language, ritual, and organization in an Umbanda cult group, traces how Umbandistas rehearse and adopt the norms and practice of power as it is wielded in the dominant society: to practice Umbanda — to submit, for example, to the demands of the medium possessed by the master spirit Seu Boiadeiro — is to accept submission to centralized bureaucratic power conceived as normal in both the material and spiritual planes. Leni Silverstein widens our focus from Umbanda to the supposedly more African Candomblé cult of Bahia.[3] Examining modes of survival in Candomblé groups, Silverstein brings out the religiously masked dependence of cult groups on white upper-class resources: the religious relationship between the cult leader (female, black, and poor — the *mãe de santo*) and the participant patron (male, white, and wealthy — the *ogã*) hides a system of lower-class survival through incorporation into an upper-class patronage system. Such a system, we may presume, works for the poor as it effectively elicits resources from the rich. But the price paid for security by the poor is precisely the sacrifice of autonomy, articulation of grass-roots perceptions and values, and independent community.

It is possible to draw evidence in support of these interpretations from most of Campo Alegre's fourteen Afro-Brazilian groups. Two cases, presented in some detail, might help us better locate Fuló and Maria Pretinha in the mélange of Campo Alegre and also map the political possibilities of Afro-Brazilian religion in Brazil.

DONA ROSÁRIA'S GROUP

Dona Rosária comes every week to Campo Alegre from Recife, thirty kilometers away. She brings, from the spiritist center in one of the city's most exclusive suburbs, a message to the poor. In her *centro* in Campo Alegre, she disperses not only enlightenment but therapy and goods to the needy. The building was originally a large barn made available to her by the local prison authorities. She has transformed it to her purposes. (Several functions of her group and differences between it and Pai Fuló's, may be read from Figure 4, which is a sort of floor plan of the center.) Two-thirds of the center is arranged as a classroom or lecture hall of the traditional kind. The top third is set apart for what Fuló would call the *cultura alta*, its personnel and its artefacts. Dona Rosária and visiting dignitaries speak from the table to an audience seated in rows. The very furniture is arranged for passive reception of messages from experts.

The remaining third of the building is reserved for other forms of dispensing from the *cultura alta*. In the cubicles, after hearing the message, Dona Rosária's audience may become clients. A client will enter into the cubicle, and an expert in spiritual currents will dispense a therapeutic pass and sometimes counseling based on the wisdom passed on from the higher, purer spirits. Then, those in greatest need may be given food and even clothing brought by Dona Rosária from the Spiritist Federation headquarters in the city.

Dona Rosária's spirit world is tidily arranged. It is elaborately structured from higher spirits, with Jesus Christ at the top; through the great departed thinkers of Western civilization; to the lower spirits, the old slaves, the cowboy spirits, the spirits of the street; then the inarticulate *caboclo* and African spirits; and finally to the evil spirits of darkness, including the African Exús. She professes the beliefs of the Umbanda cult, though among Umbandistas hers is of the kind most heavily influenced by the nineteenth-century European spiritualist Alain Kardec and the least continuous with more African cults like Fuló's Xangô or Bahian Candomblé. Her exemplar is the great white medium Chico Xavier, whose portrait hangs on the screen behind the table. Xavier has published books of prayers and revelations communicated by superior spirits. These superior spirits are not the African spirits of Xangô or the *caboclo* Indian spirits (the cowboys, the ex-slaves, and the street spirits of the Umbanda group) but spirits of departed, white, professional representatives of the *cultura alta*.

Her Saturday afternoon meetings press her points home with lectures and prayers. The spirits are not manifested — only the wisdom of the higher spirits is communicated. I was taken to the Saturday meeting for the first time by a neighbor, Maria José. Introduced as a researcher from the university, I was invited by Dona Rosária to sit at a table with her and a visiting speaker. (Fuló always made it clear to me and members of the group that I was a learner.) When we were all seated, Dona Rosária wel-

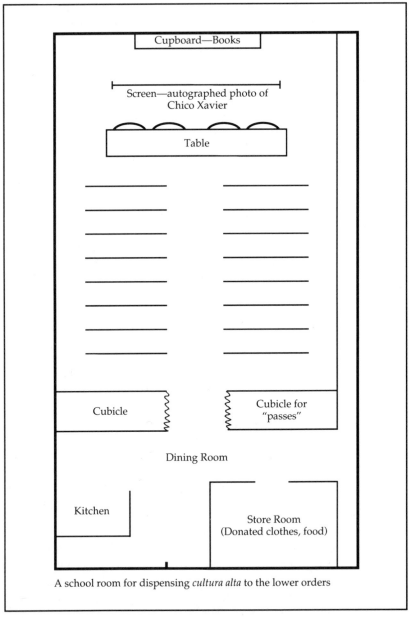

Figure 4. Centro espiritista: Dona Rosária of the Federação espiritista, Encruzilhada

comed us and then asked us to stand for prayers, which she read. The long prayers contained messages of hope: in the third millennium our children would lead better lives than we do because of the steady advance of spiritual wisdom. And there was exhortation: our bodies are like clothes, needing to be patched up and eventually discarded; but the spiritual life goes on.

Then the meeting was handed over to the visiting lecturer, a professional woman from the city, who announced her topic as "charity" but ranged over a number of themes in a very long, if charmingly anecdotal, sermon. Her points included the need for rules in life governing sex, drink, and smoking — not from any Puritanism but because rules are the basis for nonpossessive charity in relationships with others. A better world will not come through any system like capitalism or socialism — the societies of the U.S. and the U.S.S.R., both ridden with problems, show us that. Only through spiritual evolution — achieved through prayer, guidance from the higher spirits, and our practice of charity — will the world improve.

After two hours of talking, the meeting ended with a concluding prayer written by Chico Xavier and read by Dona Rosária. The visitor took a client into one of the cubicles, and Maria José went with Dona Rosária to receive a tin of powdered milk for her adopted baby. I was curious to find out what else Maria José received from the center, and what place her involvement there had in her life. She was getting old, with failing eyesight, and was no longer able to earn money as a farm laborer. She had a drinking problem, as had her husband, who had recently lost fairly steady employment when his old patron moved to the city from the last private sugar mill on the island. She was attempting to bring up two adopted children, and her life was, in many ways, a disaster. She cared for her adopted children but was unable to offer them adequate shelter, food, or medical care. The charity dispensed at the center came nowhere near to solving her problems.

But she attended for a variety of reasons, which I reconstruct from conversations with her.[4] The existence of a spirit world that impinges on this world is very real to her, but it is her experience that nothing must take you too far away from secure lines of patronage with the Brazil of the *cultura alta*. Fuló's Xangô takes you too far away and offers nothing in return; Rosária's group offers needed strength from the spirits and a line for material patronage as well. The center itself is well-lit, clean, and comfortable and offers the schooling that seems necessary to get on, but that is otherwise unavailable to the Maria Josés of northeast Brazil. Her recent biography suggests to me that Maria José goes out from the center hopeful that modernity will provide, distrustful of her judgment because convinced of her ignorance, and accepting the claims of white professional experts — the authorities — who lead in this material world and in the other world of the spirits. Through Dona Rosária, as much as through the conditions of life that are forcing her to dependence, she has made the transition from citizenship in the rural world of local patronage to a sort of compliance in modernizing bureaucratic-authoritarian Brazil. To anticipate a little: Dona Rosária's group emerges out of the destruction of the world of *coronelismo* and, in Campo Alegre's modern mélange, tends to link its members to the culture and the structures of bureaucratic-authoritarian Brazil. In Maria José we can see how Dona Rosária, gentle soul, as a medium for the learned and expert spirits is also a medium for the defeat of Fuló's sort of community and for the hegemony of expertise.

DONA PAULA AND HER CLIENTS

Dona Paula is concerned that she should be correctly located in Campo Alegre society and vis-à-vis other spiritist leaders in town. She establishes her respectability in a number of ways. One is by well-broadcast, if invidious, comparison between other groups and her own. She keeps drunkards and ne'er-do-wells out of her *toques* and *fiestas*, unlike Fuló who has drunkards barging into his — and did I know that one of the women participating at Fuló's had conspired with another woman to murder her own husband?[5] Maria, one can be sorry for, she is so poor. Where Fuló works exclusively with the noisy and uncontrollable *orixás*, she works with gentler, more controllable spirits in the "more modern" Umbanda cult: even the spirit Exú of Umbanda is more easily directed to behave and work for good than Exú of Xangô. So those respectable people who come to her group are likely to be respected rather than agitated or made to look foolish by the spirits who descend.

Dona Paula can justify her claims as she shows a visitor around her *salão*. It is a freestanding building in the backyard of her husband's house. It is larger and much more substantial than most family residences in Campo Alegre. Indeed it is much lighter, better ventilated (with the help of an electric roof fan), and better maintained than her home, which fronts on the main road of Campo Alegre and looks across a square to the temple of the Assembly of God, though it is one of the bigger and more comfortable houses in town. The largest room in the *salão* building has a maroon-painted cement floor, pale blue rendered walls, and, when the artfully installed neon lighting and the roof fan are switched on, it displays both clinical sheen and theatrical promise. With its own special lighting, a statue of the spirit currently being honored presides over the room from a plinth set in the wall opposite the entrance. To the left of the statue is a door leading into three connected rooms — one a changing room, mainly for Dona Paula's use; another the *pejí*, where the images of the spirits and other objects associated with them are kept; and a room for consultations, though these are often held in the large main room.

The *salão* befits someone of Dona Paula's attainments and connections. Her husband is *sub-prefeito* (deputy mayor) for Campo Alegre in the municipal government, and Dona Paula receives the local politicians of the government party (the PDS in 1982) into her house and often to *toques* and *fiestas* in her *salão*. She has been working as a medium in Campo Alegre for nearly twenty-five years and has a large clientele — from local fishermen to wives of successful businessmen in the municipal seat. She is not to be ignored by politicians. Her husband has retired from his position as a lower-level bureaucrat of the state government, but the family maintains contact with a wide range of small business and petty official families from the capital city and surrounding areas. One of her sons brings fellow university students back to the house. And Dona Paula, so long a successful medium, has attracted her own better-heeled clients from surrounding areas and Recife, the capital city itself.

The rituals of the *salão* are made attractive to this network of clients and contacts. Dona Paula is a careful choreographer of the social relations of ritual, even in her choice of Umbanda over the cult of the *orixás*, as the following extracts from field notes rather suggest.

28 August 1977, Sunday Night
This was to be a *toque* for Exú and a fiesta to celebrate the birthday of Dona Paula's gypsy Pombagira.[6] August 24 is the *Noite Negra*, Exú's black night. I was invited along as photographer. When I arrived, about 8.45 PM, Dona Paula handed me over to her son who was to organize the lighting. This son lives in Campo Alegre with his wife and small children, almost opposite his parents' house. He works in the aluminum-extrusion factory. He set up a 200-watt lamp to help with illumination. This was an easy job for him: he had already arranged the other lighting — the flashing lights on the statue and altar for Exú and around a statue of Our Lady-Iemanjá set into the wall. The altar lighting, cloth, and the statue itself were all the correct deep red . . . below Exú little mermaid statuettes of Iemanjá were arranged. . . .

Dona Paula initiated proceedings with a short speech. This was a night in honor of Exú. Exú was basically our friend, despite his reputation. He is powerful, and we need him to achieve the good things in life. This was also the night of the phalanx of Exú. . . .

In the early stages of the ceremony, Dona Paula spent a lot of time as a sort of roving hostess, greeting new arrivals — as though the drummers (four of them) and the fourteen women in the circle and the *pai de santo* [father of the saint] leading the *toadas* [chants] were all performers in an entertainment provided by her for her guests. The wife, daughter, and elder son of the new owner of the Main Street bakery and breadshop were welcomed as very honored guests and given some of the seats in rather short supply, which were arranged around the wall. This was the first time that any of them had been to a *toque*. Others, while allowed in, would not be given any special welcome and would have to watch standing in doorways and crowding around windows.

Reinforcing my impression that this was entertainment, Dona Paula's son invited me to leave the *toque* and come to the house and have a beer with a group of young couples who had arrived in their cars from out of town. They too had been welcomed by Dona Paula but had not taken their seats in the *salão*. One of the young men was an engineering student. Another was holding forth on what a good husband he'd been but how the worst thing he'd ever done was to get married. Some members of this group knew a lot about the folklore of Umbanda and told me what they thought would be the highlights of the *toque*. But on this occasion, at any rate, members of the group made it clear they were here for the fun. (Not without its dangers, though. Later on, back in the *salão*, one of the women became *manifestada* but did not know how to control the experience like a trained medium. Dona Paula had a lot of trouble bringing her out of trance and the woman was clearly distressed — among other things, her feet became cramped, I think.) . . .

We were called back to the *salão* for the manifestation of the Pombagira. This must have been after *toadas* for Ogun, which I missed. Dona Paula was quickly *manifestada*. Rockets were set off outside to greet the arrival of the Pombagira. We all clapped hands, and then the *manifestada* was led out through the door to the *pejí* to be suitably dressed. After some time she emerged in a fine full-length black taffeta-and-lace dress, carrying red roses in a basket. The women in the circle and some of the audience joined in the Umbanda songs of welcome to the guardian of the crossroads who comes by the light of the moon with her red roses. For over half an hour the *toque* stopped, and the fiesta of the Pombagira took over. The resplendent gypsy posed for photos with various combinations of family and friends. Then two magnums of sweet pink champagne were opened. There was a definite pecking order for the distribution of the drink: the Pombagira herself, then family and honored guests (I was called over for a share before the women in the circle were given any). Only then were they and other people inside the *salão* offered any. Finally, trays were taken out to spectators around the doors and windows.

It is precisely Dona Paula's attention to respectability and her success as a prima donna that makes her attractive to her clients. Regular clients whom I have interviewed are proud of the spectacle she provides. Poorer clients value the ambience of another class that Dona Paula invites them into, the exchanges between classes as well as the exchanges between powerful spirits and the living that she mediates. Above all, Dona Paula is valued for her powers in divining which spirits are causing harm and why. Most of her clients come with a story of specific suffering: a husband straying, illness, a string of inexplicable accidents. They come in the belief that much human suffering is caused by spirits whom the sufferer has offended or who have been turned against the sufferer by some other person. Dona Paula, as a manifestly powerful and successful medium, is able not only to diagnose but to remedy. If the sufferer has provided the provocation directly but unknowingly, she can prescribe the remedy that will appease the spirit. If a provocateur (or provocateuse) has been involved, working perhaps through another medium, it is expected that Dona Paula will be able to summon more powerful spirits or negotiate with the spirits causing the trouble so that the harmful activity is neutralized or stopped.

Biu, an occasional client and a neighbor in Campo Alegre, helps illustrate the medium-spirit-client relationship and the worldview that sustains it. Biu habitually attributes events, particularly mishaps in her life, to the actions of the spirits upon her. As an eighteen-year-old living with a young man who could gain only intermittent employment as an unskilled laborer, she became pregnant and felt very ill. Iemanjá acted upon her, she says, drawing her into the water, where she would have drowned if not restrained. Then, the child was born and was frequently ill, and she was anxious about her lack of resources to care for her child and herself. At this time, she says, a spirit kept impelling her to kill the baby. Later, when the baby was healthy, her husband had to leave her behind while he went to work in another town. She was convinced that he would not return but go off with another woman who would employ the power of the spirits to ensnare him.

In all these events, Biu sees herself as the passive victim of spirits acting upon her. In each case she goes to one or all three of her preferred mediums for help, for which she must pay a fee. She favors Dona Paula above the others, in part because she does not urge her to participate in a spiritist group but provides prompt diagnoses of the roots of the problem, appropriate remedies, and generally correct prognostications. Dona Paula has usually confirmed Biu's own diagnoses — though not in the case of the supposedly errant husband: in that case, Dona Paula divined, there was no spirit at work to draw her husband away and he'd be back. And he was. Dona Paula's authority and apparent success seem to reinforce Biu's own diagnoses and mode of dealing with crises in her life. This is the type of exchange in which the expert medium encourages the client in her predisposition to interpret her problem in individualistic terms: the private trouble and competitive relationships are emphasized, rather than any public issue that might be discerned or any communal solution that might be appropriate. The predisposition to pathos — to interpret suffering as being acted upon in such a way that the sufferer can do nothing (at least, not without expert help) — is also encouraged and enacted in the relationships described. Interpreting her problems individualistically and with pathos, Biu links herself with existing patronage structures and a mode of interpreting everyday life that precludes the articulation of critical perceptions and values.

It is easy to overinterpret along these lines, for there are such things as private troubles and appropriately individual modes of addressing them. The political sociologist must beware of judging that Biu misperceived her problems and concluding that her life will be determined by her misperceptions. In fact, over the years, it has become apparent to me that Biu has not been set in or determined by her interpretations and actions of 1977. But the example is meant neither to establish tight causation nor to assert correct political vision but only to demonstrate how a particular spiritist worldview and the social relations involved in a type of spiritist group might steer those involved away from the perceptions and responses that might be, and are, encouraged in groups like Fuló's and Maria Pretinha's.

At several other rituals I attended at Dona Paula's in 1977 and 1982, the impressions I recorded after the feast of the Pombagira were confirmed. Dona Paula's rituals have little to do with constructing the historical identity of a group, as at Fuló's; nor are they dedicated to the formation of a moral elite, with perhaps some sheer fun on the way, as at Maria Pretinha's. In ritual Dona Paula seems frankly intent on securing attachments to existing socio-political elites and establishing or reinforcing her credentials as a powerful medium. It would be going only a little beyond her own frankness to claim that, through well-managed and lavishly resourced entertainment, Dona Paula advances her business as a consulting medium: impressing and attracting customers and initiating or completing a variety of exchanges for patronage and respectability.

In 1977 I took my daughter along to the children's feast at Dona Paula's, celebrating the day of the twin child-saints Cosmas and Damian. Again there was careful attention to spectacle, with two of Dona Paula's grandsons dressed up as the saints standing on a table decorated for a birthday party. But the highlight of the afternoon was when Dona Paula, supposedly *manifestada* with an Indian child-spirit, emerged from the *peji* in a sequined ballerina outfit and tights, with feathers in her hair. Dona Paula is a rather bulky grandmother, and not nearly as physically convincing as an Indian child-spirit as she is as Pombagira, but the children did not mind for she was to distribute sweets to them. The child-spirit, however, was worldly-wise, and to my embarrassment my daughter was included in the first rank of higher-status children to receive more sweets first, while her poorer neighborhood friends were told to mind their manners and wait their turn. My daughter compounded my embarrassment by accept-

20. Dona Paula manifests an Indian child-spirit.

ing her privilege with enthusiasm and observing with eleven-year-old shrewdness that Dona Paula wasn't even in a real trance.

In 1982 I went to a *toque* at Dona Paula's with an old lady who had had a *salão* on the outskirts of Campo Alegre for many years before moving to São Paulo in 1975 to be with her children and grandchildren. The old lady asked to join in the *gira*, the circle of sons and daughters in the saint who dance and chant and manifest the spirits as they descend. Dona Paula agreed. Almost as soon as the *toadas* for Ogun commenced, the old lady was *manifestada*, and in quite a moving and spectacular fashion. One of the other women in the *gira*, a *filha de santo* who had been trained by the old lady, went over and paid her elaborate homage. Dona Paula and another participant in the *gira* seemed to regard this as an unacceptable stealing of the limelight and stopped dancing to stare with obvious displeasure on the spectacle. Soon after, the old lady left the circle and the *salão*, heading with her sister, the local health nurse, for the *toque* being held at Fuló's place. It was some days after this that Dona Paula retailed the gossip to me about how unrespectable Fuló's establishment was. She also had some questions about the old lady's reputation.

TOWARD A TYPOLOGY OF
AFRO-BRAZILIAN SPIRITISM

The establishments of Dona Paula, Dona Rosária, and Lauro (with whom Maria Pretinha once worked) loom large in Campo Alegre, their premises and the material success of their mediums highlighting the fragility of the few attempts at spiritist community building. The literature reviewed to this point suggests that as in Campo Alegre, so in Brazil. The forms of association and the political culture developed in the Afro-Brazilian centers tie participants to existing structures of power: the white conquest over black (or, more correctly, grass-roots polychrome) Brazil through the white death of the black shaman.

Roger Bastide, in his monumental *African Religions of Brazil*, shows he is well aware of this possible turn in Afro-Brazilian syncretism. But he warns us of the determinism that, of necessity, relegates Fuló and Maria Pretinha to a historical sideshow:

> It is always easy enough to see through hindsight how economic or social systems are reflected in religion, but one forgets that there was a factor of creative freedom, that substructural aspects are determinative but not compelling, and that the people confronted with them can either reject the old values that no longer seem to fit the new social situations or invent new meanings for the old symbols they do not wish to reject completely and thus be forced to find an original solution.[7]

Colin Henfrey's comparisons of Afro-Brazilian groups in Salvador, Bahia, and various works by Carlos Brandão direct our attention to the exercise of creative freedom in the Afro-Brazilian traditions and to some of its political consequences. Their case studies help the argument that Fuló and

Maria Pretinha are something more than merely aberrant. In Brandão's town, Itapira, there is a range of spiritist groups. There is a sort of Kardecian High Church spiritism for higher-class Itapirans presided over by qualified experts. Then there is the largest set, consisting of one Candomblé and two Umbanda *terreiros*, which are examples of what Brandão calls "religions of mediation,"[8] in which a mass of lower-class devotees is led by an expert who is higher up the class ladder or who draws participants into the values and practices of the dominant culture. But there is yet a third set of spiritist groups in the popular domain, in which religiously creative, unskilled, and often underemployed laborers build up small groups consisting of members from the very bottom of the class structure. These groups continue to emerge, despite the fragility of any one of them; and their members defend a culture and a way of life that is stubbornly independent of any "reproduced" in the "mediating" and "erudite" groups.[9]

The groups in Salvador differ as much as those in Campo Alegre, and on some of the same dimensions noted there and by Brandão in Itapira. There are the traditional Candomblé cult groups, beloved of tourists and tourist agencies. The members of these groups, Henfrey tells us, are descendants of slaves, still engaged in traditional occupations, servicing the households of the bourgeoisie. The religious groups (as the members do in their work) serve the upper classes in a variety of ways and have upper-class patrons as paying participants. The Candomblé groups compete for rewards provided by patrons and the Department of Tourism; and rewards are proportional to success in exemplifying the tradition as it is hallowed by the patronizing classes.[10]

Though the groups work exclusively with the African *orixás*, as Fuló does, these *orixás* accord, in considerable degree, to the memory and interests of the upper-class patrons. For members, the Candomblé groups are environments in which a set of myths and values is rehearsed that freezes the past, for the reward of an assured niche in the established social and political hierarchy. Within the groups, life is structured in ways that duplicate the structuring of life in work and everyday life outside the religious group. With mythology frozen, and ritual formalized and under the control of upper-class patrons and intellectuals, there is no room for creative freedom and adaptability. Despite exotic African appearances, these are "kept" groups.

In great contrast to these Candomblé groups, which Henfrey locates with the *"old* subproletariat," are those spiritist groups he found in the *bairro* (district) of Liberdade, a redoubt of the more independent *"new* subproletariat." Liberdade, in terms of its location, history, and the informal sector occupations of its inhabitants, is much less integrated into bourgeois society than the inner-city areas of the Candomblé groups. The cults, as well as the samba groups, reflect and maintain the distance, but not in any precisely determined way. Henfrey finds leaders and members of groups — with their diverse pantheons of spirits — creatively conserving counterculture, discerning new spirits, devising new ritual, and reinterpreting old symbols in jealously guarded free spaces. The concern of these groups with the building of autonomous communities seems, from Henfrey's account, to lead some members into political activities directed against perceived injustices in the status quo.

Clearly enough, the Campo Alegre cases of Fuló and Maria Pretinha cannot be placed in a box labeled "Liberdade"; that would do violence to important differences in religious myth and symbol among all the groups involved. Nor is there any simple identity between Dona Paula's and Dona Rosária's groups in Campo Alegre and the Salvadoran Candomblé groups described by Henfrey. Again — though it seems likely that similar forms of association and modes of address to the problems of everyday life might emerge from the Campo Alegre and Salvadoran groups — nonetheless, as religious groups, they seem too profoundly different to be located together in a useful typology.

As an ethnographer of Campo Alegre, trying to draw from its social and cultural mélange images that may help us understand the current social and cultural history of Brazil, I am drawn in two directions about typologies. On the one hand, they seem necessary to provide a framework for the comparison and contrasting required if the local is to be located in the national scene. On the other, they are useless if violence has to be done to the local facts in order to squeeze cases into a typology that helps make sense of the national literature. Here the specific problem is the danger that the religious character of the Campo Alegre groups (which is not simply ancillary to what might crudely be called the political output) might be suppressed or treated as ancillary for the sake of drawing out similarities with groups studied by Henfrey and Brandão.

The solution is not to try to place our Campo Alegre groups in available typologies — which might indeed capture their religious character, but only that. One typology would arrange the Afro-Brazilian religions on a continuum from most African (in terms of the language of chants, the exclusive reference to the *orixás*, and the practice of animal sacrifices) to the most European (in terms of use of Kardecian texts, reliance on the most "advanced" spirits, sedate white-table rituals, and an abhorrent rejection of animal sacrifice).[11] Within a typology of this sort, distinctions might be made between the various African traditions: the Dahomey stream in Maranhão, the predominantly Yoruba stream in Pernambuco and Bahia, the Bantu stream in Rio de Janiero. Further distinctions would then have to be made according to regional variations in the degree of integration in regional societies and of syncretism with Catholicism.

A typology of Afro-Brazilian religions on these dimensions might satisfy students interested only in the religions themselves. But if the interest is in following religion out of the *terreiros* and into the streets, away from the religious virtuosi and into the lives of ordinary citizens, then such a classification would not be of much use. I have not been able to devise a typology that does everything: that captures and respects religious content, tabulates political output, and allows neat placement of the local cases in the array of national cases. But it has been possible to devise a typology that includes cases in the national literature reviewed here, and that allows comparison and contrast between these cases, so that relationships between religious and political culture at the grass roots might be appreciated. The Campo Alegre cases may then be compared, in all their local untidiness, to the types evident in the literature. The aim will not be to push the Campo Alegre cases into one or another of the types but only to help locate them nationally (and perhaps to suggest that someone else should set about the construction of a more inclusive typology!).

The Traditional Kept Group

Our first type, the "traditional kept group," has been constructed with cases in mind like the Candomblé groups studied by Henfrey and Silverstein. In those studies, the religious symbols, myths, and rituals seem most African; there have even been attempts to get authentic detail right by returning to West Africa to check on the genuine article — attempts sponsored by upper-class patrons often enough. But that reinforces a point made by the new wave of critical scholars: that the religious culture of these groups is frozen, and in forms agreeable to, even constructed by, a patronal class that is neither African nor engaged in the religious articulation of the modern experience of the descendants of the African slaves. In this sort of group, syncretism with Christianity and the *cultura alta* has created myths and symbols that assert harmony in race and class religion and that legitimate patronal arrangements in which black and lower class is always dependent on white and upper class. Then, congruent with group culture is group structure — typically, as noted earlier, with religious leader (female, black, and poor) subordinate to and dependent upon participating patron (male, white, and wealthy). Sons and daughters in the saint, most of them occupationally tied into servant relationships with the middle and upper classes, are further incorporated into patron-dependent relationships through their religious engagements. For quick comparison with the other types, the features of the traditional kept group are summarized in Figure 5.

The Autonomous Creative Group

A second type, the "autonomous creative group," is drawn from Henfrey's Liberdade groups and Brandão's protesting spiritist groups in Itapira. In many of these groups, the African *orixás* are almost ignored. The blood sacrifices that the *orixás* demand are rarely found. On the other hand, something of the spirit of what Bastide regarded as the genuinely African cult of the *orixás* survives. The spirits of a varied and changing pantheon of folk heroes are believed to bring strength and wisdom to the living through the rituals and communal activities of the group. New myths, new spirits, and contrasting manifestations of familiar spirits characterize these groups. In the eyes of tourist authorities, the creativity of these groups is not at all attractive. They are found on the periphery of cities rather than downtown, and their new rituals lack the polished presentation and color of traditional Candomblé, in part because the groups lack the resources necessary for the purchase of finery. Worse still, the spirits and the mediums suggest that all is not well with race and class relationships in Brazil and seem to proclaim that truculence is a virtue in negotiating them. Nor can the message and presentation of these

Features	Typology 1
Class of membership	Old subproletariat
Form and content of syncretism	White patronal content in African forms
Ritual features	African and Portuguese language – blood sacrifices
Autonomy – structural	Continuity with patronage hierarchy in dominant society
Autonomy – ideological	Acceptance of racial/class harmony myths – frozen syncretism for acceptability
Developing perceptions and values	Articulation to conserve a space reserved – no interest in critical perceptions and values
Desired form of association	Concern to construct and maintain subgroup within accepted structure

Figure 5. Features of the traditional kept group

groups be monitored and guaranteed: typically these groups resist incorporation into the lawful spiritist federations.

In this and other ways, these religious groups — as social formations — stand apart from both the Brazil of traditional patronage and the Brazil of bureaucratic-authoritarian relationships, though they seem not to be averse to exchanges with contenders in populist politics. Their internal structure is relatively egalitarian — in the same sense in which the sectarian Pentecostal group is — with members rejecting permanent professional or expert leadership and self-consciously avoiding patronage relationships both within the group and in engagements outside the group.

Both Brandão and Henfrey consider that there are political concomitants of the cultural and structural features of these sorts of spiritist groups. The Liberdade spiritists include in their religious vision the consciousness of a long history of rebellion against slavery and defense of land and of other rights as part of their heritage. And members of the groups are frequently engaged in political struggle, drawing on their spiritist groups for support as they do so. The groups themselves, ideologically and structurally autonomous social formations at the grass roots, constitute a challenge to patronal, bureaucratic, and military order. Brandão emphasizes lower-class spiritists' consciousness of that challenge and concludes that, like the sectarian Pentecostals, they are involved in class struggle waged in the religious sphere. (The main features of the autonomous creative group are summarized in Figure 6.)

Features	Typology 2
Class of membership	New subproletariat
Form and content of syncretism	Constant variations on Afro-Brazilian forms and themes
Ritual features	Portuguese only
Autonomy — structural	Discontinuity with dominant patronage structures — internal egalitarianism
Autonomy — ideological	Rejection of harmony myths — development of African and other folk myths
Developing perceptions and values	Articulation of critical perceptions and values
Desired form of association	Concern to construct and maintain alternative community

Figure 6. Features of the autonomous creative group

The Co-opted Whited Group

The third type of spiritist group is drawn from a rich recent literature on Umbanda groups, including the works of Ortiz and Brown cited earlier. I will call this group, as tendentiously as the others, the "co-opted whited group," drawing attention (as in the naming of the others) to key political and religious features. Where the kept African groups seem to comprise members of a traditional subproletariat or servant class, and the autonomous creative groups are constructed for and by members of the new subproletariat engaged in the informal sector, this third type of group consists of new urban upward mobiles (*upward* by aspiration rather than by attainment, *new* in the sense that their class position has developed through urbanization and industrialization largely since World War II).

In the myths and rituals of these groups, the African *orixás* play a part, but they are tamed and manipulated by mediums who regard them as inferior to higher spirits ranging upward to the spirits of departed heroes or archetypes of white bourgeois culture. Structurally, these groups integrate lower-class urbanites into the patronage formations of urban middle-class Brazil. Controlled by leaders who claim professional expertise, the main relationship evident in these groups is between expert medium and consulting client. In some of the more prosperous groups, a further salient relationship is the exchange between the medium and one or more politicians, usually from a higher class than either the medium or clients. A great deal of time and energy in these groups is devoted to activities that enhance the medium's prestige as a powerful manipulator of the spirits.

Ideologically, mediums in these groups teach and rehearse in their rituals a vision of Brazilian history and a mythology of its heroes and villains that tend to legitimate upper-class patronage and the values of national security dear to the bureaucratic authoritarians. The relationship between medium and client and the way in which the spirits are manipulated—to protect or advance the individual interests of the client in battles of the spirits known as the *demanda*—seem to encourage among clients competitive, individualistic responses to the problems of everyday life.

Ortiz and other interpreters who have been influenced by the French sociologist Pierre Bourdieu have argued that members of these co-opted whited spiritist groups are "clients" of religious "agents" of dominant economic classes.[12] The clients, it is argued, have bought a religious ideology in the market of symbolic goods, which locks them into a compliant role in the dominant economic order. That seems to me to involve too much manipulation of actors into a preconceived structure. The image of a market of symbolic goods might have its uses, but there is an automatism expected of the agents and clients that is derived from still-reductionist neo-Marxist theorizing rather than from the case studies to hand. On the basis of those studies, it seems sufficient to argue that there are spiritists who, with varying degrees of interest in or consciousness of any political consequences of their choices, find meaning and social location and resolution of salient problems in everyday life, in spiritist groups of this type. Interpreters (like myself) who do not like the political consequences have to be careful that they do not set up their own dreams of transformation and of a more just Brazil as reality—which, when ignored, avoided, or misperceived, has to be judged bad faith (on the part of agents) and robotic behavior (on the part of clients). Participation in a group that is relatively less autonomous, structurally and ideologically vis-à-vis dominant classes, does not imply determined, automatic behavior. Perpetrators of the white death of the black shaman seem to be active co-constructors of their religious and political worlds, just as the black shamans were. (Figure 7 summarizes the features of the type of Afro-Brazilian religion they construct.)

Campo Alegre Spiritists and the National Typology

The three-fold typology summarized in Figures 5, 6, and 7 fails all sorts of tests, as foreshadowed. It does not easily subsume the complexity of some of the best case studies—notably Maggie Velho's

Features	Typology 3
Class of membership	New urban upward mobiles
Form and content of syncretism	White hegemony in African *caboclo mestre* symbols and myths
Ritual features	Portuguese only—sacrifices for individual clients
Autonomy—structural	Continuities with patronage and bureaucratic structures—expert-client relationships
Autonomy—ideological	Acceptance of Brazilian national-security myths
Developing perceptions and values	Articulation of received ideologies vs. articulation of critical perceptions and values
Desired form of association	Concern for advancement of individual clients and maintenance of medium's prestige before building of historical community

Figure 7. Features of the co-opted whited group

Guerra de orixá (Battle of *Orixás*). Nor, as we shall see, does it neatly subsume the cases from Campo Alegre I have described. Fuló's group, if I have got it right, challenges the timeless adequacy of our typology right away. There are elements of all three types to be found in the group. Fuló's group is as African in myth and ritual as any Candomblé group, and yet his could hardly be called "kept African" — not, at least, with any respect for Fuló's own ambivalence toward the *cultura alta*. There is some evidence that he would welcome a rich participating patron if he could find one in Campo Alegre, and he may indeed have had one in the town he lived in before coming to Campo Alegre. But even if there were such a patron, Fuló would not want his group to be "kept" in the sense that the other groups defining the type are supposed to be. As *zelador* of the *orixás*, Fuló is concerned to assert the value of a culture he recognizes as counter to the *cultura alta*. And he has been intent, though in recent years with fragile success only, in creating community to live and maintain that culture — to the point even of encouraging scorn for the pretensions of some bearers of the *cultura alta*.

In all this, Fuló and his group begin to seem religiously African but almost as politically autonomous, structurally and culturally, as the autonomous creative type. Then, to confound the coherence of the types even further, it might be recalled that some more peripheral participants in the group relate to Fuló as clients to master-medium, whether he approves or not: in that, the wider group displays some political characteristics of the co-opted whited type.

The point is not to worry about the typology but about the case in relation to other cases. But the exercise of trying to place Fuló's group in the typology suggests some reasons why, as an autonomous community, his group is so fragile in Campo Alegre and why groups like his will be rarely found and will be of little political significance in modern Brazil. It is reasonable to suppose that there is a sort of coherence constituted by the elements of the kept African type; that religious and political structural and cultural components are not randomly but dialectically related; and that this coherence accounts for incidence in the literature as well as in Brazilian society. The pure or frozen cult of the *orixás* and the patron-dependent ties of the extended bourgeois household, which developed after the abolition of slavery, feed upon one another. Religious myths and rituals preserved in an antiquarian mode require, within the preserving group and in byways of the society at large, the antique bonds of dependence between master and African servant.

In the mélange of Campo Alegre, the traditional elites have left, and the poor of the town — hawkers of labor, searchers after preferment in agencies of state and local government — have no illusions of attachment to

21. Fuló's daughters create community, sharing a ritual meal.

nonexistent traditional bourgeois households. The *orixás* of Xangô offer power and purpose only in another world. Fuló in this poor peripheral suburb has only his own considerable charisma and verve and his own meager means to create a space for the *orixás* to descend. And it is not enough. Attracted to an obviously powerful medium, most Campo Alegrenses, like Naícia and Elsa, will want to use Fuló and not sit at his feet to become part of a community whose spirits do not even wield that first instrument of survival for a Campo Alegrense, spoken Portuguese.

Campo Alegre's mélange is more representative of the contexts in which poor urbanites and suburbanites in Brazil construct their religions and politics than the traditional inner suburbs of Salvador. If my arguments about the implications of typologizing are correct, we may infer that groups like Fuló's, straddling the types, are indeed eccentric, their experiments in the building of autonomous community probably doomed to frustration and failure once the limits of a leader's charisma have been reached.

On the other hand, the exercise allows reasonable speculation that Maria Pretinha's project, though apparently fragile in Campo Alegre, might indeed take firmer root there. Maria's group is fairly close to the autonomous creative type, except that Maria is more bookish and works spirits whose characters and requirements can become as settled as the *orixás'*. However, her Zé Pelintra and Joanna de Barros are able to surprise, and they change and develop, as Maria insists they should. They dignify, and offer guidance in, a way of life that is required of many of the citizens of Campo Alegre: gleaning the pickings at the margins of urbanizing, industrializing, bureaucratizing Brazil. The dialectics between religious creativity and group autonomy seem actually to happen in Maria's group just as they do more exuberantly perhaps in Liberdade and more robustly in Itapira.

But in the mélange of Campo Alegre, Maria has her problems as she tries to create her sort of autonomous community. One she understands perfectly well herself. She is very demanding — participation in the life of her community of self-discovery asks more than the gleaners of pickings are able, prepared, or confident enough to give. Neighbors for whom spiritism in one form or another is plausible have, through their precarious engagements in an unsettled environment, problems so demanding of immediate solution that the mystifications and magic offered by a Dona Paula are much more attractive. And if the disciplines seem right and bearable, then why not the more secure mooring of the Assembly of God? Maria has herself tested that option. Furthermore, for some there is more solid hope for solutions to life's problems in the offers of the populist politicians or the achievements of the *regime militar*.

A second problem is suggested by the attempt to introduce Maria's group into the company of the groups used to construct the type. Campo Alegre, unlike Liberdade and Itapira, does not have a tradition of lower-class solidarity against invasions from on high. On the contrary, if there is any memorable tradition at all, it is the tradition of the brotherhood; and that is a tradition of inclusion rather than resistance. In Campo Alegre it is hard to have confidence that the truculence of Zé Pelintra or the scorn that his medium pours upon the powers-that-be will provide protection for a free space in which a better world might be created.

In a way, placing Maria in the autonomous creative type, rather than meeting her alone in Campo Alegre, allows us to consider her less isolated, and the political style and stands that flow from her construction of the religious life less eccentric and more apparently viable in modern urban Brazil. Even so, the exercise of making typologies also points to some of her difficulties, to the very special conditions (beyond her own extremely hard work) that seem necessary for success. And the expected future does seem to lie more easily with the co-opted whited groups.

Despite their differences, it seems reasonable to consign Donas Rosária and Paula and their groups to this type. In both groups (as suggested in the outline of the type) the mode of relating to a particular hierarchy of the spirits interacts with the structure and outward linkages of the group itself to create an environment in which a distinctive mode of dealing with the problems of everyday life is rehearsed and encouraged. This mode includes an individualistic and competitive perception of the problems, tinged with not a little pathos; the relationship of client and expert to deal with a specific problematic episode; the incorporation, or its promise, of the lower-class client into higher-class patronage networks. Citizens engaged in this mode of address to life's problems, it is argued, will tend to opt for some mix of authoritarian populist politics or the politics of the *regime militar*. In Campo Alegre, it is groups like these, especially in those cases where the medium actually has patronage to dispense, that seem to survive and prosper. Politicians find their groups at least useful nodes in patronage structures; and some seek political success by having a medium summon strong spirits to aid in the struggle. That constituency of battlers at the margins who find that Maria Pretinha demands too much and consider that Fuló offers too little too far away from the *cultura alta* flock to the co-opted whited groups. In this respect again, our exercise in typologizing suggests, as in Campo Alegre, so in Brazil, both now and in the foreseeable future.[13]

CHAPTER SEVEN

The Catholics

PADRE EDUARDO

NO LESS THAN the spiritists, the Catholics wage war on one another with rival saints and heroes, and variant representations of those they share. To a certain extent the different and opposed Catholicisms were acted out and their political implications revealed in the competition for the fiesta of Campo Alegre's patron saint. But the actors have more to say than space allowed in Chapter 1.

Pe. Eduardo had his say in sermons. On Sunday after Sunday, he made clear his personal identification with the Brazilian Catholic church's stand for social justice and the heroes of that stand. He spoke of social justice and liberation and the building of *comunidades eclesiais de base* (CEBs), grass-roots church communities, when he spoke of local issues. During much of 1977, and even in 1982, he would refer to the injustices perpetrated by the new (ex-military-officer) landowner on the large property bordering the town, as he fenced off his land and threw off sharecroppers without any care for their livelihood, scorning the law relating to due compensation. And to this attuned and sympathetic listener, at any rate, it was clear that Pe. Eduardo was not just speaking politics from the pulpit but articulating his deeply rooted religious culture.

Brief summaries of sermons on four successive Sundays in 1977 communicate Pe. Eduardo's concerns, his aims and identifications:

First Sunday: On false Christianity
To be a Christian is not to be baptized and go to mass. Christianity requires that the Gospel be lived, and that means provoking hostile reaction from those — landowners, businessmen, and others — whose interests lie in maintaining the clouds that hide reality.

165

Second Sunday: On the Gospel story of Mary's visit to Elizabeth
Mary was not like those statues found in churches, an aristocratic matron.
She was poor, a member of a poor neighborhood, aware of and involved in
suffering arising from injustices.

Third Sunday: The vanity of vanities
This is to be preoccupied with gaining the riches of this world. An example
is to be found in those landowners who use gunmen to help pile up riches
extracted from the poor. Such greed is not just a personal sin but an evil that
spreads through a whole society.

Fourth Sunday: Christianity enters into all spheres of life
Saint Paul told Philemon that to continue as a Christian he would have to
recognize his brother Onesimus as a brother and not as a slave. The bishops
of the state of Maranhão have published a statement about the treatment of
peasants in that state. They point out, like Paul, that men who throw their
brothers off the land and destroy their crops cannot call themselves Christians. Can it be that these things happen only in Maranhão? You know the
answer to that.

There are variations in the emphasis given to these themes over time.
I think I detected in the fewer sermons I heard in 1982 a shift — away from
the attempt to call on the poor of Campo Alegre to realize their abilities
and vocations as the heroes of the struggle for justice — toward the more
churchy theme: the exemplary heroism of bishops and priests who were
defying the government and the powers-that-be. In 1977 on the feast of
Saint Peter the fisherman, the sermon was delivered from the altar by the
side of the statue of Saint Peter. The image had been returned to the church
after a procession around a section of the town where most of the fishermen lived. It stood, Romanesque, patrician, papal, in cold defiance of Pe.
Eduardo's words. The real Saint Peter was not like this, preached Pe.
Eduardo, he was a fisherman, like the fishermen of Campo Alegre, his
clothes poor and torn, his skin burnt and wrinkled by the sun. He was
a simple man, just like you, a man of the people. And yet he was the rock
upon whom Jesus constructed his church, and he died struggling against
the might of the Roman Empire as the people of God struggle against injustice today.

In 1982, after the procession, the statue returned decorated with flowers
to a room belonging to the fishermen's union. Pe. Eduardo preached to
a congregation that included few fishermen, though the fisherwomen who
had been meeting with a nun for seven or eight years had turned out in
force. Chico Amorim, of the family that had dominated the old brotherhood, stood in tinted glasses with arms folded, well groomed and flanked
by out-of-town acolytes, at the back of the church. He had not been seen
in town since he failed to gain election as a municipal councillor in

1979 — angry that he had to be appointed what the people called a "bionic" councillor for the government party. As a councillor he had been sniping at the priest, for his encouragement of opposition to the local landowner, and at the archbishop, for not giving land within the patrimony of the brotherhood to the poor. But today he was back in the church. New elections were five months away.

This time Pe. Eduardo made no attempt to do battle with the absent statue. He spoke instead of Saint Peter as the first pope to be jailed by the authorities, just as priests and *posseiros* (squatters) were today being condemned up north, in the state of Pará — though there was hope that the superior tribunal in Brasilia would reverse the decision. The bishops of Brazil, he reminded us, consistently supported the struggle for justice and peace, just as the present successor to Peter seems to be doing in helping to bring peace through his visit to Argentina.

In the context of rather sad conversations I had with the nun about slow progress in building community among farmers and fishing folk and lack of movement on the issues of justice in 1976 that still dragged on in 1982, I wondered whether eternal hope had not shifted from Peter the fisherman to papal Peter. Perhaps the fishermen, like the farmers, had been, even for patient Pe. Eduardo, a little too slow to follow the real Saint Peter of the 1976 sermon. Peter the pope had got things done. His successor had reproved the head of state and rallied millions on his visit in 1981. Perhaps the fishermen, too, knew where the action was. When, at the end of mass, the fisherwoman who was secretary of the church-sponsored fishing cooperative read out names of fishermen who had won prizes in boat races that afternoon, not one was there in church to receive a prize. Everyone was embarrassed. Except Chico Amorim who, after mass, asked me why the fishermen had not come to the church. They used to in his day. . . .

But Pe. Eduardo's Catholicism is not only to be discovered in sermons and the rituals of feasts. He is a bookish man, and he will direct anyone really interested in his faith and his church to books and documents that expound the Brazilian church's modern history and currently dominant theology. In these texts we learn that the Brazilian National Conference of Bishops (CNBB) has adopted a "preferential option for the poor," spelling this out to imply that the church should assume a new identity as promoter of the liberation of the poor.[1] Analyzing why the church should have adopted this option, some (not Pe. Eduardo's preferred commentators) have seen its quest for institutional maintenance and influence as the prime motivation.[2]

By the late fifties, and thereafter at an accelerating pace, the attempt to maintain influence by institutional alliances with the state and through

22. Padre Eduardo celebrates Mass in the brotherhood's chapel that he has renovated and made "too simple" for some.

concentrating resources and personnel on the urban middle classes was failing. A marginalized church, in this view, turned to the people at the margins of society for its new constituency — the uprooted peasants, the new urban masses. And a shortage of clergy (about one priest for every nine thousand people) called forth new methods, culminating in the creation of the CEBs, run by lay leaders, to exert influence. One implication of this explanation of change in the church is that the CEBs themselves might be, after all, just a new mode of grass-roots aggregation initiated by elites for the ends of what remains an upper-class institution. Some of the ambiguous rhetoric in church documents and some accounts of CEBs as "co-opting" agencies support this position, though Pe. Eduardo's heroes, like Dom Helder Câmara, do not seem to have been motivated primarily by these considerations of strategy.[3]

Religious vision and principles, and not the quest for influence, have persuaded many clergy and laity that the building of CEBs is what the church should be doing — even at the cost of influence as usually conceived. That is Pe. Eduardo's view and the message of most of his texts. In the journals and documents of the "new church," those members who have actually practiced the "preferential option for the poor" seem (from what they say about what they do) to be motivated by religious ideas that they and a majority of bishops consider faithful to recent papal teaching, the Vatican Council, and the declarations of the Latin American bishops assembled at Medellín, Colombia, in 1968 and at Puebla, Mexico, in 1979. Those ideas include the definition of the church's mission as being to the whole person, not just to some separated spiritual part — hence the concern with issues of justice and equity. Salvation is conceived not so much in individual terms as in social terms: it is believed to involve the individual in participating in the transformation of society so that human potential revealed and called for in the Bible might be better achieved. Further, there is the belief that social transformation of the poor cannot be achieved by elites but only through the building, by the poor themselves, of communities, the CEBs, in which new understanding of the Bible informs action to change society, and vice versa. New ministries performed by laity from the lower classes are considered not simply to be filling in for the lack of priests, as would be consistent with the institutional-influence approach, but expressing a new understanding of the church as "the people of God."[4]

What is intended of the over eighty thousand CEBs, by episcopal authorities and by church clergy and laity in the field, is outlined in a great number of documents and reports going back to the early sixties with the setting up of the groups associated with the Basic Education Movement (MEB). I will cite here from one of them, an official report commissioned by the CNBB and presented to the conference by Bishop José Freire Falcão in 1979.[5]

The new communities are expected to be autonomous in several senses. They are expected not just to be recipients of religious messages but articulators and transmitters to the whole church of an understanding of the Gospel that only the poor, it is believed, can have:

> The more oppressed class, of the factory workers, the small farmer, the Indian, becomes the privileged location of the message [of God] — because it is a class more sensitive to the need for union and more open to give welcome to the Gospel's message of liberation. It is notable that in the middle class the process is more difficult; there the message is often received and applied only in the solution of isolated, individual or family problems and never arrives at the community level to become a dedication to the transformation of the whole environment in which one lives.

They are to be autonomous, too, in the sense that they will not duplicate and reproduce the hierarchical relationships of the dominant society. Involvement in CEBs converts individual members to think and act communally:

The change, or the conversion, transforms relationships. No longer is it the relationship of the expert who teaches that the student might learn; of the rich who pay that the poor might receive; of the patron who commands the passive obedience of the employee. Instead it is a relationship between brothers, sharing among themselves their own material and spiritual goods and recognizing only one Master, before whom all are students. . . . Lacking power, expertise, and riches, the communities are a challenge to the world and to the social system that dominates in our continent.

The life of the communities is expected to be directed outward:

Discovering the grandeur of life, the communities set out to restore dignity to it, uniting members, therefore, to struggle against everything that degrades and oppresses man. From the community's living of the Gospel values, members draw energy, courage, and inspiration, and, in the environment in which they live, they join with others with whom they might transform the world, in accordance with the will of God.[6]

These hopes from on high for the CEBs are shared by at least some of their ordinary members. Cláudio Perani quotes a member of a CEB in Pernambuco defining, as its purpose, "that the people might see with their own eyes, think with their own heads, speak with their own mouths, and walk with their own feet."[7] That asserts clearly enough the intent of autonomy and critical articulation of experience that Pe. Eduardo preaches as his ideal for communal Catholicism in Campo Alegre, politically involved but independent of old brotherhood attachments to *coronelismo*, of invited attachments to *populismo*, or required loyalties to the *regime militar* or civilianized bureaucratic authoritarianism.

In Chapter 2 we saw that, in the mélange of Campo Alegre, there are Catholics, like Gonçalo, attached to the cultural paradigm of *coronelismo* and to the Catholicism that sanctified it. There are opponents, too, like Chico Amorim who, though fond of Dona Paula's spiritism, would proclaim himself a Catholic, a former judge of the brotherhood, and call on the priest to return to the true priestly role and stop playing the politician. And he could count on getting Catholic votes despite, and even for, his attacks. But the varieties of Catholicism and the differences between them, in religious and political terms, are more extensive and run deeper than these static and publicly stark divisions between Pe. Eduardo, Gonçalo, and Chico Amorim.

PADRE EDUARDO AND CARLOS

Though there are others in Campo Alegre who hear and apparently understand and sympathize with Pe. Eduardo, Carlos seems nearest to being the sort of broker who might link Catholics of the old brotherhood and from Gonçalo's world of *coronelismo* to their priest.

Pe. Eduardo hoped this and believed it had been achieved. Carlos is thirty-four years old, married, with five children. He is neither very well-off nor of the poorest. (He runs the *jogo de bicho* [a gambling game] in a nearby town.) He is literate, so he can read at religious gatherings, but he does not have that priestly level of education that would place him in a world apart from his neighbors. His father was on the executive of the brotherhood, and his older brother (who runs the *jogo de bicho* in Campo Alegre) is the leader and organizer of the great folk-Catholic *promessa*-paying pilgrimages that take place in the last quarter of every year. The brother—whose front room is dominated by a huge photo of the modern saint of northeastern folk Catholicism, Padre Cícero—does not himself have any regular contact with Pe. Eduardo. But the brothers and their conjugal families maintain daily contact with one another. Through personal attributes and kin ties Carlos is well located to link priest and people. And, in some ways, he does.

Carlos, for the last five years, has been chief organizer of an *encontro dos irmãos* (meeting of brothers) congregation. These congregations exist in many dioceses in Brazil and are intended to be grass-roots awareness-raising groups; in Recife they were predecessors of the CEBs. While I was in Campo Alegre, on most Sunday afternoons, a group of from ten to thirty would gather in a private house or in a local nonchurch primary school where Carlos was a sort of voluntary caretaker. At these meetings, which Pe. Eduardo did not attend and at which up to half of those present did not go to mass, Carlos dominated. He would always summarize, usually quite accurately, Pe. Eduardo's sermon of that morning and attempt to lead discussion on it. But in these discussions, and in the meeting as a whole, it appeared to me that only some aspects of Pe. Eduardo's message had taken hold in his consciousness. At first I had only a general puzzled feeling that this was so. But after I had participated in a number of congregation meetings, some basic thematic differences became clearer.

First, with Carlos and in the congregation, Pe. Eduardo's moral values became a moralism. Moral judgments about social and public issues, which were intended to evoke social action for change, became moral judgments applied against individuals (the landowner, for example) who were singled out for condemnation. The concern in the congregation was to clarify right and wrong; to distinguish wrongdoers from sufferers from wrongdoing. And two reactions were evoked. The congregation must right wrongs by assisting those of its members who were among the sufferers. Individual members must strive to be free of whatever was being condemned in their own lives.

Second, the congregation was still operating with the notion of the church as law, *a lei católica,* rather than Pe. Eduardo's notions of the church as liberator. Carlos and the congregation were much more concerned than Pe. Eduardo about the Pill, the errors of the Protestants (false law), and so on.

Third (and as I interpret things, behind the previous two differences), the congregation operated with a basically different image of Jesus from the one held by Pe. Eduardo. His image of Jesus was of Jesus the liberator, the model of liberation who calls us forth to battle oppression. The congregation's image was of Jesus the lawgiver, the judge who orients us in our quest for salvation.

These three related differences lead, in my view, to a sort of diversion of Pe. Eduardo's prophetic messages. But Pe. Eduardo himself seems not to grasp this. He admires and feels a need for Carlos, and Carlos appreciates these responses. Each believes himself to be engaged in the same mission. Each is able to maintain this belief because so much is shared. But, in my view, what is held in common obscures from both the real divergences in religious worldview.

PADRE CÍCERO, PEDRO FARÓ, AND PADRE EDUARDO

Padre Cícero

Something must be said about Padre Cícero before introducing any more of the Catholics of Campo Alegre. For many of them define their own Catholicism and their relationship with Pe. Eduardo as though Padre Cícero were the paragon of *a minha lei católica* (my Catholic law) and the measure of a worthy priest. Padre Cícero died in 1934, at the age of ninety, in Joaseiro do Norte, Ceará, which—as parish priest, holy man suspended from priestly functions, mayor, state and finally federal politician—he had built from an insignificant hamlet to become the commercial, political, and religious center of the erstwhile "backlands" of northeast Brazil.

In many ways, as Ralph Della Cava shows in his magisterial *Miracle at Joaseiro,* Padre Cícero, as a living saint first and an unwilling politician second, was catalyst in a set of complex exchanges that put the northeastern backlands on the map in the increasingly integrated political economy of Brazil in the early twentieth century.[8] Then as now, for tens of millions of Brazilian Catholics even beyond the Northeast, *meu Padim Ciço* (as one hears his name so often spoken) is the legendary landmark around whom maps of sacred and profane are drawn. The statue erected to his memory in Joaseiro is the second largest in Brazil, after the famous Christ of Corcavado in Rio. Climbing up the stairs inside the statue, one can take in, through Cícero's eyes, the Cariry valley over which he still presides. He presides, too, in the central living room of many a wattle-and-daub hut in Campo Alegre, four hundred kilometers away, in statuette and photo. Carlos's brother Mário has both, the photograph being the largest reproduction I have seen. With tens of thousands of other pilgrims one year Mário went to Joaseiro, returning with the photograph and other mementos to become the chief organizer of pilgrimages to a more local shrine. On the bus on this annual pilgrimage from Campo Alegre, Mário and other members of his family lead fellow pilgrims in singing the hymns of Joaseiro and exchanging stories about the miracles and the wisdom of Padre Cícero. But this sociologist, known to be interested in religion, had already been taken through the repertoire on his first visit to Mário's house, when an attempted interview was scuttled by a show-and-tell of Joaseiro mementos, performances of the hymns, and Cícero stories and remembered aphorisms illustrating the padre's stern backlands moralism.

There are four interwoven stories that help us explain why Padre Cícero should preside over popular Catholicism in the Northeast in this way, and that allow an appreciation of the content of that Catholicism. There is the story of the miracle at Joaseiro and the development of his reputation as saint and messianic leader. In 1889, so the story of the miracle came to be told, the very blood of Jesus Christ issued from a Communion host consecrated and administered by Padre Cícero in the chapel where he had been celebrating mass since 1872. Ralph Della Cava tells the story in the way it is often told.

> On 1 March 1889, Maria de Araujo was among several pious women who had come to the chapel of Joaseiro to attend the mass and rituals celebrated on each first Friday of the month in honor of the Sacred Heart of Jesus. She was among the first to receive communion. Suddenly, she fell to the ground and the immaculate white host which she had moments before received became red with blood. The extraordinary event was repeated every Wednesday and Friday of Lent for the next two months; from Passion Sunday to the feast of the Ascension of Christ into Heaven, a duration of forty-seven days, it recurred daily.[9]

Della Cava also shows us how a set of events became the famous miracle. There is the prologue to the miracle, in which Padre Cícero establishes himself locally as good counselor to drought-stricken *camponeses* (peasants), as tireless crusader for moral order in a frontier land of brigandage and social breakdown, as an ascetic dispenser and mobilizer of charity in a precarious economy highly productive of victims. By 1889, though by no means alone, Padre Cícero has all the marks of one whom God and a needy people might anoint with a miracle as successor in a line of backlands messiahs. Then there are the signs after the events, which confirm that a miracle has indeed occurred. Pilgrims come in thousands, seeing for themselves the holiness of the man and the *beatas* (holy women) around him, and contributing, by their presence and in many instances by their labor, to the growing prosperity and political significance of Joaseiro. As has happened before and since in the Brazilian backlands, holy man, miracle, and political-economic development substantiate one another.

The second story is of conflict between popular Catholicism and the more urban, even urbane, Brazilian Catholic church, re-Romanized after the Syllabus of Errors and the First Vatican Council.[10] Initially, this story may be told in terms of conflict between the bishop of Crato (as representative and protagonist of the renewed church) and the supporters of Padre Cícero, about the validity of the miracle. Eventually, the conflict became less about the miracle itself and more about the holy man's suspension from priestly duties, which followed unfavorable official verdicts about the miracle and about the popular cult of Padre Cícero that grew from it. But it is not just the change in issues over forty years that makes this story complex. At odds with Rome and the Brazilian hierarchy, Padre Cícero struggles to maintain his identity and status as a Roman priest, orthodox and obedient. Characterized by the renovated urbane church as another backlands fanatic, the Padre acts, and is venerated, as a true missionary of the church — recalling the poor and the ignorant to Catholic practice and morality, defending the church against Protestant heresy, rebuilding the church, its plant, its artefacts, its designated functionaries, its prescribed rituals, its law, as the locus of the sacred. And so the end of this story is Padre Cícero become not anticlerical rebel but, for millions of northeasterners, the model of the Catholic priest, the measure and hope of the *lei católica*.

The story of Padre Cícero's rebuilding of the church, centered on the town Joaseiro, connects with a third story: a tale of two cities. At the beginning of the twentieth century, Joaseiro was part of the municipality centered on the city of Crato. By 1911, after protracted struggles involving Padre Cícero as protagonist for the interests of Joaseiro and arbiter in feuds between rival *coronéis*, Joaseiro won its autonomy, and the padre became its first mayor. The tale continues as interested groups based in the two cities do battle for economic and political control of the Cariry valley. Until his death, Padre Cícero is central to the tale. The story begins as he tries to establish Joaseiro as an ecclesiastical center away from the control of the bishop of Crato, his major antagonist in the religious question of the miracle at Joaseiro. The tale develops as a story of regional politics and economics as pilgrims, squatters, and merchants settle in the town until it becomes larger than Crato.

By the most dramatic phase in the story, in 1911, Padre Cícero has become, in Della Cava's phrase, "*Coronel* of the biggest bailiwick in Ceará."[11] From that date, the tale of two cities becomes part of a state story, in which the *coronéis* of the Cariry valley contest for recognition and power commensurate with economic fortune in the government of Ceará. In turn, that story flows into the struggle of the backlands leaders for their due share of national political power and attention to their interests in the growing national economy.

The fourth story, of Padre Cícero and the backlands struggle for inclusion in the national political economy, is protracted and complex and its details need not concern us here any more than they concern Padre Cícero's devotees in Campo Alegre. But the legacy of exchanges between protagonists in the story may still be discerned in contemporary folk Catholicism, as we shall see and as we might guess in any case from the vignette of Gonçalo. So it is important, at least, to outline them.

One key exchange in the story of the struggle for national inclusion is between Padre Cícero and the new backlands elites whose interests and institutional attachments were wider in scale, less exclusively local, more comprehensively based on a national cash economy than those of a previous generation of *coronéis*. The new elites are not political radicals, in any sense: their politics is the politics of patronage, a *coronelismo* of enlarged scale, of patron-client rather than patron-dependent retainer relationships. The new elites see they have much to be grateful for in Padre Cícero, and Della Cava shows us some of them quite self-consciously manipulating the padre in their cause. First as good counselor of the drought-uprooted poor, then as attractor of pilgrims, Padre Cícero harnesses and mobilizes labor for the projects of the new elites. Further, he becomes preacher and image maker, enjoining on the poor the norms and values required of them in a wage-earning economy. More particularly, in his daily sermons and in the stories told of him, Padre Cícero preaches and makes plausible a new law and order against the moral economy of backlands banditry. Finally, the new elites discovered that Padre Cícero, as an established holy man and revered patron, was, for their causes in the national political arena, a champion it was difficult to ignore or assail.

In 1926 Padre Cícero, now a very old man, was elected to the Brazilian National Congress. As before, when he became mayor and then entered politics in the state of Ceará, he stood as champion for the new elites in the national arena, because he hoped that his position would help him resolve the religious issue in his favor and secure the return of his full faculties as a Catholic priest. At all stages in his political career, Padre Cícero seems to be a reluctant politician but easily manipulated into becoming a symbol of the backlands' and then the Northeast's cause as formulated by the new elites, on the basis of his religious preoccupations.

The exchange between Cícero and the new elites is possible only on the basis of the second exchange—between the priest and the backlands poor. In Della Cava's account, Cícero shows himself to be well aware of what the poor have to offer in this exchange. Their devotion (even their vaunted fanaticism, which he could contain) was recognized by him, by his new elite allies, and by his enemies, as a resource in religious and political conflict. In turn, the Padre Cícero stories, still told in Campo Alegre, show the bases of that devotion in what he could give the poor. *Meu Padim Ciço* is protector of the law-abiding poor against bandits, against bosses who don't pay, against strangers who exploit simple folk or befuddle them with false law. He finds jobs for hard workers fallen on hard times. He is the instrument through whom God punishes the rich and the poor who, by their immorality, tear apart families and moral community. Through him, too, God extends mercy to the weak but goodwilled who would be obedient to his law.

In Campo Alegre, when these stories are told, it is as though the exchange between priest and poor were still available, or might be, were Pe. Eduardo to follow the example of Cícero. Perhaps the outline of the interwoven histories of the miracle at Joaseiro, of Roman or folk Catholicism, of the two cities and the backlands struggle for place in the national case economy, explains why the legend of Padre Cícero lives and continues to shape the expectations that many Campo Alegre Catholics have of their priest. The legend of Cícero mediates the separate but intertwined religious cultures of priest and many of his people.

Pedro Faró

In Pedro Faró we can see how the legend lives and helps divert even Catholics who are well disposed to Pe. Eduardo away from full participation in the struggle for realization of his communitarian vision. In 1977 it seemed to Pe. Eduardo and to me that Pedro was already a leader in the formation of a grass-roots community resisting the new landowner's expulsion order. He was the son of a rural migrant to Campo Alegre who had arrived in the fifties and achieved considerable prosperity through hard work as a cultivator of manioc and small businessman, establishing one of the two main *casas de farinha* (manioc-processing plants) in Campo Alegre. When Pe. Eduardo first arrived in town, Pedro's father was already part of the group within the brotherhood that was opposed to the old guard dominated by the Amorim family. He quickly became an ally of the priest in his quest to clean up the brotherhood. Now the old man was dead, but Pedro, who had inherited the *casa de farinha,* seemed about to develop the alliance. When the expulsion orders were delivered, Pedro led a small group of recipients downtown to inform the priest and enlist his aid in resisting the orders. Pe. Eduardo took up the cause, seeking legal aid in Recife: he urged Pedro to gather those who had received the orders and led them in discussion and learning about the moral and legal issues involved. He advised Pedro that the farmers must develop a unified response to the threatened loss of land. Pedro followed the advice and called meetings in the *casa de farinha,* some of them attended by the priest. Though threatened directly by the landowner (who showed him scars of wounds he had sustained in other battles he had won), Pedro continued for some months to provide leadership and aid to his poorer neighbors. It seemed only fitting that Pe. Eduardo should choose him to receive the banner of the saint at the conclusion of the fiesta in 1977.

But before the end of the year and even before some of his poorer neighbors, Pedro Faró accepted a poor compensation payment from the landowner and abandoned the fight. Though a small group did fight on, and something like a small community evolved in the struggle, Pedro withdrew to the sidelines and the *casa de farinha* ceased to be the epicenter of resistance. A simple explanation for Pedro's withdrawal is to be found in prudence. As he often pointed out, he had a wife and three small children to maintain at a reasonable standard of living; he would not lose everything if he pulled out (he had access to other land to grow some manioc, and his brother had not only land but a truck to bring manioc in); and he was faced with a ruthless enemy who, if provoked, could deprive him of everything. But also, on the basis of long conversations with Pedro in 1977 and 1982, I am convinced that the legend of Padre Cícero entered into the equations of prudence.

In 1982, the sense of a dichotomized world seemed much stronger, more easily articulated by Pedro than in 1977. On the one hand, threatening and looming ever larger is the *mundo desmantelado* (literally, the dismantled world). If there is any one figure who presides over that world, symbolizing it for him and investing its sensed advance with gut-wrenching dismay, it is his own mother. Corrupted by the ways of the town, as he sees it now, she abandoned her children and left Pedro's father for another man. But though he speaks bitterly of her, Pedro does not count her uniquely or eccentrically evil and even pities her in her old age. She has become simply the personal paragon of the vast majority of people who are *cheio de mundice* (full of worldliness), taken over by the pursuit of self-interest.

Sometimes, when he populates the *mundo desmantelado,* Pedro sounds

23. Pedro Faró hard at work pouring manioc flour into a sack.

as radical as the communitarian clergy. That world is dominated by the rich who, for individual gain, have abandoned their responsibilities to the *nação dos pobres* (the nation of the poor). Lawyers, judges, big landowners, city bureaucrats, sugar-mill proprietors, politicians of the government party, all are singled out for special criticism. Lawyers are the frontline of the attack against the *nação dos pobres:* even those who seem on the side of the poor are out to make money from their troubles that only the

24. Peeling manioc in Pedro Faró's manioc house.

government might resolve if the minority of good politicians could gain control of it.

That will be difficult to achieve, however, because most of the poor are themselves *cheio de mundice* and, as such, contribute to the making of the *mundo desmantelado*. They "follow the wrong path" and dismantle moral order. "If there's a mass on Saturday night in the church, few will go. But if there's a dance at Pasmado then the road will be packed even if it's a rainy night and people have to go on foot." Or "they flock to the beach which is full of half-nude women." The priority given to satisfaction of the senses in these examples is considered by Pedro to show in leisure time what is evident to him in the world of work. There the pursuit of self-interest leads the poor to "take issue against the *nação dos pobres*."[12] Without any sense of, or care for, the ability of small businessmen like himself to pay, the poor demand higher wages and better conditions. The rapid consequence is that the small businessman has to close his doors, big business takes over, the poor lose employment and participation in a locally controlled economic order. Having abandoned the moral sense and the rules that are necessary to keep families, communities, and nations together, they fall into the hands of the equally corrupt lawyers and landowners, to the destruction of the community that the likes of his father were building in Campo Alegre.

In Pedro's analysis there is much of the beleaguered loneliness of the abandoned-son-become-small-businessman caught between desperate poor and extractive rich. But there is more than raw experience and more than lament in what he has to say. There is also a sense of a real and possible world that might still be rescued from the ruins of the *mundo desmantelado*, if only a true leader like Padre Cícero might be found. Padre Cícero, Pedro tells me, led the *nação dos pobres* in the Joaseiro of his day out of the destruction that was threatening it. He made possible the world of the small, independent *roceiro* (farmer) and businessman in which his father had prospered and which he had tried to establish in Campo Alegre. Padre Cícero's basic and essential contribution to that world was his success in teaching, to the poor especially, the values and the morals that make for an ordered and just society — the opposite of the *mundo desmantelado*. Padre Cícero knew that the intact family — with the father instructing children in correct behavior and the faithful wife nurturing the whole family — was the basic building block in the independent community of the poor. But he also preached the honesty, the cooperativeness, and the obedience that the good citizen must live if the *nação dos pobres* was to prosper.

In Pedro's view, Padre Cícero succeeded as a teacher because he was strong, manifestly holy, politically astute, and because of the miracles that showed God wanted what he preached. But, he believes, it would be hard even for Padre Cícero to achieve what he once did if he were alive today. Perhaps only the pope (this said in 1982, one year after Pope John-Paul II's visit to Brazil) would have the *força* and the authority to bring back the people from the *mundo de mundice*. That conceded, Pedro's expectations of a priest remain high. Unlike Maria Pretinha and the *crente* Teresa, who share much of Pedro's moral vision and moralism, Pedro believes a strong priest is essential if the battle against the *mundo desmantelado* is to succeed. But that priest must have all the qualities of Padre Cícero and more — the ability to confront effectively the ever more powerful generals and bureaucrats of our times.

Padre Eduardo

Padre Eduardo could hardly measure up. In part, his was a failure of presence; in part a divergence of views about priestly leadership that already separated priest and the Pedros of his flock when he was invited to become a Padre Cícero in the battle of the quit notices in 1977. Disqualifying presence and divergent conceptions of leadership are evident in Mary Aitken's description of one of the meetings of affected farmers in Pedro's *casa de farinha*.

> Inside, the manioc house was surprisingly re-ordered and strangely subdued. Long benches had been brought in and drawn up in a rough semi-circle. At

the head, near the spot where one of the groups of women usually scraped the manioc root, stood a wooden chair, a table covered with a neat cloth and a vase containing two paper flowers. Some thirty or forty people sat expectantly awaiting the arrival of the priest. There were more younger women than old, and more older men than young. Dress was simple but tidy. The women . . . had donned their best dresses, carefully combed their hair and perfumed their necks and wore thongs or sandals. . . . The men generally wore ill-fitting trousers but their painstakingly laundered short-sleeved shirts and the Sunday hats placed respectfully on their laps testified to the formality of the occasion. . . .

Eventually, the priest drove up in his car. He too wore long trousers and a short-sleeved shirt, but of better quality and fit than the men around him. He addressed the meeting, sitting formally on the chair, earnestly developing the text of the day — the importance of sharing this world's goods with one another, especially the needy; the great promise that the poor would inherit the earth, so clearly prefigured in Christ's washing of his disciples' feet. This feast would be celebrated during the coming week, the priest reminded his listeners, and he personally planned to wash the feet of six farmers and six fishermen at the local ceremony. Now and then the priest elaborated his lesson, coaxing his audience to suggest examples from their own lives which paralleled the Gospel story. For most of the time the audience was silent, now and then shuffling feet. Occasionally, one of the men would mutter a comment or suggest an example, his eyes hardly leaving the ground in front of his feet. Often, the priest's questions remained rhetorical. The restrained conduct of the audience and their halting speech contrasted oddly with the animated debates about prices, wages and bosses, the jokes about manioc-roots and marriage, and the incessant bustle that normally took place in this space.[13]

For Catholics like Pedro, superimposing Joaseiro on to Campo Alegre and gazing through the eyes of the great priest-politician over their own lives and prospects, Pe. Eduardo was a disappointment. They did not want a priest of the sort pined for by Gonçalo, the holy intermediary through whom one could bargain with the great saints and established *coronéis*. But they did want a priestly leader who would, at one and the same time like Padre Cícero, lead a revivalist moral crusade among the poor and a campaign on behalf of the poor against the established, unjust powers. The priest who had vanquished the old brotherhood, who spoke of the need for new community, who had proven himself a gifted administrator of the *património* of the church, who was clearly a holy man — such a priest could be expected to be a leader in the mold of Padre Cícero.

But at the meetings in the *casa de farinha*, Pe. Eduardo demonstrated a temperament and proclaimed a vision that disqualified him from such leadership. He would disappoint Pedro just as he disappointed the opposition politicians of the MDB in the negotiations about the fiesta. He neither would nor could have truck with populist politics, however good the cause. Once this was clear to Pedro he stopped participating in the small community Pe. Eduardo had tried to establish. In 1982 he wondered whether it wasn't the *crentes* who had got moral teaching right; and his political hopes were lodged with the PMDB.

That the farmer's group fell apart cannot be blamed simply on Pe. Eduardo. Some of the reasons have to do with resources and networks within the group of farmers, which alone, to an outsider, might suggest that any sustained communal response to the landowner's actions was unlikely. Pedro Faró as natural leader of the group was nonetheless separated by interests and resources from poorer farmers, especially those who worked for him; and his own prudential calculations suggested that he should cut his losses, abandon the fight and any claim to actual leadership in the community of farmers the priest hoped would develop. Some of the farmers who had worked for and traded with Pedro had been urged by members of their families to pull out if Pedro should continue to confront the landowner. The daughter of one of these, active herself in local opposition politics, told me she had gone to Pedro and begged him not to send her father out to work on Pedro's plot on the landowner's property because he would be killed by the landowner's thugs.

But expectations about priestly leadership and assessments of Pe. Eduardo's inability to measure up to the possibilities embodied in the Cícero legend often enter into such considerations of loyalty and prudence. For some small farmers, given the well-appreciated bases for disunity within the group and the even-better-appreciated strengths of the landowner, only miraculously strong Cíceronian leadership from Pe. Eduardo would have made it worthwhile to stick with the group and fight it out. When it was clear that their priest was no Cícero, the fragile bases of unity in religious hope and material interest collapsed. For most, but not for Angelita.

ANGELITA

By 1982, very few of about ninety of the families affected by the expulsion order, six years earlier, continued to hope and struggle for their land. One small group continued to meet to talk about their own and similar cases of injustice in the light of the message of the Bible. Members of the group helped one another in the crises of everyday life. And, against the background of exchanges of news about successful land invasions nearby and in other parts of Brazil, the group was planning to regain lost land by organizing an occupation by men, women, and children, which would be well covered by the media so that the landowner would not dare to use his gunmen. A nun, one of three who worked mainly with the fisherwomen, was a member of the group and helped with the invasion plans. But the acknowledged leader of the group was a married woman in her forties called Angelita. Her tiny house, rather than Pedro's *casa de farinha*, became the center for informal and planned meetings of a small grass-roots community of ex-farmers.

The two nuns not involved in the group, Pe. Eduardo, and lay leaders who had worked with him since the battles to reform the brotherhood were appalled on prudential grounds at the invasion plans. Angelita, in their view, was imprudent in two ways. She was focusing too exclusively on the immediate land issue and did not appreciate how an invasion could prejudice other church projects for justice, which worked slowly within the law. She was also being rash, failing to consider the physical danger into which she would lead the invading families. One of the nuns recalled Angelita's experiences in 1977 as an explanation for rashness. Angelita had not only farmed on the large property but had her house on the land. When she made it clear that she was not going to comply with the landowner's wishes he brought in a bulldozer, knocked down the house, and razed her crops. She lost everything. That was the basis in desperation and anger for the imprudence of 1982, according to the nun.

Angelita, when I interviewed her in 1982 (we had met only a few times in 1977 when we both attended the *congregação* meetings led by Carlos), rejected both the prudential interpretation of the situation and modified the desperation interpretation of her own actions in a significant way. It is worth quoting at length from her response to my simple question, "Why did you struggle and others gave in?"

> Because Jesus gave me the *força* that I needed to resist. So Jesus Himself is the reason, Jesus Himself. It's Jesus Christ who gives us strength – and the hunger and the need in a place like this where we live starving. . . . And the church helped, the brothers and sisters from other places [Angelita is referring here to members of the church-based grass-roots communities in Campo Alegre and neighboring areas].[14]

She returns to her theme by way of a reflection on what is necessary if victory is to be achieved on the land issue.

> Union among the people is necessary. We had nothing, not a potato, a *macaxeira* (cassava root), or a yam, and now we've got support from justice in the capital. . . . What we've got to do is reunite all the people and go out and work the land. But even though the media are ready to give publicity, people have been full of fear. . . . Religious differences don't cause disunion, though some *crentes* affected in the past kept out of the struggle . . . and there are some of them who have another attitude: they think it's only God who will win justice in heaven. . . . But I don't think that way. Jesus Christ told us to

go out. Who dies of fear doesn't know that he is dead. It's fear that kills people. . . . Many say that it's wrong to make an issue when things go wrong. My reply is that those who can play with a full belly don't have the need to struggle. And if they say that Jesus said it's not good to make an issue, I say that they're not ready to work to survive. . . . Whoever hopes always achieves; whoever calls on God never gets tired. For God, in the end, remains on the side of those who struggle for justice. The landlord who has kicked us off cast a shadow over many people. But not over me. Nor will he ever. For he is not more than God. Only Jesus Christ has that power. To the landlord there is this reply: that he is dominated by Jesus Christ. None of us is anything unless God has granted it. And from God comes nothing that is evil. Evil comes only from the Devil. . . . I don't have a drop of fear.

Angelita agrees that her own extreme suffering at the hands of the landowner and the experience of an empty belly have driven her to struggle. But, in her view, hunger and deprivation are not sufficient explanations for her defiant actions and her persistence. It is her faith in the God who is with those who struggle for justice and who gives strength to those who have nothing that explains why she has continued to struggle when others have given in. The rhetoric of her explanation, its very linking of the deprivation of the poor in everyday life with the continuing struggle of the Biblical God for justice for his people, here and now, echo the language and the theology of the church of the grass-roots communities.

There are many ironies in this. In many ways Angelita and her small group seem to have taken in Pe. Eduardo's message; or, rather, in Angelita we can see the possibility of a marriage between the church's communitarian vision and a stream of myths and symbols in folk Catholicism. Angelita's Catholicism is of a kind that nurtures the fierce independence and zealous sense of justice among the poor that the priest's vision requires. Yet, though open to clerical inspiration, she is not at all inclined to wait for Padre Cícero or even Pe. Eduardo's prudential moment. She seeks and takes note of clerical help and good counsel in dealing with the problem of everyday life, but, in this instance to the point of clerical discomfiture, she rejects the old moral economy according to which the price for counsel was obedience to its dictates.

It is more common in Campo Alegre to find folk Catholics for whom Padre Cícero is a revered but less central figure than for Pedro Faró and Mário, keeping any priest at a distance and attending to life's problems episodically without recourse to the clerical church. Where Padre Cícero stands small, there is no search for a priestly savior. In this strain of folk Catholicism a priest is needed but confined to specific life-cycle functions and a ministry of the extraordinary. Wisdom about the affairs of everyday life and efficacy in dealing with the private troubles of daily existence are sought in lay religious functionaries. There are the *rezadeiros* (literally, those who pray), men and women who say the prayers that restore health when the Evil Eye has caused illness. There are the *curandeiros* (healers), men and women who know the herbal and other remedies for the Evil Eye and other forms of bewitchment.[15] Hundreds of Catholics in Campo Alegre negotiate a world as haunted as medieval Portugal was with werewolves and malign forces — natural, human, and supernatural — with the aid of these artisans of health and well-being. And, as they do so, they keep the priest in his place, insulated from ministry and communication with the people in their everyday lives. As the communities sustaining this stream of folk Catholicism have broken up, as in Campo Alegre, leaders of the newer spiritist groups like Dona Paula seem to be replacing the *rezadeiros* and *curandeiros*. The valency of this stream of folk Catholicism seems to engage it with Umbanda rather than with Pe. Eduardo's communitarian church. And yet this is the stream from which Angelita seems to come.

Possibly, in this stream, an emphasis on the high God, who is with his people as they struggle for justice, may overcome what is otherwise a focus on remedies for private troubles. The emphasis on a wisdom passed down through generations of the laity may prepare for the church of the CEBs. In any case, Angelita's Catholicism has room for the new priest without destroying his project, as Pedro Faró's Catholicism would, by setting him up as a Padre Cícero. But therein lies the irony. In living — and perhaps especially in a situation of crisis like that confronted by Angelita — a people's prophetic communitarian Catholicism can be a challenge to the more prudential communitarian Catholicism that comes from the presbytery.

PADRE EDUARDO'S PROJECT

Pe. Eduardo's communitarian vision is not easy to realize in Campo Alegre, even though there are individual Catholics who share it and groups that seem to manifest it from time to time. It has remained only a vision, in part, because of structural and cultural mélange in Campo Alegre. The farmer's group, to be led by Pedro Faró, falls apart as its members retreat under fire to preexisting support networks and attachments based on diverse origins and ranges of resources for survival. The community formed around Angelita becomes isolated from any larger community linking the CEBS of Campo Alegre, as her strategy for working on the larger polity clashes with the strategy pursued by the group of fisherwomen and endorsed by Pe. Eduardo himself. Catholics like Gonçalo, attached at least notionally to the world of the *coronéis*, will have nothing to do with the pursuit of the communitarian vision. Catholics like Pedro, with an actual stake in the reemerging networks of populist Brazil, abandon communitarian experiment as unrewarding and uncongenial.

There is also the problem of communicating the vision and the project that flows from it. As the story of Carlos suggests, this is a complex problem. It includes unequal competition between the messages contained in Pe. Eduardo's words and the stronger messages issued by his disposition in the symbolic landscape that tends to determine relationships between priest and people. The problem also includes the chances for misunderstandings that arise because religious symbols, shared by priest and people, may nonetheless vary among individuals and groups in salience, significance, and power to shape choice in everyday life.

Above all, there are elements shared across the variety of religious cultures (often referred to as "folk" or "popular" Catholicism), which pre-empt engagement in the communitarian project.[16] In all three of the cases discussed there are signs that any priest, whatever his gestures or mode of delivery, would have great difficulty in engaging the Catholics of Campo Alegre in the realization of the church's vision of a communitarian Brazil. Gonçalo, Mário, and Pedro Faró know clearly what they want of a priest and what is the precise quality of priestly leadership. The images of the world they would like to construct with a priest as a leader among them are informed by Joaseiro and Padre Cícero. The images of priest and community contained in the communitarian project are simply not admissible and cannot be assimilated into a religio-political culture powerfully integrated around the Cícero stories.

That religious-political culture has historical roots well beyond local history, reaching back to a past centuries older than Padre Cícero. The roots of a complementarity between priests' and people's religion, which is fixed and difficult for either party to modify, go back to colonial times. One of the modern historians of the church in Brazil, Eduardo Hoornaert, characterizes the patterned exchanges through the paradigm set when the conquering ecclesiastical religion required of the Indians and their descendants that they "take refuge in the world of non-verbal expressions in order to keep alive a sense of dignity; in order to live and struggle and defend the heart against the invasion of despair."[17]

During the years of African slavery, the ecclesiastical church presented itself to the illiterate slave as the source of literary culture. The statues of Saint Anne the mother of Mary, to whom devotion was encouraged, invariably depicted a white, beautifully dressed Portuguese matron teaching from a book to the child Jesus in her arms. The church, its clergy, and its high saints on the one hand and the blacks and Indians on the other were as far apart and as locked in with one another as master and slave.

The local priest, from the point of view of the descendants of the Indians and the slaves, had a certain circumscribed role in popular religion. He was expected to represent the ecclesiastical church and to perform some, but by no means all, key religious functions. These functions required him to be a person apart: a holy man, taking care of the holy places, legitimating the great moments of individual and communal life cycles, and preaching and enforcing the law for correct living. Other religious functions, including the rituals of healing and counteracting the Evil Eye, would be performed by other religious functionaries such as the *benzador* (blesser) or the *rezador* or the *pajé* (healer in the shamanic Tupi-Guarani Indian tradition).

In the northeast of Brazil this legacy, which places any priest within a cage of expectations and requirements from which it is difficult to escape, emerges in the religious categories of everyday speech. Hoornaert's compilations of such speech, together with my own, allow the construction of a sort of model of beliefs, perceptions, and expectations that corresponds to a model for negotiating everyday life followed by many northeastern Catholics.[18] In my reconstructed model, the elements are beliefs about man in the cosmos, beliefs about salvation, beliefs and perceptions about the church, and beliefs and expectations about the priest. In Hoornaert's interviews, in particular, there is strong evidence that these elements interact, each lending a plausibility to the others, such that the role of the priest, for example, is implied in the notion of salvation.

First, there are beliefs and images about humans in the cosmos. These include the notion that the cosmos is ruled by God who is *todo poderoso* (all-powerful). Each man and woman, in God's order, is born into an ordained place and fate (*todos tem que nascer pela sorte*). Each person, then, has an obligation to conform to his place and his law that teaches correct living (for Catholics this is *minha lei católica*). This can be difficult because all of us are buffeted by evil forces beyond our control, like the Evil Eye, illness, or Satan himself.

Second, there are beliefs about salvation. Salvation is a reward to those who conform to place and law. It is a breaking through the limits of fate to life in heaven with God. Salvation is also a reward for *promessas* faithfully observed. These vows are usually made to the saints.

Third are the beliefs about the church, the images and expectations about its functions. The church is the guardian and administrative agency of God's law. It provides and maintains holy places in which God may manifest himself and in which his lieutenants, the saints, might be sought. The church provides, occasionally, exemplars who call people back to the law and show what life lived according to the law might be.

Fourth are images and expectations of priests. The priest is the guardian of the holy places and images through which access to the saints is possible. The priest officially validates ordained relationships, administers the law, and proclaims the conditions of salvation by virtue of his outside training in the law. The priest, ideally, exemplifies the lawful life (like *meu santo Padim Ciço* does). Again ideally, the priest is *um bom conselheiro* (a wise counselor) who, drawing on his outside knowledge, gives good advice for dealing with forces usually beyond control (including agencies of the state).

Any priest in Campo Alegre will find it difficult to negotiate this assigned and culturally embedded role of the priest as *animador* (animator) of his church's communitarian project. Even Pedro Faró — a competent negotiator of Campo Alegre's social mélange, remote from the worlds of slavery and *coronelismo* that shaped the religious culture outlined above — tends to reanimate that culture and confine the priest to the role required of him. The image and myths of Padre Cícero show that the role might be lived in a more modern world and that it is worth pressuring the priest to conform to the measure. So, where the *animador* should be all things to all men, the priest must be the holy man apart; where the *animador* is co-constructor of a new community, the priest ordains an existing order; where the *animador* is to be a prophet helping his people to discern the signs of the times, the priest is to preside over a tradition and care for its monuments.

In the case of Pe. Eduardo, as we have seen, the priest has made his own contribution to confinement within the role assigned to him. Only a fairly small minority of the Catholics of Campo Alegre hear his sermons in which the prophetic communitarian vision unfolds; fewer still see him as *animador* in his dealings with Carlos and some of the more highly educated young people in the town. Most have seen him restoring the old church and building a new presbytery. He is known as a firm and competent administrator of the church patrimony. By reputation, he is a holy man. He does not move around the town very much, partly because he is shy and retiring and partly because he is often in Recife attending diocesan meetings and seeing to matters related to the institutional maintenance of the church. In short, his personality, his use of time, and his chosen confinement to church space make it easy to read him as a traditional priest. When his mode of dress, his words, or his pursuit of communitarian vision run counter to that reading, he becomes an enigma. And an enigma cannot be an *animador*.

As we look from the Catholics of Campo Alegre to Catholicism in Brazil, it becomes important to ask how crucial Pe. Eduardo's character-istics and choices have been in the containment of communitarian vision. Initially it must be stressed that, within Campo Alegre, the realization of his church's vision did not depend exclusively on Pe. Eduardo. For sev-eral years, Campo Alegre has been one of the centers of pastoral work among men and women engaged in small-scale, artisanal fishing. This work — led by a priest who lived for two or three days a week in Campo Alegre as he moved up and down the coast, and a full-time resident nun — was given enthusiastic support by Pe. Eduardo. The aims of this "pastoral of fishing" are consciously attuned to the realization of the communitarian vision. And the personal styles of the priest and the nun are in marked contrast to Pe. Eduardo's. They are both people apart from the fishing folk in education, dress, and mode of speech, and they do not try to be anything but different. But they have an ease of manner and a chosen in-dependence of administrative involvements that have allowed them to act and to be seen as *animadores* rather than traditional clergy.

Over a period of about ten years, these *animadores* have been able to count some successes. A cooperative for the selling of fish has been established and is now run successfully by an elected board of fishing folk (women rather than men having emerged as better administrators, as they are more willing or able to connect their activities in the cooperative to the wider community-building concerns of the pastoral). The nun can point to a group of women she has worked with for twelve years, which has produced some of the most successful leaders of the cooperative and has become an important community-aid group — organizing the rebuilding of houses undermined by the rains, providing emergency services for dis-tressed families, initiating small-scale health programs — in the poorest areas of the town. Some of the women in this group speak of their lives and of Campo Alegre and enunciate their religious faith with all the strength and fervor of Angelita. The myth of Padre Cícero has no purchase in this group.

But the nun herself has reservations about what has been achieved. In 1982, in conversation, she worried about continuing dependence on her as leader of the group. The small number of women and families di-rectly involved was also a cause for concern. Most fishermen, she con-sidered, had been unable to break out of their dependence on patrons who owned boats and nets and on the intermediaries who controlled and ma-nipulated the price of the catch. The church groups had been able to spread a greater awareness of rights and drives to get fishermen to obtain the documents necessary for pensions had been relatively successful. But the fishing folk had not, over the years of her work, been formed into a grass-roots community of the kind that fulfilled her ideals and the ideals of her church. This sad assessment by the nun suggests to me that Pe. Eduardo's own contribution to failures in communication and the lack of realization of his church's communitarian project ought not be exaggerated. Any priest is likely to have encountered his problems and found difficulty in overcoming them.

Accounts of popular Catholicism in other areas of Brazil also suggest that Pe. Eduardo is by no means a special case. If one of the goals of the communitarian church is to achieve "fraternal dialogue" between popular Catholicism and the theology of liberation,[19] then a number of recent studies suggest just how difficult this is, for reasons quite independent of a priest's personality or strategy. Marjo de Theije's study "Brotherhoods Throw More Weight Around than the Pope" suggests very limited basis for fraternal dialogue where an organized and autonomous popular Catholicism persists. Papers by van den Hoogen and van Halsema show how popular Catholicism — tightly linked to the institutional church in its pre-Vatican II form — is rather closed to fraternal dialogue with the church of the CEBs.

THE COMMUNITARIAN PROJECT OF THE CATHOLIC CHURCH IN BRAZIL

Many other studies support and help elaborate this conclusion that the Catholic church's communitarian project comes up against a range of linked cultural and social-structural obstacles. My own previous work on clergy in the northeastern diocese in which Campo Alegre is located shows how "new priests" of the communitarian church are received at the grass roots very much as though they were priests of the old dispensation.[20] Together with their commitments to institutional maintenance, this reception at the grass roots has made it very difficult to realize communitarian projects.

Thomas Bruneau

The work of Thomas Bruneau allows us, up to a point, to place Campo Alegre, its diocese and region, into a pan-Brazilian context.[21] Bruneau's surveys of dioceses in several different regions of Brazil allow us to assess what was the fate of the communitarian vision by the end of the seventies.

In a section on the archdiocese of São Paulo, Bruneau shows us the church with its programs and priorities committed to internal change and social action, diametrically opposed to the aims and tendencies of state policies. Against state repression, co-optation of the lower classes in corporatist institutions, or simple unconcern, the church turned its resources to the development of the anticorporatist CEBs, the defence of human rights, and the extension of the "workers pastoral" and the "pastoral of the periphery." When the state moved against individuals or groups dedicated to these goals, the church demonstrated a tremendous capacity for mobilization in their support.

In São Paulo, Bruneau points out, the church is not only strong in programs for a new church and an alternative Brazil but, in his terms, seems to be actually influential. The demonstrated capacity to mobilize support, the growth in the number of base communities in the peripheries, the extraordinary sales of books dealing with the church, all are indicators of actual impact. At the conclusion of his chapter 5 Bruneau asks "Who would have expected such interest in the church ten, or even five years ago?"[22]

In the rest of the book, though, Bruneau wants to remind us that there is more of Brazil to be influenced than São Paulo, and there is more to being influential than attraction of interest. His wider and deeper investigation of the new church's influence consists of two projects. The first is a survey of eight dioceses: two in the South, two in the Northeast, two in the Center, and two in the state of São Paulo. The point of the survey is to find out, simply, the extent to which ideas and programs that flourish in the archdiocese of São Paulo — and to which the Brazilian bishops, collectively, have committed themselves — are actually implemented throughout Brazil. He and his research team spent about a week in each diocese, interviewing the bishop and other key figures, reviewing documentation, and generally observing.

The researchers systematically collected data on three dimensions of church life. The first was church leaders' conceptions of the church's role or mission — the "normative dimension."[23] The point was to note where diocesan leaders stood in comparison to the norms for change espoused by the bishops collectively. The second and third dimensions concerned structure, process, and programs — how each diocese was organized, more as a traditional, centralized, clerical hierarchy or with effective lay participation in the flatter structure based on the CEBs.

On the basis of the data obtained in this survey the eight dioceses were classified and systematically compared. The results of the comparison comprise a cautionary tale for those who would read an effectively radical Brazilian church from the pronouncements of the Conference of Bishops or from any single diocesan case.[24] Two of the eight dioceses — one in the state of São Paulo and the other in the southern region — were massively traditional: on all dimensions they, in effect, defied the Conference of Bishops and departed from the example of the archdiocese of São Paulo. Bruneau estimates that these two dioceses represent perhaps one-third of all Brazilian dioceses.

On the other hand, two dioceses — one in the northeast region and another in the central region — were innovative on all dimensions. Their leaders were fully committed to service of the poor through nonpaternalist means; and conflict with the powers-that-be was defined as a normal concomitant of the struggle for Christian liberation. In these dioceses, there was much experimentation in structuring the church so that communications, participation, and the flow of influence were full and open. Appropriately, the central focal structures in these innovative dioceses were the CEBs; and the laity, in and through them, had taken over a great deal of pastoral action. Bruneau estimates that probably one-half of Brazilian bishops would have things as they are in these most innovative dioceses.

Most dioceses in Brazil seem likely to be similar to the four between the two completely traditional and the two radically innovative dioceses surveyed. Some have leaders persuaded that they should lead their institutions to innovation; but through lack of resources, an overabundance of them, or lack of innovative ability, the commitment to change has come to nought, or very little. Bruneau looks back over his comparisons and asks why there is so much variation. He locates a set of prerequisites for innovation: the personal commitment to innovation on the part of the local bishop or his core advisers; the development of a local, concrete, pastoral plan; a socioeconomic context that stimulates or even provokes most sections of the church seeking innovation. In rural southern dioceses, Bruneau argues, innovation is difficult to achieve even if promoted by church elites, "since older clergy and conservative elements in society would see no reason to change the existing structures of society or the church."[25]

Bruneau's second, and more ambitious, project was to study, by sociological survey, the attitudes and self-reported behavior of lay Catholics in the eight dioceses. In each diocese Catholics from two parishes, one close to the diocesan center and the other more on the periphery, were asked to respond to a long questionnaire. The sample was a quota rather than a probability sample — a choice well described and defended by Bruneau in the first of his two excellent methodological appendixes. The aim of the project was to test whether the church, as its innovating elites defined and attempted to construct it, was successfully influencing Catholics at the grass roots. Bruneau, through his survey of individual Catholics, hoped to trace the links between institutional changes and change in the religiosity of individual believers.

The data from this survey suggest that both the fears of Brazil's national security network and the more exaggerated claims of innovators are without solid foundation. The influence of the innovating church, on the basis of this evidence, seems really rather slight. That conclusion unfolds in several stages of Bruneau's analysis.

First, Bruneau describes the patterns of religiosity found in his sample. Drawing on his knowledge of Brazilian Catholicism and using the technique of factor analysis, Bruneau isolates four patterns of Catholicism: popular Catholicism, spiritism, orthodox Catholicism, and social Catholicism. The latter pattern is what would be expected in grass-roots Catholicism in proportion as the innovating elites in the church had been successfully influential. I do not recall that Bruneau ever reports the frequencies for the patterns of religiosity variables; but it is clear that social Catholicism is very much a minority pattern. The new institutional church, by this measure, has a long way to go in influencing religiosity at the grass roots.

Bruneau presses the point. We would expect that if the innovators did not influence globally, the impact of their ideas and programs should at least register among Catholics in the innovating dioceses where they are institutionally dominant. So, in chapter 7, Bruneau correlates patterns of religiosity and sociopolitical attitudes with type of diocese. Once again, the results must alarm those who assume actual influence at the grass roots on the basis of episcopal pronouncements, from institutional data, or from the content of pastoral programs. Bruneau finds (as we would expect) that there is a relationship between social Catholicism and progressive sociopolitical attitudes (he is careful not to infer a causal relationship here). But his major finding is that innovative dioceses as a group, when compared to traditional dioceses, seem not to be succeeding in promoting the social Catholicism pattern. There is more likelihood of finding people who adhere to the spiritist pattern than in more traditional dioceses, but no more likelihood of the social Catholicism pattern. Only in the exceptional case of São Paulo, where there was a three-decade-long history of commitment and effort toward realization of social Catholicism, is there some evidence of success.

That raises the question of the means appropriate for promoting social Catholicism, and Bruneau pursues the question in chapter 8. In the third and final part of the analysis of his survey, he reports the proportion of respondents in CEB-type groups, analyzes the modus operandi of these groups (as compared to others to which respondents belonged), and cross-tabulates type of diocese with CEB membership. Bruneau points out that, up to the sixties, the church of the radical declarations lacked the sort of groups necessary to anchor new orientations of church elites in the church at the grass roots and, in that way, to a rapidly changing Brazilian political context. By the seventies there were signs that the anchor had been found in the CEBs. There were, at least, reported cases of CEBs that showed some of them were structurally appropriate to the vision they were meant to embody, and actually effective as means for achieving social justice at the local level. Hence the interest in investigating their diffusion. Bruneau warns us of the limits of his survey for this project.

> The reports indicate that the CEBs are found on the "margins," that is, in rural areas and the peripheral, poor areas of the cities. By the very definition of margin, it is extremely difficult to pick up these people in a survey; they are not easily found, are normally isolated, and cannot be sampled in sufficient numbers in a project such as this to produce clear results.[26]

Nevertheless, some interesting data is reported. And this time the trend of the data should provide some encouragement for innovators in the Brazilian church. Examining respondents' reports of the major activity of the religious groups to which they belonged, Bruneau is able to distinguish between CEB-like groups and more traditional groups. He finds that the CEB-like groups are indeed found in the more innovative dioceses. Furthermore, members' reports indicate that the CEB-like groups are distinguished from more traditional religious groups by a much higher degree of lay member control. Finally, there is an indication that those involved in CEBs were more progressive in terms of religious beliefs and practices. Bruneau, once again, warns us that his data do not allow easy inference about cause and effect. But on the basis of his data, read in context with the many other reports he has read, he is prepared to conclude that the specific strategy of realizing innovative goals through the encouragement of CEBs does work. In general, the influence of the innovators, working in a church structurally geared to achieving other goals, has so far been slight. But effective influence, real purchase at the grass roots, may be achieved in and through the CEBs.

It is always easy in a large ambitious survey of the sort undertaken by Bruneau, to point to the limitations imposed by the sampling design, the choice of questions, the superficiality of the survey as a research instrument. On the other hand, a survey as well designed, carefully administered, scrupulously described, and intelligently analyzed as this allows the reader to critically assess what has been learned. In this case, in my view, much has been learned, and the limitations of the survey, most of them raised and well appreciated by Bruneau himself, serve rather more to point out to other researchers what further work needs to be done than to undermine the author's conclusions.

Nevertheless, it is appropriate to review the relative strengths and limitations of the study. As a survey of the influence of the teaching of the church of Cardinal Arns (the archbishop of São Paulo), on the religious and political thinking of attenders at mass and not-so-marginal Catholics, Bruneau's work is excellent: there is no other survey in that area so competently designed, administered, and analyzed. As such, it is an indispensable contribution to the study of church influence in Brazil. But it does not deal with the issue of religious influence in all its complexity. It does not "analyze the relationship between change in the Brazilian church and patterns of religious behavior and practices" relevant to Brazilian politics in any exhaustively comprehensive way.[27]

A major limitation is conceptual. Of two conceptions of religion, which I shall call the broad and the narrow, Bruneau adopts the latter. The narrow conception focuses on explicit norms, dogmatic formulas, and specifically religious practice as the content of religion. Proceeding from this conception, religious change is observed in believers' statements about new religious rules governing behavior, in agreement to new doctrinal formulations and in accounts of new forms of observance. Attention is concentrated on notional assent to religious content: to the believer's statements of agreement or disagreement with verbal formulations of beliefs and norms.

The broader conception of religion, by contrast, focuses less exclusively on explicit verbal content. Religious content includes the interwoven (though not necessarily logically homogeneous) webs of symbols, myths, and rituals, which at once enunciate a cosmos and shape the conduct of everyday life. In the investigative approaches proceeding from this conception, prime attention will be given to real, rather than notional, assent: to the informing of the whole being of believers, with their religious vision understood as being to a variable extent independent of the formal verbal expression of its notions. So religious change, under this rubric, will be sought less in agreement or disagreement with verbalized norms and beliefs, and more in variations in the conduct of ritual, in the hierarchy of religious symbols, in the pantheon of saints, in the detail of myth, in the gestures relating clerics and lay persons.

I am suggesting the possibility that Bruneau's narrow, survey-oriented conception of religion, compounding his difficulty in surveying more marginal Catholics, may have caused him to underestimate the influence of the innovating church in Brazil. Adopting the broader conception of religion I wonder whether the last thing to change, as the church of the innovators gained influence at the grass roots, would be responses to questions about formal belief and practice.

Among the Brazilian poor, I would suggest, there is a looseness of fit between stated religious practice and doctrine on the one hand and, on the other, the range of symbolic statements about the human condition that move and motivate people to action, including political and economic action. A northeastern farmer of irregular attendance at mass might, while participating in a CEB, continue to make vows to his saints and to express folklore verities culled over generations from the more formally stated doctrines of the old catechism of Saint Alphonsus Ligouri. But if the pantheon of saints should expand to include some of the saints of liberation, if old saints be invested with new characters, and if myths and miracle stories should include the triumphs of collective action, then a deep religious transformation with profound consequences for the political action of the faithful will have occurred. But this would be missed in a survey cast in the mold of a narrower conception of religion, which placed forms of observance and doctrinal statement at its heart. This line of speculation does not amount to any sort of dismissal of Bruneau's study. It merely maps one area of research where, with more qualitative methods, issues raised by Bruneau's work might well be pursued.

My own work in Campo Alegre might be considered one such study. But the Catholics of Campo Alegre, as we have seen, do not allow support for the hypothesis that qualitative research, in areas where the communitarian project has been attempted, will show a deeper purchase of the communitarian vision at the grass roots than survey research leads us to expect. If anything, the Catholics of Campo Alegre — studied qualitatively, with my notion of religion and its traces in mind — send us back to question whether the project of the CEBs could have taken root anywhere in Brazil. Carlos, in whom Pe. Eduardo (the bearer of that vision) had hoped, suggests to me that there may well be shifts in verbalized norms and beliefs that look like a seeding of the communitarian church at the grass roots, but which mask a continuity of belief and practice at odds with the communitarian vision. Examining Pe. Eduardo's frustrations and hearing the nun's sadness, we might wonder whether the limited triumphs Bruneau has allowed the church of the CEBs might indeed relate more to notional than to real religion, to outward forms rather than to a profound sea change in the religious construction of everyday life that might achieve the communitarian Kingdom of God.

Rubem César Fernandes

Other case studies, also of the more qualitative kind, might suggest to Pe. Eduardo and the nun that there is hope for their vision. Rubem César Fernandes studied themes and variations in Brazilian popular religions, through the case of the pilgrims to the shrine of the Good Lord Jesus of Pirapora, in the state of São Paulo: he was a participant observer with a group of pilgrims who set out for Pirapora in the traditional manner, on horseback. He draws attention to distinct Catholic, Protestant, and Afro-Brazilian religious cultures. Like Carlos Rodrigues

Brandão, he draws attention to "dominant" and "popular" streams within each tradition. But among the popular Catholics he finds an even greater range than I found in Campo Alegre. It may be, he concedes, that there are pilgrims to northeastern shrines of the kind found by Daniel R. Gross who, in their exchanges with their saints, sacralize patron-client relationships and humbly accept their permanent status as subordinate clients.[28] But Fernandes shows his *promessa*-paying pilgrims as a long way, in their proud individualism, from cementing any such relationships. Then he describes another group of pilgrims at this shrine of what many have read as a homogeneous popular Catholicism.

Today, there are motorcycle pilgrimages, but it is worth recalling another horseback pilgrimage which arrived at Pirapora from Vargem Grande on July 11, 1981. The procession to the sanctuary followed the customary pattern. The Mass, however, was exceptionally lively and, judged by the movement in the church, it seemed that the whole group went up to receive Communion. A black read the passages from the Bible, the music led by three guitars played by two young men and a girl seated behind the altar. The hymns recalled Protestant choruses with that easy and rather sentimental style that characterizes most of the songs that come from the CEBs. The priest who accompanied the pilgrimage (dressed as a layman) opted to say the Mass, exercising a right which is not always taken up by the "spiritual assistants" who arrive at Pirapora. He spoke to his congregation with a tone of intimacy, mentioning names and experiences of members of the group. He dedicated the Mass, and the whole pilgrimage, to three "intentions": the sick and deceased, the family, and . . . to the unemployed workers of Brazil. I transcribe some passages from his homily:

> We ask, all of us together, of the God Jesus of Pirapora a great grace: that our life as parishioners, as Christians, might always be similar to the life of Jesus. . . . He came into the world to do good for all and, in a special way to the most reduced, to the poorest, the most humble. . . .
>
> Next we ask for the grace to be ever more united. Our parish is three years old. It's like an infant, crawling and learning to walk. . . . Then we pray for our sick. . . . Each one of us has, in our families, those who are ill. . . . But the compassion of God is not like a bird which flies from on high. . . . The compassion of God takes birth in the compassion of people for one another. . . .
>
> Next we pray for the families. Some from the parish are to marry before the end of the year. . . . *Everything* depends on the family. . . .
>
> Next we pray for the workers. Our Brazil is passing through a very difficult moment. It is only the beginning. Don't imagine that the worst is over. We are entering a deep recession. Unemployment will increase. . . . So we ask that those who govern us cease to stick on the side of the privileged and start to turn their eyes to those who come last in our society. So that every Brazilian should receive his daily bread with dignity. So that all in

this Brazil who call themselves Christians can pray together: Our Father, give us this day our daily bread.

The priest concluded the sermon with a prayer in which each phrase was repeated in one voice by all present.[29]

Fernandes interprets this liturgy as a display of something almost the opposite of what I found in the case of Carlos and Pe. Eduardo. These pilgrims *together with* their priest, in an old devotional form, have re-interpreted old symbols and appropriated them for the communitarian project. We do not know how this was achieved, through what conjunc-ture of ecclesial circumstances, priestly creativity, and lay experience. But Fernandes assures us that the ritual described is a sign of a people's Ca-tholicism that not only rejects patronage but embarks on a "strike of the knees" against the prevailing government, much as Polish workers have done.[30]

Scott Mainwaring

Of course, on the evidence presented, other interpreta-tions are possible. Do the responses in one voice imply one vision? Is the priest in lay clothing still so vested with traditional authority that the communitarian project in its deepest religious moorings is still preemi-nently his and not a joint project, as the vision itself requires? Scott Main-waring's exhaustive critical review of all available reports on and from the CEBs restrains the skeptical response to these questions that would be prompted by Campo Alegre.[31]

Mainwaring's materials do not allow him to explore how a mutually transformative conversation has taken place between a variety of folk Catholicisms in a variety of places and "pastoral agents." But his analysis of the voluminous literature leads him to conclude that it has. Noting cases to the contrary, he argues that the emphasis on promoting popular leader-ship has been pronounced in the CEBs and that the development of demo-cratic social practices fostered through them has already begun to form citizens motivated, willing, and able to challenge authoritarian political structures. He finds evidence that, in many CEBs, there are many indi-viduals who seem to have discovered a sense of human worth and ac-quired skills in demystification. Where bonds of solidarity are under threat from a variety of social, economic, and political pressures for fragmenta-tion, the CEBs, in a wide variety of circumstances, have achieved among the poor a new sense of community.[32]

Mainwaring alerts us to the fragilities of the achievement and argues against naive exaggeration of the immediate political effects of the CEBs. He points out that "democratization of social values (however important at the human level) does not inherently produce democratization of the political order."[33] He refers us not only to disputes about the role of the pastoral agents but to a great range in practice among those agents (Pe. Eduardo and the nun do not nearly exhaust the variation to be found). There are extremes of veneration for popular culture, on one end, and dismissal of alienated popular Catholicism, at the other, that seem to preclude any serious investigation, in specific instances, of potential for dialogue between a Catholicism of the grass roots and the agents' communitarian vision. There are different ideas about pace of change and mode of entry into the political arena. There are differences of emphasis on the religious versus the explicitly political aspects of pastoral work. These variations make it difficult to assess the impact of the CEBs on Brazilian institutions and the projects of the state up to the early eighties; and the task of plotting the trajectory of the communitarian project itself is rendered difficult.

Nonetheless, Mainwaring concludes that in many different circumstances there has been a meeting of priests' project and people's religion, to the transformation of each; and out of that continuing encounter arises a new political force, which has at least local and occasionally national impact. In some instances, the encounter has resulted in institutional change in the Catholic church, which, as a relatively well-organized and competent national body, has been able to set up agencies capable of confronting and sometimes outmaneuvering agencies of the state in specific areas of policy. For example, out of small local initiatives in the development of the communitarian project, the Pastoral Land Commission and the Indian Missionary Council emerged as national church agencies; and these agencies have had a notable effect on the course of the land reform struggles and the survival of indigenous groups respectively. In other cases, the encounter has issued in the formation of a local citizenry, moved, motivated, and equipped to participate in local struggles for social justice. Mainwaring presents us with a detailed case study of the political impact of the CEBs in the diocese of Nova Iguaçú, which illustrates this point.[34]

Priests' and People's Catholicisms

There is no easy explanation why the encounter between priests' project and people's Catholicism sometimes issues in religious and political developments favorable for the former and sometimes in a priest's frustration and a nun's sadness. It is tempting to attribute success or failure to resources available both to pastoral agents and people, along lines suggested by Bruneau. Another possibility is that, in conditions of worsening absolute poverty, CEBs — even should they be formed — are unlikely to fare well. A report on the CEBs in the extremely poor area of Tacaimbó, Pernambuco, makes the point:

> The poor do not believe that they can emerge from this situation in which they are living. They cannot believe in improvement. They can only believe in worse conditions until the end. . . . People are now observing the poor uniting but it remains to be seen whether the unity is merely a pretence. The poor person does not have a chance in the local society. The society is made for those who have prestige, those who have a name, an education or money. The little people have no place in it. A better society for the poor has yet to appear. It will occur when a poor person gets along well with others, and, together, they become associated with one another.[35]

In Campo Alegre, I think, we have a similar situation with the fishermen. Their extreme destitution and dependence render implausible the claimed benefits of community building. The commercialization of fishing without benefit to the fishermen themselves, if it encourages any selection from among the array of paradigms for living in grass-roots Catholicism, turns fishermen away from the more communal forms and meanings to a religion and a life made possible through private deals with the saints and spirits. In situations such as this, a pastoral agent without the resources of a network of contacts, outside and upward, of time, energy, health, and money would have little hope of reaching and communicating with the desperate and privatized poor.

But resources of people and pastoral agent cannot be a sufficient factor in an explanation of the linkage between priests' and people's Catholicisms. W. E. Hewitt's study of CEBs in São Paulo warns us that resources must be only one element, complex itself, in a complex equation.[36] Hewitt, in this study, focused on six of the least affluent of the CEBs in a larger sample of twenty-two. The six are within the region that Bruneau found to be the most favorable environment, in terms of resources available to pastoral agents, in Brazil. And though the neighborhoods in which the CEBs are located are poor, the degree of poverty is not nearly as absolute as that to be found in Tacaimbó or among the fishermen of Campo Alegre. In this relatively well-resourced environment, however, all is far from well with the CEBs. It has been possible for these groups, most of which were instituted for religious ends to struggle for local improvements like garbage collection, street lights, running water, and health posts. But a plateau seems generally to be reached, disillusion sets in, and a certain degree of disintegration becomes evident.[37]

There are external sources of the problems these groups establish. There is lack of community recognition, in some cases connected with the fact that residents are angry with their neighbors in the CEBs who have initiated changes that they have to help finance. Local officials and politicians, anxious to deaden local initiatives to preserve their own power and patronage, seek to co-opt individual members of the CEBs with bribes and favors; and at election time installations are made leaving some CEBs without solid local issues.

But the problems of these CEBs seem also to be associated with internal problems that our Campo Alegre investigations might lead us to expect. More politically radical participants complain of the restraints placed on them by clergy — particularly proscriptions against direct links between the CEBs and political parties. On the other hand, clergy complain of the religious traditionalism among the membership. As one nun put it, "In the religious sense, they remain as they always were."[38]

It is here that the Catholics of Campo Alegre help us with a necessary element in our complex equation. They do not provide us with a complete explanation of the variable purchase of the church's communitarian project at the grass roots. Still less can we confidently generalize from Campo Alegre about the future course of Brazilian politics or even the Catholic church's role in the shaping of that future. But as we look back over Pe. Eduardo's negotiation of a fiesta and his relationships with Pedro Faró, Carlos, and Angelita, we can see how the content of a variety of folk Catholicisms, the history of a place, and the hazards of symbolic communication and miscommunication must be taken into account in an attempt to provide such explanations and forecasts. Campo Alegre is not representative of the variety of situations in which the church's communitarian project is attempted.[39] Nor does it display the whole range of folk Catholicisms. But the encounters between Pe. Eduardo and some of the Catholics of the town represent to us how what I would call the valencies of several folk Catholicisms might affect the chances of the communitarian project at the grass roots.

There is the folk Catholicism in which *curandeiros* and *rezadeiros* are still the most important religious functionaries in everyday life. The priest, when available, was once an important figure in this sort of folk Catholicism, but only for life-cycle events and extraordinary needs. This sort of Catholicism seems to need the priest less than in the past and seems to be associated with private devotions and the seeking of individual solutions to life's problems. In the mélange of Campo Alegre, where saints, spirits, and religious functionaries proliferate, the former visitor to the *rezadeiro* for some problem arising from the Evil Eye will tend to become a client of a Dona Paula rather than a member of Carlos's *congregação*.

25. Padre Cícero appropriated in a Jurema spiritist *pejí*. Popular Catholicism may link with projects other than the priest's.

The life-cycle functions of the priest, where there is now a bureaucrat to attend to everything, seem less important now than they used to. So, where the priest was once locked in to specific functions and heard only on special occasions, he now tends to be locked out altogether from the lives of many Catholics and heard not at all. The valency of the Catholicism of the *curandeiro* allows linkage with clientelistic spiritism and its politics rather than with the priest's communalist project.

Other folk Catholicisms leave the individual much less alone with private troubles and seek communal solutions to communal problems. Carlos and Pedro, whatever else their differences, not only assume that there is some fault in local society that contributes to their individual deprivations but that some form of group action can set things better, if not right, in this life. Carlos sees a past in which the Catholic church, clergy, and faithful laity together have slowly closed the gates of hell and achieved a better life for all. Pedro knows, through the historical achievement of Padre Cícero, what a priest-led people can accomplish against the forces of injustice. Neither is predisposed by religious myths or symbols to expect much from technocrats or to believe the stories of those who preach salvation through compliance with the growth policies of the modern state. But, as we have seen, when Padre Cícero haunts this communal vision or the moralizing missionaries of Catholic dogma dominate in it, there will be only very partial and selective attention to the message and vision of a priest from the church of the CEBs. Only partly understood, he is likely to be rejected (and that is easy, given Campo Alegre's absorption into a marketplace of religious and political leaders) when he fails the tests of true leadership. Probably, a priest representative of those sections of the Brazilian church who are hostile to the "new way of being church" that is spelled out in the CEBs project would be much more congenial to Pedro and Carlos. And the church in Campo Alegre, with such a leader, would almost certainly resume one of its modern roles as legitimator of morally respectable and church-respecting populism.

There is no need to review Gonçalo's Catholicism, or to reassemble the church of the old brotherhood, to make the point that popular Catholicism is multivalent in at least two senses: religiously, in the sense that some streams in a modern terrain bear their devotees to spiritism, others to Pentecostalism, few to the vision and practice of the CEBs; politically, in the sense that there is scope for linkage in one or other of the folk Catholicisms with all the contending political economies of modern Brazil. That, especially when multivalency is not understood in its local manifestations and creative permutations, is an important element in explaining why a priest's communitarian project might fail.[40]

CHAPTER EIGHT

The Kingdoms Come

SKEPTICISM FROM ON HIGH AND SKEPTICISM FROM THE FIELD

I WENT TO Campo Alegre because I imagined it to be small, isolated, and simple enough for the intersections of the religious and the political, there in the lives of its inhabitants, to be understood. And Campo Alegre, although it was not to be a microcosm, was to be the locus in which the political implications of the religious constructions of everyday life in Brazil could be grasped. It is time to recall the hopes expressed in Chapter 2: Campo Alegre was to be studied for its representations of linkages between the local and the national. Through the lives and associations of its citizens, the religious constructions of distinctive paradigms for living were to be traced; and within the variety of Pentecostal, spiritist, and Catholic paradigms, the elements of distinctive political cultures would emerge. As they used, debated, and lived their religiously constructed political cultures, the citizens of Campo Alegre would represent for us how modern Brazil's great political-economic projects — *coronelismo*, populism, the bureaucratic-authoritarian, and the communitarian — are variously subverted, rendered viable, crafted, or reassembled at the grass roots of Brazilian society.

Surveying Brazil from on high, a political economist might be forgiven some skepticism about the achievement of these ambitions so far. Looking from what Brazilians call the *cúpula* of society down, the struggles of Pe. Eduardo to achieve a new communal politics, Severino's quest for *crente* justice, Dona Paula's contributions to authoritarian populism, all must appear inconsequential. When the Sunday *culto* of the Assembly of God, the priest's mass on the feast of Saint Peter, and Maria Pretinha's performance of Zé Pelintra are read as the jostling of rival political economies, the political economist must suspect mere metaphor. From on high, there must seem to be but little articulation between such local jostling (if that is how it is to be characterized) and the dynamics of a bureau-cratic-authoritarian polity, in its military or civilian forms and over-determined by its debt problem.

Some concessions must be made to this skepticism. There can be no doubt that when we put the state back into the picture, and move from the everyday local to an era of national history, *coronelismo*, populism, and the Catholic church's communitarian vision and praxis do not jostle on equal terms, whatever might seem to be the case in given localities at particular times. The Brazilian state, during the time span covered in this study (from the seventies through the mid-eighties), has been able to in-vade local worlds, set agendas for the contest between rival political econo-mies, force conversions, and exact compliance from those who can only act as though their worlds of meaning were intact and enactable on any-thing more than a local and discontinuous basis.

There can be no doubt that the hegemonic political economy — carried by agents and agencies of the state, even into daily life in Campo Alegre — is the bureaucratic authoritarian, even during the "transition" to civilian democracy. As the military regime relaxed the extreme repression of 1969–1974 and finally moved over for the present civilian government, the bureaucratic-authoritarian project of the state has remained largely in-tact. That project includes the maintenance of a strong centralized execu-tive able to protect its internationally oriented technocrats from the vagaries of electoral politics; the continuation of export-led economic growth poli-cies; the subordination of equity and social-justice considerations to the exigencies of growth and debt management as they are understood by modern economists; the maintenance, in the name of growth, of complex alliances between transnational corporations and large state enterprises; the exclusion of the popular classes if not from electoral politics then most certainly from participation in policy making or any real control over the distribution of national resources. And, if less stridently and with more concessions to populism than in the darkest days, the state has continued to evoke and promote versions of a national security ideology for the le-gitimation of its policies and strategies. The might and economic muscle of the state, in a sense, have been deployed to make the jostling of politi-cal economies in Campo Alegre irrelevant to its functioning.

But that is to concede neither that the state has succeeded nor that it is as monolithic as the discourse implies. Nor is it to concede that only the methods of macro political science are adequate to the investigation of modern Brazilian politics. Indeed from the field, from Campo Alegre, arises a skepticism about the methods, key concepts, and substantive claims of the approach from on high. From Campo Alegre, exclusive focus on affairs of state and the use of concepts like hegemony and alienation to marginalize the local and religious construction of political reality seem rather to beg questions about how the dominance of the state is achieved and to assume the absolute triumph of the state and the political economy it carries into existence. Even the strict setting apart of the state from civil society seems to preclude on a priori grounds a dialectics for which there is some evidence in Campo Alegre.

Skepticism from the field, too, demands its concessions. At the very least, the state must not be spoken of as some sort of metasocial force. From Campo Alegre it seems not to be so. Rather, the state can be seen in those who act it into existence in national day parades, who teach its partly hidden curriculum in local schools, who offer and withdraw employment in reaction to the flow of monies from state agencies. From the field, the state can and must be seen as sets of actors who, with varying degrees of private endorsement, publicly act as bound by the shifting rules of the bureaucratic-authoritarian political economy, as persuaded prose-lytizers for the state's legitimating ideology, and in extremis as enforcers of compliance to its projects. In local everyday life these sets of actors seem to see themselves as contestants and as negotiators for the future, not as absolute victors over a robotic population. They must persuade, cajole, manipulate, and occasionally coerce Pedro Faró, Severino, Maria Pretinha, and Pe. Eduardo. But they do not always win outright, and outright victory is not always the goal.[1]

Against such contestants as these, they fail at least to gain robotic acquiescence, and they have occasionally to modify their projects. At a minimum, skepticism from the field — armed with confidence borrowed perhaps from Severino — demands from macro analysts that they acknowledge a certain vulnerability of the projects of the state before the religious projects of the grass roots. The rehearsal of rival skepticisms suggests the possibility of a fruitful truce. Taking account of both critiques, we might refine the agenda set in Chapter 1. Instead of the general questions about relations between the religious and the political posed there, we shall take a more specific question arising from concern about trends in politics at the national level, and we shall review how local religious constructions of reality might impinge on that concern. Our question, to be elaborated below, is this: how do local religious constructions of reality impinge on chances for a deepening of democracy in Brazil?

RELIGION AND THE DEEPENING OF DEMOCRACY

Even as Brazil returned slowly to formal electoral democracy and civilian rule in the late seventies and early eighties (the famous transition), many commentators on the national scene reflected on the historical shallowness of Brazilian democracy and questioned whether the changes would involve any deepening. Some political historians conceived of political trends over fifty years as a pendulum oscillating between authoritarianism and populist democracy and noted that, wherever the location of the pendulum, the lower classes were always excluded from the political arena except on terms manipulated from above.[2] Drawing convincingly on data concerning the state of Pernambuco, Aspásia Alcântara de Camargo has argued that the pendulum tends to swing toward populist democracy when elites whose power depends on a strong central state seek a new equilibrium because conflicts among upper-class groups supporting authoritarian rule have become irreconcilable. She considers that "the State's duplicity, accomplice of decadent elites and fortuitous ally of popular movements, reveals its supremacy over civil society."[3]

Simon Schwartzman, in the conclusion of a study focusing on São Paulo, paints a similar picture. He analyzes the shallowness of democracy in what he characterizes as two alternating political systems in Brazil: the liberal system and the authoritarian system.[4] The liberal political system in Brazil, as elsewhere, has been grounded in the economics of private capitalism. The centralized authoritarian political system is conditioned by the need for a strong state to mediate between disunited capitalist interests and to promote the national growth that the private sector, relatively weak and dependent in the international economy, is unable to achieve.

The liberal political system is most obviously characterized by representation as its major form of political participation. The claim of its champions is that it guarantees participation of ever-widening sectors of society in politics and, through that participation, the possibility of an increasingly just distribution of resources. There is historical justification for the first part of the claim, but there are also ample grounds on which to challenge the second part.[5] Representative politics in Brazil has often, perhaps mainly, functioned to guarantee established interests over and against sectors of society, especially the rural poor, who are less able to articulate their own interests or back them with political resources. (In gossip about the forthcoming elections in 1982, many Campo Alegrenses concurred. For them, elections were mere interludes in rule by one or another group of Them, when They pay short-term costs of democracy for long-term spoils of office.)

The centralized authoritarian system, Schwartzman notes, is bureaucratic in form and in its principles of legitimation. When citizens are not merely called on to comply with bureaucratic expertise (as in the more authoritarian phases of the system such as 1969–1974), they participate as co-opted members of a vast and pervasive patrimonial bureaucracy (as throughout the democratic phase, 1945–1964). The claim of the champions of the centralized authoritarian system — explicit in the declarations of Getúlio Vargas during the Estado Novo (1937–1945) and in military justifications of the 1964 coup — is that the authoritarian system remedies characteristic defects of the liberal political system. The centralized political system, it is said, guarantees that the general will and the national interest prevail over minority, sectional interests. (Severino, trying to provide for his family on $110 per month backs this claim, as we have seen: in his view, only the military have sufficient muscle to ensure that his wages arrive on time and intact and that his few rights can be protected against the institutionalized avarice of the local rich.) But Schwartzman (again with endorsement from Severino!) notes the historically evident defect of the system: that the distribution of the social product unduly privileges those groups deemed necessary and sufficient consumers of national growth while excluding other groups from political participation even more drastically and effectively than the liberal system.

Schwartzman hopes that the state and society might develop in such a way that the virtues of each system might be realized and the vices attenuated. This would be "to de-bureaucratize, for the action of the State to become less authoritarian and clientelistic, for representative politics to become less oriented to private interest and less conservative."[6] But those changes, he understands, cannot be engineered into existence through manipulations of political institutions; they imply profound changes, cultural as well as socioeconomic. In particular, if political change is to eventuate, it will be "in proportion as society develops the capacity for participation by citizens in a variety of different areas, effectively reestablishing the link, lost and hidden by the liberal tradition, between state and society; that link in which the electoral system can . . . establish its rationale as the visible and structured manifestation of social values."[7] Here is one version of the call, expressed so often in the period of transition to civilian rule, for a deepening of democracy in Brazil.

It seems to me that Schwartzman, perhaps more explicitly than other critics of shallow democracy in Brazil, recognizes that a necessary element in any deepening would be the emergence of new forms of group life at the grass roots. Unrepresentative representative politics and bureaucratic-authoritarian politics that exclude most citizens escape challenge and succeed one another for as long as lower-class marginalized interests and values are not effectively articulated. But effective articulation requires collectivities at the grass roots, where private troubles may be seen as public issues, where lower-class identity, values, and visions can be lived and rehearsed. I would call these collectivities "intermediate groups." Intermediate groups are not just any grass-roots groups. They must be autonomous: unlike the official unions granted the working classes by Getúlio Vargas, which incorporate while extending state control; unlike Campo Alegre's old brotherhood, which incorporated the poor in the patronage of local landed, commercial, or clerical elites in return for a respectable burial. The members of intermediate groups must actually be engaged in the articulation of grass-roots identifications, values, and interests, rather than in the transmission of hegemonic ideas from the state and the dominant culture. Finally, intermediate groups must operate as inclusive communities rather than as closed hierarchies or expert-client relationships that reflect and reproduce the dominant society and its politics.

A pessimistic view of Brazilian society — easily adopted if one views that society from the top down or from the perspective of an economic determinist — might conclude at this point that there was no hope for intermediate groups. After all, shallow democratic political systems do work for the upper classes and can be worked by the lower classes. Working or being worked, they tend to destroy the bases for their overcoming. It is not easy to persuade a worker of the unsecured virtue of a deeper democracy when he knows the destitution that awaits him outside the umbrella of the corporatist union. Articulation of the values of the poor seems to promise little to those who see that chances for the good life improve through assimilation to the values of the rich. Community must seem elusive to the uprooted in occupationally diverse neighborhoods where one's neighbor is a rival for land or for a job in the informal sector. Then the economic achievements of authoritarian Brazil, as they involve the uprooting of the urban poor and the creation of urban neighborhoods of extraordinary complexity, would seem inexorably to undermine anything like intermediate groups. And the political achievements of populist Brazil must preclude intermediate groups as they massify and co-opt.

It would be possible, contemplating these processes, to engage in the pessimism of overdetermination and to conclude that the pendulum will go on swinging, that the deepening of democracy in Brazil is a pipe dream because the system is so solid — as controlled *abertura* and the transition to civilian rule demonstrated. But from the field — from Campo Alegre, Itapira, Liberdade, and the *bairros* where Willems talked to followers of the new faith — arise questions skeptical of such pessimism. Among the sectarian Pentecostals, in Pai Fuló's Xangô group, and among the nun's fisherwomen, can we not see the lineaments of intermediate groups? In Severino and Maria Pretinha, are there not signs of limitations of the state's colonization of everyday life? In negotiations over the feast of the patron saint, is it not clear that there are free, undetermined spaces in Brazilian society where the projects of the powers-that-be must contest with the projects in search of other Kingdoms?

If nothing else, my previous chapters have established a basis for these questions. It seems reasonable, now, to push on a little by posing questions that can be seen to include them all: what is the potential in the "popular religions" in general, or the variable potential in different religious constructions of reality, for the formation of intermediate groups? First, this entails a review of our evidence, to determine whether there arises from the religions any political culture that counters easy conquest by hegemonic ideas at the grass roots. Second, our review must examine to what extent autonomous social formations that are not merely reproductive of dominant social structures are to be found in the religious groups. Third, if there are such autonomous formations we must determine their viability in the face of the many economic and political pressures tending to undermine them.

THE NATIONAL SECURITY CODE AND GRASS-ROOTS RELIGIONS

I think I can assert with safety, without being able to establish it here, that the projects of the state and the bureaucratic-authoritarian political economy have been legitimated through a loosely integrated set of myths, symbols, and propositions, sometimes characterized as the "national security code."[8] This is not to assert that the code as enunciated by an erstwhile éminence grise of the military regime, the late General Golbery e Couto, corresponds exactly to constructions of historical reality enjoined on the citizens of Campo Alegre on public occasions and in a variety of public institutions. It is to assert that some mixture of the provisions of that code, as summarized below, has been presented to Campo Alegrenses as a structure for memory and a map for common-sense citizenship—not only during the military period but even in the mixed market of ideologies throughout transition. These provisions include: (1) the image of the good citizen as one who accepts and obeys rational, bureaucratic authority and understands the necessity of a system of status and rewards grossly favoring those with formal qualifications over those with few qualifications in the modern, urban sectors of the economy; (2) the equation of the state, the nation, and the society as being but different names for the same organic entity, proceeding from the one pure stream of history toward the single destiny of the successful national security state; (3) the belief that loyal citizens and legitimate groups will identify above all with the nation state and only secondarily or not at all with class, region, or ethnic group; (4) the belief in formal, instrumental education as the source of all worthwhile wisdom and the means of progress away from individual and collective ignorance and poverty;

(5) the belief that civilization and Brazil's destiny as a world power can be achieved through the triumph of white-ness, European-ness, and hygiene over darkness, Indian-ness, African-ness, and dirtiness; through the triumph of science and modern technology over emotionality and ignorance; through the taming and tapping of nature, above all Brazil's wild, unused hinterland; (6) notwithstanding the above, the conception of Brazilian history as one of unique harmony between its disparate class, racial, and regional elements; (7) the conception of Brazilian history as essentially in accord with the history textbooks, in which the remembered heroes are great military commanders, conquerors of the hinterland, modernizers, and defenders of order.

From each of the religious traditions there emerges a range of predispositions toward these encodings of Brazilian historical reality, from adoption and rehearsal to explicit rejection of key provisions. Among the spiritists, perhaps, the emergent political cultures are most divergent. On the one hand, recall Maria Pretinha, Fuló, Henfrey's Liberdade groups, the spiritists of the popular domain in Itapira. The religiosity associated with these names in teaching and ritual calls citizens to become members of a distinctive historical community. This is not the national community of the *cultura alta* celebrated in the national security code but a community of the poor, the relatively un-Europeanized, the independent, and occasionally truculently critical. Fuló and Maria Pretinha (the former more ambivalently than the latter) reject the claims for duly qualified expertise that are part of the code, just as they conceive of themselves as communicators of communal wisdom rather than as experts in the esoteric or as agents of a higher culture. Their followers are enjoined not to be passive, if diligent, followers of the nation's recognized heroes in confronting life's problems, but to conceive of themselves as having some responsibility for suffering and to take an active part in dealing with it.

This type of spiritist religiosity provides a vocabulary of motives, alternative heroes, interpretations of experience and meanings that predispose men and women to make their social worlds other than the worlds the powerful desire. Afro-Brazilian reality of this type does not train revolutionaries to do battle with generals and bureaucrats but constructs a sensibility that is incredulous before the claims of the national security code, whether advanced by the invited colonel in the town square or the populist politician on the hustings.

This is probably a minor stream in Brazilian spiritism (though Reginaldo Prandi's report, noted in Chapter 6, gives me pause on this). Numerically, in Campo Alegre, it certainly is. There, groups like Dona Paula's attract the numbers. In such groups, followers are involved as competitors to harness the power of the spirits to private ends. The individual mem-

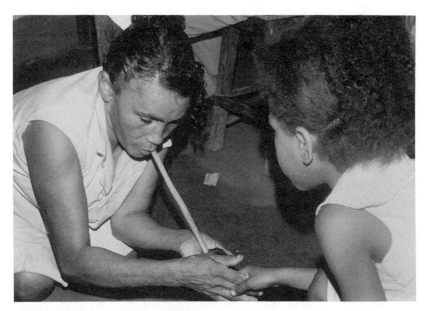

26. An old slave spirit passes across the generations a sensibility that is incredulous before the claims of the national security code.

ber seeks development by gaining competitive advantage and defensive cover through the expertise of the medium, whose interpretations of misfortune and chosen remedies connote a disposition of pathos: the sufferer has been acted upon by forces beyond normal personal control, and restoration is sought in therapies in which the client is passive. Leaders are primarily experts in the therapeutic techniques. The spirits themselves are called on to serve for specified goals, rather than to draw participants into a way of life.

In these groups, much of the national security code is endorsed and sacralized. Brazilian history as harmony is celebrated in ritual; the social and technical hierarchies of the code are replicated in the hierarchy of the spirits (perhaps even more in the case of Dona Rosária than in that of Dona Paula). Spiritist religiosity of this type at once predisposes toward acceptance of the national security code, if not always in toto, and parades its successful hegemony, if sometimes incongruously. It does not seem too provocative of the skepticism of the field to suggest that here is a sort of Gramscian movement in which the powerful in Brazil, through their control over symbols and over the means of survival and success, are powerful even over the spirits. And, as the spirits are transformed — from exemplary historical heroes into colorful "inside-dopesters" — so they come to serve the powerful and to subordinate the less powerful in a bureaucratic-authoritarian state. What that skepticism does insist on, however, is that we listen, as her neighbors listen, to Maria Pretinha as well as to Dona Rosária.

In the case of the Pentecostals also, we have seen a range of predispositions that affect responsiveness to the national security code. Severino is resistant. As a package (and Severino is one of the few citizens of Campo Alegre who perceives such a package), the code is idolatrous. His universal moral critique does not award automatic moral, political, or economic ascendancy to anyone, with or without qualifications, or to any class. His devotion to the Bible and God's law, as revealed directly to him, stands in the way of his awarding supreme loyalty to the state, science, or the learned doctors. The creation story and salvation history make the history of official heroes pale to insignificance. If Severino does not follow Manuel da Conceição in confronting the powers-that-be, it is not because he takes the restraining national security code any more seriously but because no political engagement of that scale can be taken seriously within his religious vision.

In his overview of the Pentecostal "explosion" in Latin America, David Martin defines a sort of ideal type of the Pentecostal (rather close to Severino).[9] This ideal typical Pentecostal is the bearer of deep democracy, a capitalist, probably, but essentially subversive of both traditional clientelism and the projects of the centralized secular state. Martin's Pentecostal, just as Severino has done, emigrates from the relatively undifferentiated, clientelistic, authoritarian, established order in which the Catholic church is still seen as providing the sacred canopy. In the receiving Pentecostal world it is possible to express and experience criteria of worth and power that are the reverse of those that have helped confine him (and especially her) to the lower rungs of the order prevailing outside. The migrant, truly Protestant, rejects all mediations between himself and God, acquires a sense of individual responsibility and the discipline to realize it, learns the skills of participation in a voluntary association, and develops a new and binding sense of purpose and meaning in life. Such Pentecostals in their increasing millions, though they might vote conservatively or, like Severino, avoid direct political involvement, nonetheless rehearse political, economic, and social revolution. As they fashion a new Pentecostal psyche and a new social order in the religio-cultural sphere, they achieve that differentiation of politics and economics from religion that has been essential in the North American religious liberal-democratic revolution. In the longer term, if we might extrapolate from Martin, their peaceable revolution should prove subversive of a centralized state that claims moral authority for secular experts, as the national security code does. The skills, disciplines, and values that transform individual and collective life within the Pentecostal world may eventually become available to the whole society in direct political action. As Martin puts it, "The latent may be made manifest and the limited free space devised by religion may suddenly be enlarged as it was in the Civil Rights Movement led by Martin Luther King."[10]

If Severino helps persuade me that Martin successfully typifies one type of Pentecostal and a historical potential for one type of Pentecostalism, then Madalena, Valdo, and indeed most members of the Assembly of God in Campo Alegre persuade me (as we saw in Chapter 4) that we need at least one other type. Those I call the church *crentes* nurture a political culture quite different from that of the sect *crentes*. Among the church *crentes*, the private meaning given to suffering, the role assigned the church and its increasingly professional clergy in addressing the problem of salvation, the intense desire for respectability to ensure the triumph of the church in the institutional marketplace, the assumptions about legitimate authority, all mesh in a political culture in which many of the provisions of the national security code are congenial. The political culture that arises from church-*crente* religiosity is not identical with the national security code, and it could not be easily argued, on the basis of our Campo Alegre case, that it was a political culture manipulated into existence by cunning formulators of the code. All that can be argued is that the *crente* who comes out of the Sunday *culto*, enthused in the rightness of what his church and his often-quite-authoritarian and increasingly professionalized pastor are doing for him, will be predisposed to see normality and rightness in the more authoritarian forms of shallow democracy. The claims of the qualified expert, the rational, rule-abiding administrator, and the president who allows his religion to flourish will have been blessed in his imagination.

It may be that we need yet a third type of Pentecostal, a type I have not described because I did not find any examples in Campo Alegre. This is a type that could be described if we had case studies of the followers of the Pentecostal televangelists and mass-rally healers. We know quite a lot about leaders like Bishop Edir Macedo, founder of the Universal Church of the Reign of God.[11] We have the basic statistics for his church — its five hundred thousand followers built up in only thirteen years, its rally in June 1990 of one hundred fifty thousand faithful that filled Rio's Maracaná Stadium. But ethnographies on the followers are missing. Insofar as we can infer anything of the beliefs and dispositions of followers from the public positions assumed by their leader, I would guess that the politics of the followers of this most spectacularly successful Brazilian Pentecostal televangelist are even closer to positive endorsement of the national security code than those of the church *crentes* and an electronic age away from Severino's skeptical conservatism.

Among the Catholics, Pe. Eduardo and the participants in the communitarian project that he espouses explicitly reject, and seek to counter, hegemony achieved through socialization in the national security code. Every one of its provisions is challenged on the basis of the priest's interpretations of Biblical story and message. The People of God, discussing their readings of the Book of Life in the light of the Book of God's Word, are the formulators of national needs. The society of the poor stands apart from and above the state and its agents. God's law and one's neighbor exact loyalty before the national state. Wisdom and qualifications are not the same thing, and both church and state, to act wisely, must listen to the voice of the poor. The achievements of white, scientific, hygienic Brazil are to be criticized for the injustice and oppression they have engendered. The myth of harmony is dismissed, and a more Marxist vision of conflict and exploitation is adopted. New saints, heroes of justice and peace, are substituted for the heroes of conquest and modernity.

Several forms of Catholicism co-exist with the priest's Catholicism, however, and in Campo Alegre at any rate it has been difficult to engage any but a small number of Catholics in the making and living of so radically transformed a vision. Most Campo Alegre Catholics are like most of Rubem César Fernandes's pilgrims: the priest has an important place in their religious vision of the world, but it is a place circumscribed by images and myths of the good priest as a holy man apart, who connects an intact and separate order of the everyday life of the people to the higher order of the life-cycle, the *cultura alta*, and the highest entities of the supernatural. He must not trespass into the roles of those who work Catholic magic for dealing with the ills of everyday life — the *curandeiro*, the *benzadeira*. He must maintain and cultivate his lines of influence with the powers that be. Thus constructed by his people, the priest will not easily enter into their religious world to transform its other constructions of reality. And those constructions, if Pedro Faró is any guide, predispose their constructors to accommodate the changes coming from that wider world over which the little man has never had control. From Pedro's type of Catholicism comes not a positive endorsement of the national security code but a quasi consensual accommodation. A Pedro Faró will behave as though he accepts the national security code, if that is what is necessary to get the best deal in a changing world for the true values that Padre Cícero taught and the real community he showed was possible. Relatively untouched by the priest's message, Pedro looks for leaders and institutions to link him to the ineluctably invasive world of the big people. He does not feel called by the rules and models for survival his father gave him to construct alternative community.

Even if we were to take the hazardous step of generalizing from the single case of Pedro to a Brazilian folk Catholicism, we are a long way from arguing that there is some sort of Weberian elective affinity between the national security code and that folk religion. At most, we might want to suggest that folk Catholicism provided no vocabulary of motives, no quest that might move groups of Brazilians at the grass roots to resist the claims of bureaucratic authoritarian Brazil as simply preposterous. However, on the basis of other cases even within Campo Alegre, but certainly in other locations, that milder suggestion, too, might seem to underestimate the potential for resistance to the code from grass-roots Catholic religiosity. Other priests, elsewhere, have got through and encountered Angelitas who have helped inform the Catholic church's explicit critiques of the code. The political culture emergent in at least those CEBs that approach the ideal type is not just a set of propositions opposed to the provisions of the code but consists in an articulation of grass-roots identifications, values, and interests that, apparently, move hearts and minds away from the projects of the rich and powerful.

In all three of the religious traditions, we have found signs of a potential to resist the cultural hegemony of the national security code triumphant. More positively, alternative proposals about authority, hierarchy, the nature of the good citizen, and the possible and desirable future emerge from some, albeit minority, streams within each of the traditions. Quite apart from any intrinsic value of these alternatives, their vibrant existence suggests that at least one of the ingredients for intermediate groups emerges from the religious traditions.

It could still be argued that to set up the national security code for comparison with emergent political cultures at the religious grass roots is to set up a straw man. A faithful Gramscian might argue that cultural hegemony for the various forms of modern capitalism is achieved through a more fundamental shaping of perceptions, expectations, and sentiments than is enunciated in the provisions of the national security code. Those provisions would be mere and optional accidentals to a deep, hegemonic, capitalist culture. What the religious traditions must be measured against, in this view, is the project, advanced through a variety of institutions and biting deep into individual consciousness, whereby citizens of all classes become predisposed to accept the primacy of market relations over other domains of life. The realization of that project is what is basic to the maintenance of the state, shallow democracy, and the bureaucratic-authoritarian political economy. What really counts is the extent to which religions are able to counter that project, rather than aid and abet it.

I do not concede the straw-man argument but would argue that this proposed assessment of religions leaves us with much the same conclusions reached in the prior paragraph. In each of the religious traditions we have seen models for living that challenge the primacy of relations of production — market or state-directed — over other domains of human existence. Maria Pretinha, Severino, Pai Fuló, and the nun engaged in the pastoral of the fisherwomen struggle, in their different ways, to counter what they perceive as a humanly destructive invasion of everyday life by linked economic, political, and cultural powers-that-be. Each has managed to create a space (or, more accurately, a reenchanted space and time) for the living of an explicit critique of the hollowness of market-dominated relationships and the quest for wholeness in community. Each has established a beachhead for another Kingdom in prayer and in ritual where a communally achieved salvation and fulfillment in a cosmic career achieves priority over the constructions of time and horizons for living that are embedded in prevailing relations of production.

On the other hand, some of the religious actors we have seen — Dona Rosária in one way, the devotees of Padre Cícero in another, Pastor Moisés and the *ogãs* of the Salvadoran Candomblés in yet other ways — enhance and hasten the invasion of established political economies. We have seen them resacralizing certain secular market relations and the power structures within them. Some religious institutions, the ever-more-churchy Assembly of God and, if Renato Ortiz is right, the emergent church of Umbanda both parallel and help achieve established forms of national domination through a powerful sacralization of secular time and hierarchies. The magician-client relationship — cutting across religious traditions and appearing now in the *curandeiros* curing after the Evil Eye, now in Dona Paula doing battle with the spirits who assail Biu — also asserts the Kingdoms of modernity. Manifesting and reinforcing an episodic analysis of life's problems and solving those problems in appointed space and time, the magician's consultation helps achieve the market-dominated fragmentation of time, its attendant individualism, and even a certain social isolation before the power of the technocrats and the state.

RELIGIOUS GROUPS, THEIR VIABILITY, AND THE RELIGIOUS CONSTRUCTIONS OF POLITICS

These reproductions, counterproductions, refurbishings, and subversions of political economies in and through religion are not achieved only at the level of individual mental life. In Campo Alegre and in some of the other community studies of lived religion, we have seen particular forms of group life and particular modes of relations between social strata arising out of collective religious practice. And these forms and modes, I argue, are important in the reproduction and creation of the Brazilian political economies.

There is as much intentional construction of political and economic life involved in the competition for the feast of the patron saint of Campo Alegre, as there is in the great procession of Montpellier described by Robert Darnton's eighteenth-century observer of transition.[12] Pe. Eduardo attempts to choreograph a set of events in which small farmers and fishermen can see and feel themselves actors in a struggle of communities-in-the-making for a more just Brazil. He fails, largely because the choreography is too much and too exclusively his. But the failure is not just Pe. Eduardo's: the group life of Catholics in Campo Alegre is so intermittent and fragmentary that it cannot even, of itself, embody and sustain the clientelistic projects of the majority of actors in it, let alone the communitarian project of a priest.

In the *congregação* meetings that Carlos runs, in the fisherwomen's group, and in the small band of resisters around Angelita, there are signs perhaps that the communitarian project is more than a dream of priests and nuns. Articulate lay leaders work with their peers, drawing on the rich liberation mythology and the personnel and communications network of their church, to define public issues and devise a citizens' praxis for acting on them. They are fragile groups though, and their potential for challenging or replacing the blocs of clients activated by populists or the compliant, privatized mass of nationalists required by the authoritarians seems, in Campo Alegre, to be very slight. The potential for collective expression and embodiment of the communitarian project is seen less in achievement and viability in Campo Alegre and more by association with the robust CEBs described by Mainwaring and others.

In Campo Alegre, older formations are sustained by an older Catholicism; but they too are fragile, lacking the clerical leadership or the organized patronage that once provided élan, energy, and continuity. The group of farmers around Pedro Faró might be a formidable force in local "new broom" populist politics and might even preserve a relatively prosperous niche for small, landed, local, market-orientated *agricultores* (farmers) and food processors, if only the group could find its Padre Cícero.[13] And it might yet. Similarly, in the case of the annual busload of pilgrims from Campo Alegre gathered together to make or pay *promessas* to the most powerful patron saint of the region, the common language is found in the Padre Cícero hymns. The common task (strikingly evident in the utterly private devotion at the shrine) is the establishment or cementing of an individual-client tie with the saint for specified individual ends. Collective rituals, like mass, are drawn on as a resource from the past to seal private pacts.

These sorts of Catholic groups have several features in common. They are temporary associations, lasting only so long as some sort of union serves often diverse individual ends. Their discourse is oriented to a celebrated past that was good, has been dismantled, and (it is fervently prayed) will be restored. But though this discourse seems to connect members on a temporary basis, the group lacks the sort of collective project that, in the mélange of so many Brazilian towns and suburbs, is probably necessary for long-term viability (and that, in any case, may not even be desired). Internal cohesion is weak because a, or sometimes the, principle of unity is the search for the shared memory of the leader/patron who will solve the group's (that is, the individual members') problems.

Such Catholic groups often seek and will be picked up by populist politicians. Pedro made common cause with conservative politicians of the PMDB opposition party, and 1982 was a bumper pilgrimage because it was a year for municipal elections and politicians provided travel subsidies. But that sort of exchange is only the most obvious tie between these Catholic groups and populism. More important is the way in which this sort of group at once manifests and achieves a particular sort of construction of civil society. As citizens move in and out of such groups, they are making a civil society in which private troubles can be expressed and dealt with more easily than public issues and concerns. They are living a form of association that, mocking the not-too-distant past dear to Gonçalo, prejudices increasing density of association between members of polyclass neighborhoods. They are constructing a society in which public leadership at the grass roots is provided by outsiders of higher class and status rather than by insiders and peers. It is through these constructions that Catholic groups like the annual pilgrims of Campo Alegre achieve an elective affinity with the economic and political projects of populism. The CEB groups, for all their fragility in Campo Alegre, stand out in stark contrast: they are already structuring a very different society in which there is a high density of association at the grass roots — despite, and even on the basis of, mélange — in which leadership on public issues is generated at the grass roots rather than introduced from higher classes and the established political arena.

On the basis of the stories told here about the Catholics of Campo Alegre, one would have to conclude that the major political construction emerging from popular Catholicism is of the kind congenial to the populist projects. Further, in the later eighties, there have been vigorous attempts from within the Catholic church itself to dismantle the communitarian experiments of the Catholicism of the CEBs. Looking at the Catholic church in Brazil as a whole, in 1990, it is quite clear that powerful bishops like Dom José Sobrinho of Recife-Olinda, backed by the Vatican, are moving with purpose and effect to halt the communitarian constructions of church and society emerging from the CEBs.[14]

In many other dioceses, pressures against the CEBs have so far been resisted, but the return to civilian democracy has posed new issues and problems for the communitarian project. In turn, the variety of responses has revealed divergent agendas within the project that, in practice, would shape civil society in different ways. One agenda would have the CEBs develop very much as basic units within the church — building local communities and avoiding engagement, on the part of members, in secular supralocal party politics (which are judged to be corrupt and corrupting). At another extreme, the PT (the workers' party, for which Lula stood as nearly successful presidential candidate in 1989) is regarded as created by the CEBs, and engagement in party politics for the PT's electoral success is seen as the main way in which a new church should achieve a new Brazil.[15] The first agenda is very much Pe. Eduardo's, and its attainment, doubtful as we must be about that possibility, runs the risk of creating small, local havens for participatory democracy, which are institutionally incapable of transmitting their vision and practice to the wider polity. Conversely, the second agenda, as feared by Pe. Eduardo, risks the absorption and destruction of local, church-nurtured, democratic groups in yet another national party machine; though that is a fear, not a demonstrable outcome as yet.

What is clear even in Campo Alegre, though in greater degree elsewhere in Brazil, is that in the later eighties contests between a profusion of rival forms of Catholic group life and organization involve political stakes that are well understood by contenders. They understand and proclaim themselves not only to be contesting church governance but rival modes for the construction of civil society. In this sense, a religious contest engaged in thousands of localities throughout Brazil is, at the same time, the contest between Brazilian political economies-in-the-making.

Among the crentes, too, we have seen contesting constructions of civil society. A review of my account of the crentes of the Assembly of God in Campo Alegre and of case studies done elsewhere in Brazil hardly supports Emílio Willems's expectations of two decades ago or David Martin's more recent speculations. The group life of the followers of the new faith cannot be construed as an effective prototype of a new civil society in Brazil, a civil society akin in some respects to the vision of the Catholic defenders of the CEBs, replete with peer-led, democratic groups independent of the dominant institutions of church and state. In Campo Alegre there are hints — in the congregação groups, the informal networks linking crentes in everyday life, and in the closed-door rituals of the Spirit of God — that many members of the Assembly, seeking faithful apartness from the world, do create the sorts of alternative groups at the grass roots that Willems had in mind. But, as the local Assembly has become more integrated into the hierarchically organized regional and national Assembly church, the sect-type grouping tends to be subsumed. On the national scene (if we may generalize from the case of Itapira) there may be a tendency for sect group and church to generate one another: as *crente* churches professionalize, bureaucratize, and consolidate, so they breed their opposites in small, local, autonomous sects of the poor.

So there is within Protestant Pentecostalism, as in the Catholic church, a contest between modes in the construction of daily life at the grass roots. When *crentes* order their lives as church *crentes*, they enter into social formations that link the poor and relatively powerless to agents and actors of the ruling classes in an authoritarian and non-negotiable mode. When *crentes* order their lives as sect *crentes*, they form groups even more autonomous than the Catholic CEBs, free of the structures of control that are worked by higher strata. However, these groups of sect *crentes* are much more hermetic than the CEBs; their experiments in new ways of naming and addressing the problems of life at the grass roots stay locked within the group because they lack the horizontal linkage to poor neighbors of other faiths and the vertical linkage to individuals and organizations with more direct access to the means of cultural production.

The stakes in the contest of church and sect may be clarified through the formulation of hypotheses that seem reasonable conclusions to the studies reviewed. As *crentes* continue to increase at present rates of conversion and the church formation advances over the sect, it is to be expected that lower-class neighborhoods will increasingly be characterized by a one-way flow of communication helping incorporate the poor into centralized, authoritarian, state projects. Conversely, as the sect formation advances over the church and local independent sects continue to emerge, it is to be expected that lower-class neighborhoods will resist incorporation into such hegemonic communications networks, but also that these neighborhoods will display a low capacity for horizontal mobilization in the pursuit of locally defined interests and projects.

Among the devotees of the spirits, we have seen that the types of groups, in terms of internal structure and both horizontal and vertical linkages, are very diverse. At one extreme are the traditional kept groups, wherein the internal hierarchy, financial links, and social ties with traditional upper-class families at once replicate and (in certain inner-city areas) reproduce, at the grass roots, the relations of urban patrimonialism, a sort of urban *coronelismo*. At the other extreme are the autonomous creative groups. These, though not as self-consciously democratic as some of the CEBs, seem to be rather flat in structure, as members of the groups virtually negotiate their preferred spirits into existence. In terms of linkages, they are as insistently autonomous of vertical class ties as the sect-*crente* groups but much more open to horizontal movement and alternative attachments of their members.

If an area like Liberdade were to develop many such groups, to the point where they became a major form of association incorporating a substantial proportion of the adult population, then that area would have a social structure very like that uncovered by Luther Gerlach and Ruth Hine in certain religious organizations in the United States.[16] That peculiarly resilient and effective form of organization, difficult to perceive for those who equate all organization with bureaucratic organization, is characterized as SPR — segmentary (many autonomous groups or cells), polycephalous (many leaders), and reticulate (the component groups maintain a network of personal contact and communications through cross-membership and visitation). A lower-class *bairro* organized in this SPR manner would be quite the opposite of that old, discredited stereotype of the *favela* as a fragmented mass open to manipulation by populists and tight control by bureaucratic authoritarians. Rather, it would be resistant to such projects, fertile and effective as a local public, curiously close to the realization of the grass-roots society toward which the communitarian clergy work.

There is no escaping use of the subjunctive mood, though, when we try to generalize about any general trends in social and political construction through religious life in the neighborhoods of the Brazilian poor. We do not yet know enough about particular cases. On the basis of trends in the spiritist family in Campo Alegre, I have been inclined to speculate that the most common form of neighborhood construction emerging from spiritist practice is neither the SPR union of intermediate groups nor the formation of patronage shafts in which the urban poor are vertically integrated into the world of the preindustrial bourgeoisie, as we saw in the case of the practice of the traditional kept groups. More common, I expect, is the social structure emerging from the co-opted whited groups. In these groups there is the hierarchy of expert over apprentices in the spirits and over a mass of mere clients; and there are linkages, through leaders, with modern urban patronage structures, military protectors, and generally conservative politicians.[17] We may expect that a neighborhood in which this sort of group is the most common form of association will display an elective affinity (in all senses of the phrase) with urban populists as diverse in platform but similar in political style and modus operandi as Jânio Quadros on the right and Leonel Brizola on the left.

Moving out from Campo Alegre to the whole of Brazil, we have seen a variety of constructions of civil society emerging out of the various ways of using and living spiritism, Pentecostalism, and Catholicism at the grass roots. Within each of the traditions, different and often publicly rival visions and projects for individual and collective life seem to entail, in the living, the formation of groups that vary in internal democracy, viability, and linkage outward, both horizontally within neighborhoods and vertically up the class structure. The argument, emerging from information culled from my previous chapters, may now be made more explicit.

As Pentecostals, Catholics, and spiritists at the grass roots construct experience, making sense of past and present and rehearsing their futures, they enter into distinctive forms of association. These forms are often the major (and always an important) element in the social structure of whole lower-class neighborhoods and *bairros*. In turn, neighborhood structures, somewhere between the polar opposites of SPR organization and fragmented mass, will powerfully affect the chances of the jostling populist, bureaucratic-authoritarian, and communitarian political projects.

For example, the associations of church Pentecostals, as they shape the structure of whole neighborhoods, help establish and reproduce a one-way communication flow, through which the bureaucratic-authoritarian project flourishes. The co-opted whited spiritist groups seek out and provide structural opportunity for the patronage exchanges between populist leaders and urban masses. The CEBs and the autonomous creative spiritist groups may provide the forms of association necessary to resist one-way flows of communication and other aspects of the populist and bureaucratic-authoritarian or national security projects; and, conversely, they are themselves the structural expression of the communitarian project at the grass roots.

So conflicts within and between religious traditions for the hearts and minds of the Brazilian poor involve a double contribution to the construction of Brazilian politics. The first contribution can be seen in the way different religious paradigms for living move and motivate believers so that they become distinctive sorts of citizens. The condition of poverty and insecurity is religiously constructed as private trouble or as public issue; the condition of relative powerlessness is religiously constructed into the experience of subjection to legitimate authority, evidence of the need to withdraw from an incorrigibly corrupt order, or as challenge to create new people's power at the grass roots; the condition of exploitation in work is religiously constructed into the experience of challengeable oppression within a class system, a test to be borne for the sake of salvation and the glory of God, or a natural state of affairs to be negotiated with the aid of strong helpers from among the spirits. And religiously constructed experience moves citizens toward indifference or concern, acceptance or subversion, action or passivity, before the political projects of *coronelismo*, populism, bureaucratic-authoritarianism, and communitarianism. The second contribution is the focus of this section: the construction of neighborhoods in the collective living of religious paradigms such that the poor and powerless are more or less vulnerable to hegemonic manipulation, more or less capable of carrying their own projects to success in the political arena.[18]

Both these modes through which I claim Brazilian politics is constructed in religious practice at the grass roots require that Campo Alegrenses and Itapirans do indeed have what we might call the freedom to experience. There is always the possibility, defined as probability in some traditions of cultural anthropology and sociology, that condition (including imposed culture as well as social relations) determines experience. Forms of association, effective solidarities, paradigms for living, the conduct of everyday life (says the voice of doubt from many a textbook) may be overdetermined by political economic systems, and especially among the poor in places like Campo Alegre.

THE SATURDAY *FEIRA* CRISES OF FAITH AND THEIR RESOLUTION

In the opening chapter I declared that I entered the field and left it with a sort of faith that the theories and methods that begin and end inquiry with overdetermination lead us astray as they divert attention from the construction of experience at the grass roots. I would have nothing of that "metaphysical pathos" of the sociologists or the "pastoral myth" of anthropologists, which would have Campo Alegrenses telling only stories of regret for a lost past and going into a future constructed for them. In Chapters 1 and 2, I assert a faith that through the case study of Campo Alegre we might see Brazilian citizens at the grass roots constructing individual and collective experience in lived religious allegories — with effect — that is, in such a way that their stories of self and social world enter into the unending making of Brazilian history.

If Severino and Maria Pretinha have helped convert anyone to this faith, it is only fair to the cause of proper social-science skepticism to return in this final section of the final chapter to the challenge to the faith that Campo Alegrenses presented to the author every Saturday morning. This was the challenge of the *feira* (market), which, as I came to understand its working and to know many of those who bought and sold in it, seemed to me to display and achieve the very condition of Campo Alegrenses and their determination by that condition.

Every Saturday morning most Campo Alegre adults come to the town

27 and 28. The Saturday *feira:* a flotilla of stalls in the square—harbor of a colorful but strictly ordered capitalism.

square to buy food, textiles, and other household goods that are produced elsewhere, channeled through the central wholesale markets of Recife and sold to them — increasingly, though not yet exclusively — by outside retailers of the greater-metropolitan *feira* circuit, at prices standardized for the region. There is a dwindling band of locals selling or, very rarely, bartering their own produce — fish, yams, manioc products, or salad greens. A few more locals, from the kerbside rather than the covered stall rented out by the municipality, resell, to the very poor, very small portions of goods (a slice of pumpkin, half a bunch of *quiabo* (okra) to add to the beans) bought in greater bulk from professional retailers. But for the most part, the *feira* is not a place, any more than an urban supermarket, for exchanges between locals according to local rules. And in the *feira*, Campo Alegrenses are reduced to their condition as determined by cash income, their present roles and future prospects manifestly determined by their lowly position in interlocking educational and occupational hierarchies ordered according to rules over which they have no control. The hard decisions that have to be made when total disposable income for the week will only just, or not at all, cover the cost of basic needs put individuals and their families on show as *presos* (imprisoned), their life chances determined radically by unchallengeably low income.

Even the expression of the smaller worries of the marginal local sellers seemed to me to be elements in a regular ritual of condition. As the sun got hotter, kerbside sellers would worry about their tender greens, the coriander, spring onions, lettuces, and capsicums they had brought in from their small plots or in bulging baskets from the central wholesale market in the capital. No need to worry, they would explain to anyone with time to listen, if you are selling yams. They move quickly and the sun doesn't do too much harm to their elephant skin. But it's another matter with these greens. Perhaps it would be better to hire a table and awning like those with more produce. But that costs money, and people here pay so little. . . .

I remember the questions, amounting to a crisis of faith, that troubled me as I thought about what I heard and saw at the *feira*. Given this weekly display of determining condition, can this town be a place where history is made, where the rival models and projects for Brazil's future are traded along with coils of molasses-cured tobacco, beans with more or fewer tooth-shattering stones, luscious mangoes, and flyblown offal? Is this town such a mélange without boundaries where so much is contested, when it is here assembled, between 6.00 and 11.00 AM, haggling over prices within a narrow known price range, all aboard a flotilla of stalls in the same square harbor of a colorful, noisy, but strictly ordered, capitalism? Here in the market you might spot *crente* women by dress and hairstyle, and there might be a slight tendency to try prices first at a co-religionist's stall; but in this place where the trajectories of lives seem set by regional, national, or even international, market value, is it not the case that religion makes no real difference at all?

During the rest of the week, a goodly number of the market-goers, as they led me a little further into the living of their faiths, would restore my faith in the hunches I expressed in Chapter 1. The *feira* would become a reminder of determining condition, of limits to the constructions of experience. But I would be drawn into those other moments of existence when everyday life is endowed with significance and located, sometimes a long way from the confines of the marketplace, in the storied worlds of the spirits, the saints, the Savior, the Liberator.

Against the great Saturday rehearsal of condition, the religious constructions of experience seemed the more valiant to me even when, in my view, some of those constructions locked their makers in to their condition. The religious construction of experience will have moments of sheer enjoyment — frisson, exhilaration, catharsis, the sense of belonging, discovery — but, under the constraints of the condition of poverty, it is hard work. The public display of condition every Saturday, I was shown through the rest of the week, does not deny or negate the religious constructions of experience but only makes them more marvellous.

Quite often I have been inviting readers to share a sense of marvel before what I would evaluate as the work of tragedy. Much of the religious work we have reviewed builds the Kingdoms of the powers-that-be, within which the workers are to be contained by their condition. But we have seen something too of the construction of the Kingdoms of challenge. In either case, Brazilians at the grass roots have perhaps made more plausible my opening claims that they, in their living religions, are active contestants in a continuing political transition. If I have represented them correctly in their religious work, they are making a claim on those who would analyze Brazil's, and perhaps many another nation's, politics: that analysis should start again with the religious Kingdoms constructed at the grass roots.

APPENDIX

NOTES

BIBLIOGRAPHY

INDEX

APPENDIX

RANDOM SURVEY DATA

TABLE 1
**Residential Origins of 104 Randomly Surveyed Heads of Household,
Campo Alegre 1977**

	Number	Percentage
From properties on the island and the immediate hinterland	19	18
From the northern sugar zone of the state, but including residence on properties of the immediate hinterland	17	16
From more distant rural areas, but including residence on properties of the immediate hinterland	4	4
From another coastal fishing settlement	9	14
From local or northern sugar-zone urban areas	15	10
From the capital city or other large city	14	13
Always Campo Alegre	26	25
TOTAL	104	100

TABLE 2

Career Paths Between Sectors — 79 Economically Active Heads of Households

Career Path	Number	Percentage
Always rural	14	
Always UNI (urban nonindustrial)	12	
Always fishing	7	
Always industrial	0	
SUBTOTAL	33	42
Rural to UNI	17	
Rural to fishing	3	
Rural to industry	2	
Rural to mixed UNI	3	
Rural to industry and industry to rural	1	
SUBTOTAL	26	33
Fishing to rural	0	
Fishing to UNI	1	
Fishing to industry	0	
Fishing to mixed UNI and industry	3	
Fishing to other to fishing (permanently or as interlude)	3	
SUBTOTAL	7	9
UNI to rural	1	
UNI to industry (both administrative)	2	
UNI to fishing to UNI	1	
UNI to fishing to industry	1	
UNI to industry to UNI	2	
SUBTOTAL	7	9
Sailor to fishing	1	
Sailor to boat building	1	
Industry to UNI	4	
SUBTOTAL	6	7
TOTAL	79	100

TABLE 3
Present Main Occupations of all Working Members of
104 Randomly Surveyed Households*

	Number	Percentage
Rural		
Self employed on rented plot	2	
Rural laboring	23	
Manioc house work	6	
SUBTOTAL	31	18
Fishing and related activities		
Boat fishing (all male)	20	
Mud-flat fishing (all female)	9	
Fish buying and selling	6	
Other activities related to fishing	10	
SUBTOTAL	45	26
Urban nonindustrial		
Construction work	12	
Small local commerce (except fish selling)	18	
Clerical	6	
Services	21	
Transport	3	
General urban laboring	7	
Service station owner, main highway	1	
Professional and semiprofessional	12	
SUBTOTAL	80	46
Industrial		
Factory workers (unskilled)	9	
Factory-machine operators	9	
SUBTOTAL	18	10
TOTAL	174	100
Working-age and older adults not receiving income for work	26	
Retired on pension	39	
	65	(=27% of all individuals surveyed)
TOTAL	239	

*Not all main occupations are full-time. In certain occupational categories (such as rural laboring or construction, for example) unemployment and underemployment are common. Fishing occupations follow the tides, and many women take in washing and ironing as well.

TABLE 4
Religious Affiliation and Practice in Campo Alegre 1977

	Number
Catholic families	
Little or no formal practice by family members	44
One or more members, moderate to frequent practice (moderate = 3–4 masses a year; frequent = at least weekly mass)	16
SUBTOTAL	60
Assembly of God families	
Little or no formal practice by family members	2
Only one member practicing; others lapsed or now practicing Catholic	8
All family members belong and practice (practicing = at least weekly attendance at cult)	4
SUBTOTAL	14
Afro-Brazilian spiritist families	
One member moderate but irregular practice	8
One member frequent practice	7
Two or more members frequent practice	4
(Moderate = 3–4 cult sessions a year and consultations; frequent = at least monthly cult sessions and consultations)	
SUBTOTAL	19
Other religions and more complex mixtures	
(includes families where interviewer was unable to nominate the main religion of the family; Baptist and Jehovah's Witnesses families; mixtures of three major religions)	7
TOTAL	100*

*Four interviewees were unable to give clear information about affiliation and practice.

NOTES

1. STARTING AGAIN

1. R. Ireland, "The Catholic Church and Social Change in Brazil."

2. R. Ireland, "Catholic Clergy in the Northeast of Brazil: An Elite for Modernization?"

3. A group of articles on popular Catholicism was published in *Revista Eclesiástica Brasileira* 36 (March 1976).

4. I decided to use a fictional name for this town, to provide some measure of protection for the identities of those few citizens, like the priest, who are known outside the town and who would be easily identified once the name of the town were known.

5. The differences between a sociology of social system and a sociology of social action are well defined in A. Dawe, "Theories of Social Action."

6. Clifford Geertz, *The Interpretation of Cultures,* chapter 1.

2. RELIGION AND POLITICS IN CAMPO ALEGRE

1. An excellent description of Brazilian lay brotherhoods is provided by Marjo de Theije, in an article on their contemporary role in a town in Minas Gerais, where they have been of vital importance since the beginning of the eighteenth century. Looking across the ten brotherhoods and confraternities of the town of São João del-Rei, Theije generalizes:

> A brotherhood is an association of Catholic men and women. Most of them are lay persons, but some of them may belong to the clergy or to religious orders. Their main goal is worshipping the patron saint or, in general, promoting public worship through organising Masses, processions or novenas in a church or chapel of their own. Apart from that, the brotherhoods look after their members' funerals and the consequent rituals and Masses. Each brotherhood in São João del-Rei except for one has its own cemetery that falls under its supervision. Sometimes they also perform social duties. These may vary from mutual help in the case of illness or poverty to setting up orphans' homes and hospitals, depending on the means available to the brotherhood. ("'Brotherhoods Throw More Weight Around than the Pope': Catholic Traditionalism and the Lay Brotherhoods of Brazil," 190)

The word *worshipping* does not seem to me to be appropriate to indicate the honor bestowed on patron saints, though perhaps it captures something of the extreme devotion to the patron saint found in some members of the brotherhood. Apart from that, this definition will do nicely for the brotherhood of the saint in Campo Alegre. Thieje outlines strong opposition between local brotherhoods and the reforming clergy.

2. My sources for the history of the brotherhood include the *Livro de atas* (minutes) of the brotherhood from 1870 to 1972 (with some gaps); the *Livro de tombo* (parish log) of the parish church in the municipal seat; and a considerable amount of oral evidence.

3. It is worth noting that a priest not wearing his *batina* (soutane) or vestments at any sort of public religious gathering is saying something and will be interpreted as saying something. He is saying, "I am not your traditional priest with an entirely separate priestly ministry, a person apart from the laity." Traditional and older, but not theologically traditional, clergy like Dom Helder Câmara always wear the *batina* in public. Traditional Catholic laity complain about priests who fail to wear the *batina*.

4. Mary Aitken Ireland's "Leaseholds on Life: A Study of Land and Lives in Northeast Brazil" includes a more detailed history of the town and surrounding areas than that presented here. Memories of old-timers, summarized here and at the beginning of the chapter, are reconstructed from interviews and from responses to a question in a random survey, in which respondents were asked to compare the town now with the town of the past as they recalled it.

5. It is too easy to characterize this as the general replacement of a landed elite by a commercial elite. Some of the top businessmen bought into land and some mill owners had a hand in commerce.

6. My research on town history was limited to these minutes, the parish *Livro de tombo*, and selected cashbooks of the brotherhood. Mary Aitken Ireland's much fuller history is based on a greater variety of sources.

7. The problem of passing inspection of the books is evident in disapproving notes written by the monsignor and the canon on the cashbooks of the brotherhood for 1908 and 1930. Shortage of funds is a point frequently raised. On 2 July 1871, the treasurer complains that income is not being collected. On 5 April 1936, the treasurer complains about expenses for the priest's meals. The meeting of 5 May 1918 deliberates on the problem of collecting back dues and the non-payment of rents. On 18 May 1919, the treasurer threatens to resign because of the lack of funds to cover expenses on the chapel and complains that he needs an assistant. On 7 January 1940, all nominees refuse the job of treasurer.

8. For the changes elsewhere, see Manuel Correia de Andrade, *A terra e o homen no nordeste*, and P. Eisenberg, *The Sugar Industry of Pernambuco*.

9. Between 1940 and 1950, the total population of the district of Campo Alegre (including elements classified as rural and urban) almost doubled, from 4,565 to 8,025. In 1950 the urban element was 4,710; by 1977 that had increased to about 12,000.

10. Clifford Geertz, *The Social History of an Indonesian Town*, 10.

11. Ibid., 12.

12. *Livro de atas*, extraordinary meeting, 7 April 1946. Also *Livro de tombo*, 7 April 1946. In the same year, the parish priest noted that the fiesta of the saint

in Campo Alegre had disgusted him, and that he had not even been paid for his expenses.

13. See Richard Graham, *Patronage and Politics in Nineteenth-Century Brazil*, for the history of the emergence of *coronelismo* and for definitions of *coronéis* and *coronelismo*. Graham shows that by the end of the century, *coronelismo* was firmly in place as the political system linking local and central governments in the new Republic. In the epilogue to the book, Graham describes the system in these terms: "The country boss, or *coronel* — the rubric derived from the imperial National Guard — usually a landowner, received carte blanche to make decisions locally and wield a heavy hand against his opponents, as long as the electoral results from his county favored the candidates chosen by party leaders" (268–69).

14. All quotations from Gonçalo come from a pen-and-paper interview with the author on 13 July 1977.

15. For a historian's description of the sort of priest and the world that Gonçalo is idealizing, see Eul-Soo Pang, "The Changing Roles of Priests in the Politics of North-east Brazil, 1889–1964."

16. The best history of the rise of populism as political system and style is to be found in Michael L. Conniff, who discusses various perspectives in *Urban Politics in Brazil: The Rise of Populism, 1925–1945*. He outlines his own perspectives in chapter 1, especially pp. 10–19.

17. Paulo Guerra was a Federal senator at the time of the interview. His power base and some of his property were located in this area. He had been vice-governor of the state of Pernambuco at the time of the military coup in 1964.

18. *Recenseamento geral do Brasil: Censo demográfico, Pernambuco*, 1940.

19. C. Wright Mills, *The Sociological Imagination* (chapter 1) develops this distinction.

20. The phrase and the idea are taken from Harvey Cox, *The Seduction of the Spirit*.

21. This sort of hypothesis has been brilliantly developed by Carlos Rodrigues Brandão, *Os deuses do povo*, 138–39. References to other hypotheses will be given when they are considered in detail.

3. THE *CRENTES*

1. All quotations of Severino in this chapter are from interviews with the author taped on 23 August 1977 and 2 June 1982. Other untaped conversations in 1977, 1982, and 1989 are alluded to in this text and are noted in my research journals but are not quoted here.

2. In many Latin American countries, wage-earners are awarded a thirteenth-month's pay at Christmas.

3. All quotations from Teresa and Zé are from interviews that the author recorded on 27 May 1977 and 11 June 1977. Conversations in 1982 were noted in research journals but not taped.

4. This paraphrase and all quotations of Valdo are drawn from an inter-

view with the author taped on 7 May 1977. Other conversations with him and members of his extended family are noted in the research journals of 1977 and 1988.

4. THE ASSEMBLY OF GOD

1. I did interview Alfonso in 1977, but this phrase is not recorded. Alfonso uses it frequently in exhortations and in conversations noted in the 1977 research journal.

2. Quotations come from conversation with Valdo and other members of his family taped on 5 June 1977.

3. From the Sunday School primer *Lições bíblicas*, October–December 1977, 13. The text is Joshua 3:5.

4. For details of the growth of Pentecostal groups, see Francisco Cartaxo Rolim, "Igrejas pentocostais," 29–59.

5. These estimates are reported in *Latin America Press*, 20 September 1990, and the source cited there was the National Council of Christian Churches. In the report, the figure of thirty million by the year 2000 is repeated. These estimates support David Martin's use of the word *explosion*. They should, however, be considered against the analysis and arguments of two Canadian scholars, Brinkerhoff and Bibby, who report on surveys of Pentecostals they conducted in cities in Bolivia, Brazil, and Peru. They note failure to hold numbers and to pass religious commitment from one generation to the next. They also consider that reaction of a renewed Catholic church might succeed in reducing the number of Catholics who convert to Pentecostalism. Their conclusion is that the establishment of what they call a "self-sufficient evangelical pool" is unlikely. See M. B. Brinkerhoff and R. W. Bibby, "Circulation of the Saints in Latin America: A Comparative Study," 54.

6. Emílio Willems, *Followers of the New Faith: Culture, Change and the Rise of Protestantism in Brazil and Chile*, 249. Emílio Willems, "Religious Mass Movements and Social Change in Brazil."

7. David Martin, *Tongues of Fire: The Explosion of Protestantism in Latin America*, 229.

8. Ibid., 44.

9. A summary statement of Rolim's position is contained in Francisco Cartaxo Rolim, "Pentecostalismo de forma protestante," 81–91.

10. Rolim, "Igrejas pentecostais"; Francisco Cartaxo Rolim, *Religião e classes populares*, chapters 5 and 6; Francisco Cartaxo Rolim, "Gênese do pentecostalismo no Brasil."

11. Regina C. Reyes Novaes, "Os escolhidos. Doutrina religiosa e prática social." Rolim's commentary is in "Gênese do pentecostalismo no Brasil."

12. Manuel da Conceição, *Essa terra é nossa: Depoimento sobre a vida e as lutas de camponeses no estado do Maranhão*.

13. Rolim, "Igrejas pentecostais," 59.

14. Judith C. Hoffnagel, "The Believers: Pentecostalism in a Brazilian City."

Hoffnagel finds *crentes* much more widely distributed in terms of class and sector than either Rolim or Willems does. In Recife, growth has occurred in rural and urban areas (though whether rural society may be said to exist in the area studied is debatable).

15. Regina C. Reyes Novaes, "Os pentecostais e a organização dos trabalhadores."

16. Brandão, *Os deuses.*

17. Brandão advances this claim at several points in *Os deuses* (see, for example, pp. 111–15). It should always be noted that Brandão, never a reductionist, stresses the historical complexity of exchanges between erudite and popular religions and the variety of political outcomes from these exchanges.

18. Brandão, *Os deuses*, 125.

5. THE AFRO-BRAZILIAN SPIRITISTS: AGAINST THE STREAM

1. Roger Bastide, *The African Religions of Brazil.* Incidentally, I do not want to suggest in any way that the symbolic masking is either mechanical or cynical.

2. Here, and at several other points in this section of the chapter, I am paraphrasing passages from an interview taped on 8 April 1977. But I am also drawing on conversations noted in my research journals for 1977 and 1982.

3. This account is my summary of a fuller account taped on 17 June 1982. Naícia was telling this story as much to me as to the Catholic wife of one of Campo Alegre's best-known festive Catholics who played the accordion at all the folk Catholic festivals. Naícia gained obvious approval from her Catholic friend for shopping around, for her final resolution, and for telling a good story. The story and this situation suggest the existence of a common folk religion cutting across the boundaries of the separate religious traditions.

4. The author taped an interview with Elsa on 1 November 1977. All quotations are from this interview.

5. Statements by Gregório are quoted and paraphrased from an interview with the author taped on the evening of 18 July 1982.

6. This and subsequent quotations are from an interview with the author taped on 20 July 1982. The paraphrase of her views and beliefs has been constructed from this interview, a taped interview on 14 May 1977, and many long untaped conversations summarized in my research journals of 1977 and 1982.

6. THE AFRO-BRAZILIAN SPIRITISTS: THE MAINSTREAM?

1. This is the title of two of Ortiz's analyses of Umbanda: Renato Ortiz, *A morte branca do feiticeiro negro — Umbanda: Integração de uma religião numa sociedade de classes;* and the article of the same name in *Religião e Sociedade* 1 (May 1977): 43–50.

2. Ortiz, *A morte branca*, 197. Compare Maria Helena Villas Boas Concone, "Ideologia umbandista e integralismo." Concone draws out the very considerable overlap between Umbanda and integralist ideologies in the thirties. Many elements of those ideologies are alive and well in the national security ideology of the modern military and in modern Umbanda.

3. Diana Brown, "O papel histórico da classe média na formação de Umbanda"; Patrícia Birman, "A celebração do poder: Um ritual umbandista"; Leni M. Silverstein, "Mãe de todo mundo: Modas de sobrevivência nas comunidades de Candomblé de Bahia," *Religião e Sociedade* 4 (1979): 143–69.

4. I did not tape an interview with Maria José, but my wife, Mary Aitken, taped an interview with her, and during 1977 she was an almost daily visitor to our house in Campo Alegre. I have noted some conversations with her in my field notes, and Mary Aitken has many more in hers. Maria José took me to Dona Rosária's center on 17 September 1977.

5. These comparisons were made in an untaped conversation on 1 July 1982 and were summarized in my research journal entry for that date. I taped an interview with Dona Paula in 1977 (undated).

6. Within Umbanda, the female Pombagira forms part of the phalanx of spirits known as the People of the Street, male members of the same falange including Exú. This falange (one of seven, each ruled by one or two *orixás*) is ruled by Ogun. They are thought of as spirits in evolution and, one is often told by Umbandistas, "like snake poison, serve to kill and to cure." It all depends on the intentions of the medium, the spirits themselves being neutral. A Pombagira is a gypsy, incurably flirtatious, devious, a heavy smoker and drinker. She is not, at least in this group, perceived as "developing" as Maria Pretinha considers Zé Pelintra to be.

7. Bastide, *African Religions*, 397.

8. Brandão, *Os deuses*, 121.

9. Ibid., 106–8, 144–45.

10. Colin Henfrey, "The Hungry Imagination: Social Formation, Popular Culture and Ideology in Bahia."

11. See Cândido Procópio F. de Camargo (ed.), *Católicos, protestantes, espíritas*, part 4.

12. Ortiz does not, as far as I am aware, designate Umbanda leaders as "agents" as some others do. But he leaves us in no doubt that the role of Umbanda leaders in the market of symbolic goods helps achieve the hegemony of the dominant classes. In return, Umbanda is awarded the status of a legitimate religion by the powers-that-be. (See Ortiz, *A morte branca*, 177.) His analysis of ritual, organization, and belief in the context of a modernizing class society is subtle and compelling. But some other students of Umbanda criticize a certain determinism in the analysis, as I do here. See Lísias Nogueira Negrão, who complains that Ortiz and others miss variety in Umbanda presuming the disappearance of the charismatic under the challenge of the modern, the magical and the prophetical in the face of institutional religion (Lísias Nogueira Negrão, "A Umbanda como expressão de religiosidade popular").

13. Reginaldo Prandi reports a trend for a dramatic rise, in São Paulo during

the eighties, in the numbers forming and being attracted to Candomblé groups, at the expense of declining Umbanda groups. See "Sincretismo afro-brasileiro em São Paulo: Da Umbanda ao Candomblé." One interpretation of this trend is that ethnic and class identity other than that required by the dominant white industrial culture is being asserted through religious choice. This would be opposite to the process of hegemony through religion predicted by Ortiz.

7. THE CATHOLICS

1. The phrase "preferential option for the poor" begins to appear in church documents in Brazil in the late 1970s. Throughout Latin America, it gained official blessing at the 1979 Latin American Bishops' Council at Puebla, Mexico, where the bishops affirmed "the need for conversion on the part of the whole Church to a preferential option for the poor." (Third General Conference of Latin American Bishops, Puebla: Evangelization at Present and in the Future of Latin America. Washington, D.C.: National Conference of Catholic Bishops, 1979. Para. 1134.)

2. The most important contribution to the influence approach, but one which is subtle and sympathetic to reformers in the church, is Thomas C. Bruneau, *The Church in Brazil: The Politics of Religion.*

3. Jether Ramalho, "Algumas notas sobre duas perspectivas de pastoral popular." The theme of co-optation of grass-roots groups by upper-class religious functionaries (and not just Catholic clergy) is well analyzed in Brandão, *Os deuses.*

4. Almir R. Guimarães, "Comunidades de base — busca de equilíbrio entre ministérios e comunidade Cristã."

5. *Comunidades eclesiais de base no Brasil: Experiências e perspectivas* 23.

6. Ibid., 20, 14, 15.

7. Cláudio Perani, "Comunidades eclesiais de base e movimento popular," 28.

8. Ralph Della Cava, *Miracle at Joaseiro.*

9. Ibid., 31.

10. By the middle of the nineteenth century many authorities in the Roman Catholic church felt besieged by the powers and ideas of secular liberalism and subverted from within by lack of discipline and fidelity to doctrine. Pope Pius IX's Syllabus of Errors (1864) anathematized the doctrines of secular liberalism, and the First Vatican Council (1870) attempted to restore centralized order and doctrinal purity in the church.

11. Della Cava, *Miracle at Joaseiro,* 125.

12. All these quotations come from my second recorded interview with Pedro taped on 12 June 1982. I had previously recorded an interview with him on 11 June 1977. Several untaped conversations are noted and summarized in my research journals for 1977 and 1982.

13. Mary Aitken Ireland, "Leaseholds on Life," 374.

14. These quotations are from an interview with the author taped on 27 June 1982.

15. For a superb analysis of this type of folk Catholicism through an investi-

gation of the categories used for religious functionaries, see Regina de Paulo Santos Prado, "Sobre a classificação dos funcionários religiosos da zona rural da Baixada Maranhense."

16. There is an extensive literature on popular religion in general, and popular Catholicism in particular. A useful bibliography of studies available up to 1978 is provided in B. Beni dos Santos and Roberto M. Roxo, eds., *A religião do povo*, 135–44. I have found various works by Riolando Azzi especially helpful: *O catolicismo popular no Brasil;* "Elementos para a história do católicismo popular"; and "Religiosidade popular." The various works of Eduardo Hoornaert have also been indispensable.

Scott Mainwaring has provided us with a useful definition of popular Catholicism:

> Popular Catholicism is a set of widespread traditional religious practices and beliefs that emphasize the devotional elements of faith, such as paying tributes to the saints; asking for favors and paying thanks through material means; using private symbols, devotions and extra-official rites. The sacramental elements of faith controlled by the institutional church are de-emphasized. These popular religious practices are found outside of and often in opposition to the institutional church. The relations between the individual and God (or saint) are direct rather than mediated by the clergy; in this sense, popular Catholicism is a somewhat private faith. These popular practices have generally been associated with passive, fatalistic political views and, as a result, have often been seen as alienated. (*The Catholic Church and Politics in Brazil, 1916–1985,* 174)

Some of the recent case studies of popular Catholicism remind us of variations, including quite different relationships with the institutional church, in different parts of Brazil. See Lisette van den Hoogen, "The Romanization of the Brazilian Church: Women's Participation in a Religious Association in Prados, Minas Gerais"; Ineke van Halsema, "Religious Developments in a Peasant Village in Rio Grande do Sul, Brazil: Women, Men and Catholicism"; and Marjo de Theije, "'Brotherhoods Throw More Weight Around than the Pope.'"

17. Eduardo Hoornaert et al., *História da igreja no Brasil,* 369.

18. See Eduardo Hoornaert, *Verdadeira e falsa religião no nordeste.*

19. José Comblin quoted in Mainwaring, *The Catholic Church,* 176.

20. Ireland, "Catholic Clergy in the Northeast of Brazil."

21. Bruneau, *The Church in Brazil.* In my review of Bruneau's work here I draw on my review article "Catholics and Politics in Brazil." Many paragraphs from that article are reproduced verbatim.

22. Ibid., 92.

23. Ibid., 97–102.

24. The National Conference of Brazilian Bishops (CNBB) consists of all the Catholic bishops of Brazil. Every two years there is an assembly of the CNBB, which elects a president, an executive, and the heads of various pastoral commissions. The assembly also debates and passes resolutions on a range of matters. In between assemblies, the executive and the heads of commissions make pronouncements not only on internal church matters but also on issues of social justice. By reputation, the CNBB is the most radical of national bishops' conferences around the world; but Scott Mainwaring and others have noted a more conser-

vative trend in the 1980s. See Scott Mainwaring, "Grass-Roots Catholic Groups and Politics in Brazil," 171–72, and *The Catholic Church*, chapter 11.

25. Bruneau, *The Church in Brazil*, 113.

26. Ibid., 132.

27. Ibid., 30.

28. Rubem César Fernandes, *Os cavaleiros do Bom Jesus: Uma introdução as religiões populares;* Daniel R. Gross, "Ritual and Conformity: A Religious Pilgrimage to Northeastern Brazil."

29. Fernandes, *Os cavaleiros*, 142–43. On Brazil's national day, September 7, in 1988 I attended the second workers' pilgrimage at the huge basilica of Nossa Senhora de Aparecida in the state of São Paulo. With several thousands of pilgrims, a great many speeches on class and racial liberation, and a mass celebrated by a dozen bishops led by the president of the CNBB, this was the liturgy described by Fernandes writ very large indeed.

30. Ibid., 144.

31. Mainwaring, *The Catholic Church*, part 3.

32. Ibid., chapter 9.

33. Ibid., 212.

34. Ibid., chapter 8. In another work, which is to my mind the best single essay on the Catholic church and politics in contemporary Brazil, Scott Mainwaring warns of the limitations of conclusions about the CEBs that are based on single-case studies, or on information limited to one point in time. "Too often analysts present a static picture of the activities and perspectives of grass-roots groups. In fact, these groups continuously evolve as they face new questions within the church and within society at large" (Mainwaring, "Grass-Roots Catholic Groups," 157).

35. Alvaro Barreiro, *Basic Ecclesial Communities: The Evangelization of the Poor*, 56.

36. W. E. Hewitt, "Strategies for Social Change in Brazilian CEBs."

37. Hewitt completed further fieldwork in the archdiocese of São Paulo in 1988. He reports a continuation of trends noted in the earlier work. Partly as a result of declining institutional support from the church, the CEBs surveyed seemed less than ever involved in direct political struggle for local improvements. On the other hand, there is a trend toward increased homogeneity and harmony within the groups: "members' attitudes have become much more uniformly liberal over time." (W. E. Hewitt, "Religion and the Consolidation of Democracy in Brazil: The Role of the Comunidades Eclesiais de Base [CEBs]," 145.)

38. W. E. Hewitt, "Strategies for Social Change in Brazilian CEBs," 26. See also Mainwaring, "Grass-Roots Catholic Groups" for a full discussion of these problems.

39. See Marcello de C. Azevedo for a typology of CEBs according to social context. The contexts are: frontier rural areas where there are violent conflicts over land; rural areas, or small- and medium-sized settlements, with problems of subsistence, and/or climate, and institutional absence or neglect; areas affected by major projects (such as hydroelectric works or agribusiness) or "by the sordid politics of bossism (*coronelismo*)"; the metropolitan peripheries; the "bedroom

cities." (Marcello de C. Azevedo, S.J., *Basic Ecclesial Communities in Brazil: The Challenge of a New Way of Being Church*, 3-5.)

40. In this book I focus on local and cultural problems confronted by "agents" of the communitarian project. I do not attempt to do what Scott Mainwaring has done so well—to assess critically certain ideological weaknesses (such as the conflation of a peculiar Brazilian capitalism with capitalism in general) and political naïveté as sources of relative failure. See "Grass-Roots Catholic Groups," 176-86.

8. THE KINGDOMS COME

1. Pedro Jacobi and some other Brazilian students of social movements in the eighties have criticized static conceptions of agents of the state. Jacobi's studies of local health movements vindicate his claim that, in more recent times, movements and state agencies have transformed one another. Agencies of the state have been flexible and accommodating, often to a degree that is at once surprising and disturbing to those who expect the state to be monolithic and insatiably co-optative. See Pedro Jacobi, "Movimentos reivindicatórios urbanos, estado e cultura política: Reflexão em torno da ação coletiva e dos seus efeitos político-institucionais no Brasil" (São Paulo: CEDEC, 1988).

2. See Conniff, *Urban Politics in Brazil.* Conniff writes of the "macabre dance" between populism and authoritarianism (he explains this image on page 136).

3. Aspásia Alcântara de Camargo, "Autoritarismo e populismo: Bipolaridade no sistema político brasileiro," 23. I do not know what Camargo thinks about the eighties' phase of *abertura*.

4. Simon Schwartzman, *Bases do autoritarismo no Brasil.* A version of this outline of Schwartzman and of my analysis of prerequisites for a deepening of democracy in Brazil is contained in my essay "Catholic Base Communities, Spiritist Groups, and the Deepening of Democracy in Brazil."

5. Only once has redistribution through representative politics seemed a real possibility, and that ushered in the present authoritarian phase. One of the factors precipitating the authoritarian coup against the representative political system in 1964 was the social security law of 1960, which gave labor leaders a secure position of influence on the governing councils of all social security agencies. In 1963, the pro-labor labor minister Almino Afonso assisted labor leaders in extending their influence, so that ability to effectively redistribute and destroy the control function of the corporative system was briefly attained. See Kenneth Paul Erickson, "Corporatism and Labor in Development."

6. Schwartzman, *Bases do autoritarismo*, 146.

7. Ibid., 147.

8. José Comblin, *The Church and the National Security State* (chapter 4), provides an outline of the origins and content of the national security ideology (NSI) promoted in modern Latin American military regimes. I consider that the ideology actually transmitted to the grass roots in Brazil is not the complete NSI, which Brazilian generals such as General Golbery e Couto have helped to formu-

late, but a mixture of elements from that ideology together with ideas and perspectives that elite modernizers have been formulating and teaching since at least the thirties.

9. Martin, *Tongues of Fire*, chapters 11, 13.

10. Ibid., 288. Martin concedes that there is a process of "Latinamericanization of Protestantism" accompanying the North American–style revolution through evangelical faith. Autocratic leadership by pastors and partial retention of patronage networks (as noted by Christian Lalive D'Epinay) mean that there is no simple equation to be drawn between the Methodist achievement in North America and the Pentecostal potential in Brazil. But, in Martin's view, there is a common genealogy and, more important, distinct signs of a parallel historical role, in which the "symbolic affirmation and realisation of liberty and equality in the religious sphere" (*Tongues of Fire*, 44) creates a new citizen and ultimately a new politics. And that new citizen, distrustful of a centralized church, will reject a centralized authoritarian state.

11. A useful interview with Bishop Edir was published in Isto É Senhor (20 June 1990). Reports on Edir's group and other Pentecostal groups are to be found in *Veja* (16 May 1990). An article in *Veja* (25 April 1990) reports that Edir's church has seven hundred temples spread throughout Brazil, fourteen radio stations, a press, and a television station (TV Record) in São Paulo. Edir Macedo has a residence in New York where he has already constructed four temples.

12. Robert Darnton, "A Bourgeois Puts His World in Order: The City as a Text."

13. In Brazil, the symbol of the new broom sweeping away corruption is associated with Jânio Quadros, the conservative populist who was elected governor of São Paulo state in 1954, having been mayor of São Paulo city in 1953. He was elected president in 1960, but he served only a short time before resigning. In 1986, he was again elected mayor of São Paulo city. In all his campaigns from the 1950s, his symbol was the new broom.

14. Scott Mainwaring, Ralph Della Cava, and some Brazilian commentators note a decline in the influence and momentum of the church of the CEBs going back to the early eighties. Mainwaring attributes this to the combination of conservative pressures within the church and the dynamics of increased democratization. See chapter 11 of *The Catholic Church*, which is entitled "The Decline of the Popular Church, 1982–1985."

15. The PT did not grow out of the CEBs directly or exclusively. In his *Quando novos personagens entraram em cena*, Eder Sader has traced the convergence of new unionists, new Catholics, and new secular left intelligentsia, in the period 1970–1980 in Greater São Paulo. The PT emerged from this convergence. On the other hand, as Scott Mainwaring has pointed out, "it is difficult to even imagine the existence of the PT had grass-roots church groups not existed. The PT was inspired by progressive Catholic ideas emphasizing popular participation, grass-roots democracy, popular organization, and basic needs" ("Grass-Roots Catholic Groups," 174). In the same essay, Mainwaring gives a more complete account than mine of the range of strategy and vision among grass-roots Catholic groups in the late eighties.

16. Luther P. Gerlach, "Movements of Revolutionary Change: Some Structural Characteristics."

17. Similar expectations and conclusions arise from a study of Candomblé in Alagoinhas. See A. D. Willemier Westra, "Paradoxes and Power: Structural Tensions in the Symbolic System of the Candomblé Religion in Alagoinhas (Bahia, Brazil)," a paper presented at the 46th International Congress of Americanists, July 4–8, 1988, in Amsterdam.

18. Implicit in this argument (which links religious practice to the construction of neighborhood, and the construction of neighborhood to effective shaping of agendas for national politics at the grass roots) are a number of ideas from the literature on social movements. One of these ideas is that close ties between out-groups and in-groups in a society will reduce the likelihood of a social movement arising from the out-groups; whereas, conversely, groups that are not well linked to other segments of society may have an advantage in organizing for collective action (see A. Oberschall, *Social Conflict and Social Movements*, 118–24). Another idea is that the group base for political activity may vary across societies. Brazil, like the U.S. (but perhaps unlike Chile and Western Europe), may be especially dense in religiously based social organization but weak in union membership. And we might expect that, in Brazil, mass movements will be rooted organizationally in the churches, just as the civil rights movement was in the U.S. (see M. N. Zald and J. D. McCarthy, "Religious Groups as Crucibles of Social Movements").

BIBLIOGRAPHY

1. ARCHIVAL MATERIALS

a. Archive of the Brotherhood.
   Compromissos da Irmandade, 1870, 1929, 1942, 1972.
   Livro de atas: 1. 1870-1903
               2. 1916-1932
               3. 1934-1942
               4. 1946-?1960 (incomplete)
               5. 1964-1967
               6. 1967-1972
   Livros caixas (cashbooks) 1908, 1930.
   Membership Lists: 1870-1871, 1967.
   Planta do Patrimônio, 1939.
b. Archive of the Parish.
   Livro de tombo: 1903-1949; 1966-1968.

2. GOVERNMENT PUBLICATIONS

Plano de desenvolvimento integrado, região metropolitana do Recife. Recife: FIDEM, 1976.
Recenseamento geral do Brasil: Censo demográfico, Pernambuco. Rio de Janeiro: IBGE, 1940, 1970.
Sinopse estatística do município de Igarassú. Rio de Janeiro: IBGE, 1948.
Sinopse preliminar do censo demográfico: Pernambuco. Rio de Janeiro: IBGE, 1960.

3. BOOKS, ARTICLES, AND OTHERS

Adriance, Madeleine. *Opting for the Poor: Brazilian Catholicism in Transition.* Kansas City: Sheed and Ward, 1986.
Alves, Rubem. *Protestantism and Repression: A Brazilian Case Study.* New York: Orbis Books, 1979.
Andrade, Manuel Correia de. *A terra e o homen no nordeste.* São Paulo: Brasiliense, 1964.

Araújo, João Dias de. "Igrejas protestantes e estado no Brasil." *Cadernos do ISER* 7 (1977): 23–32.

Azevedo, Marcello de C., S.J. *Basic Ecclesial Communities in Brazil: The Challenge of a New Way of Being Church.* Translated by John Drury. Washington D.C.: Georgetown University Press, 1987.

Azzi, Riolando. "Elementos para a história do catolicismo popular," *Revista Eclesiástica Brasileira* 36 (1976): 95–130.

———. *O catolicismo popular no Brasil.* Petrópolis: Vozes, 1978.

———. "Religiosidade popular," *Revista Eclesiástica Brasileira* 38 (1978): 73–102.

Barreiro, Alvaro. *Basic Ecclesial Communities: The Evangelization of the Poor.* Maryknoll, N.Y.: Orbis Books, 1982.

Bastide, Roger. *The African Religions of Brazil.* Baltimore: Johns Hopkins University Press, 1978.

Betto, Frei. "Práctica pastoral e práctica política." *Cadernos do CEDI,* supplement no. 26. Rio de Janeiro: Tempo e Presença, 1980.

Birman, Patrícia. "A celebração do poder: Um ritual umbandista." *Ciências Sociais Hoje* 1 (1981): 403–8.

Boff, Leonardo. "Comunidades de base – povo oprimido que se organiza para a libertação." *Revista Eclesiástica Brasileira* 41 (1981): 312–20.

Brandão, Carlos Rodrigues. *Os deuses do povo.* São Paulo: Brasiliense, 1980.

Brinkerhoff, Merlin B., and Reginald W. Bibby. "Circulation of the Saints in Latin America: A Comparative Study." *Journal for the Scientific Study of Religion* 24 (1985): 39–55.

Brown, Diana. "O papel histórico da classe média na formação de Umbanda." *Religião e Sociedade* 1 (May 1977): 31–42.

———. *Umbanda: Religion and Politics in Brazil.* Ann Arbor: UMI Research Press, 1986.

Bruneau, Thomas C. *The Church in Brazil: The Politics of Religion.* Austin: University of Texas Press, 1982.

———. *The Political Transformation of the Brazilian Catholic Church.* New York: Cambridge University Press, 1974.

Burdick, John. "Gossip and Secrecy: Women's Articulation of Domestic Conflict in Three Religions of Urban Brazil." *Sociological Analysis* 51 (1990): 153–70.

Cacciatore, Olga Gudolle. *Dicionário de cultos Afro-Brasileiros.* Rio: Forense-Universitária, 1977.

Camargo, Aspásia Alcântara de. "Autoritarismo e populismo: Bipolaridade no sistema político brasileiro." *Dados* 12 (1976): 22–45.

Camargo, Cândido Procópio F. de, ed. *Católicos, protestantes, espíritas.* Petrópolis: Vozes, 1973.

———. *Kardecismo e Umbanda.* São Paulo: Livraria Pioneira, 1961.

Castro, Josué de. *Death in the Northeast.* New York: Random House, 1966.

Christian, William A. *Person and God in a Spanish Valley.* New York: Seminar Press, 1972.

Comblin, José. *The Church and the National Security State.* Maryknoll, N.Y.: Orbis Books, 1979.

———. (coordenador). *Teologia da enxada.* Petrópolis: Vozes, 1977.

Comissão Arquidiocesana de Pastoral dos Direitos Humanos e Marginalizados de São Paulo, *Fé e política*. Petrópolis: Vozes, 1981.

Conceição, Manuel da. *Essa terra é nossa: Depoimento sobre a vida e as lutas de camponeses no estado do Maranhão*. Petrópolis: Vozes, 1980.

Concone, Maria Helena Villas Boas. "Ideologia umbandista e integralismo." *Ciências Sociais Hoje* 1 (1981): 379–95.

Conniff, Michael L. *Urban Politics in Brazil: The Rise of Populism, 1925–1945*. Pittsburgh: Pittsburgh University Press, 1981.

Cox, Harvey. *The Seduction of the Spirit*. New York: Simon and Schuster, 1973.

Curry, D. E. "Messianism and Protestantism in Brazil's Sertão." *Journal of Interamerican Studies and World Affairs* 12 (1980): 416–38.

Darnton, Robert. "A Bourgeois Puts His World in Order: The City as a Text." In *The Great Cat Massacre and Other Episodes in French Cultural History*. New York: Vintage Books, 1985.

Dawe, A. "Theories of Social Action." In *A History of Sociological Analysis*, edited by T. Bottomore and R. Nisbet. London: Heinemann, 1978.

De Kadt, Emmanuel. *Catholic Radicals in Brazil*. London: Oxford University Press, 1970.

Della Cava, Ralph. "Catholicism and Society in Twentieth-Century Brazil." *Latin American Research Review*, 11 (1976): 7–50.

———. *Miracle at Joaseiro*. New York: Columbia University Press, 1970.

Deren, Maya. *The Voodoo Gods*. St Albans: Paladin, 1975.

Doimo, Ana Maria. *Movimento social urbano: Igreja e participação popular*. Petrópolis: Vozes, 1984.

Droogers, André. "Brazilian Minimal Religiosity." In *Social Change in Contemporary Brazil: Politics, Class and Culture in a Decade of Transition*, edited by Geert Banck and Kees Kooning. Amsterdam: Cedla/Foris Publications, 1988.

Dumoulin, Anne. "Popular Faith in North-east Brazil," *Lumen Vitae* 42 (1987): 48–59.

Dzidzienyo, Anani. "African (Yoruba) Culture and the Political Kingdom in Latin America." In *The Proceedings of the Conference in Yoruba Civilization Held at the University of Ife, Nigeria, 26–31 July, 1976*, edited by I. A. Akinjogbin and G. O. Ekemode. Ife: University of Ife, 1976.

Eisenberg, P. *The Sugar Industry of Pernambuco*. Berkeley: University of California Press, 1974.

Erickson, Kenneth Paul. "Corporatism and Labor in Development." In *Brazil: Issues in Economic and Political Development*, edited by H. Jon Rosenbaum and William G. Tyler. New York: Praeger, 1972.

———. "Populism and Political Control of the Working Class in Brazil." In *Ideology and Social Change in Latin America*, edited by June Nash, Juan Corradi, and Herbert Spalding. New York: Gordon and Breach, 1977.

Estudos da CNBB 23. *Comunidades eclesiais de base no Brasil: Experiências e perspectivas*. São Paulo: Edições Paulinas, 1979.

Fernandes, Rubem César. *Os cavaleiros do Bom Jesus: Uma introdução as religiões populares*. São Paulo: Brasiliense, 1982.

Forman, S. *The Brazilian Peasantry*. New York and London: Columbia University Press, 1975.

———. "Disunity and Discontent: A Study of Peasant Political Movements in Brazil." *Journal of Latin American Studies* 3 (1): 3–24.

———. *The Raft Fishermen*. Bloomington: Indiana University Press, 1970.

Frase, Ronald. "The Subversion of Missionary Intentions by Cultural Values: The Brazilian Case." *Review of Religious Research* 23 (1981): 180–94.

Freire, P. *The Pedagogy of the Oppressed*. Harmondsworth: Penguin Books, 1977.

Fry, Peter Henry, and Gary Nigel Howe. "Duas respostas à aflição. Umbanda e pentecostalismo." *Debate & Crítica* 6 (1975): 75–95.

Furuya, Yoshiaki. "Caboclo Spirits in an Afro-Amazonian Cult." Paper presented at the 46th International Congress of Americanists, 4–8 July 1988, in Amsterdam.

Gaxiola, Manuel J. "The Pentecostal Ministry." In *Ministry with the Poor: A World Consultation in Latin America*. Geneva: Theological Education Fund, World Council of Churches, 1977.

Geertz, Clifford. *The Interpretation of Cultures*. London: Hutchinson, 1975.

———. *The Social History of an Indonesian Town*. Cambridge, Mass.: MIT Press, 1965.

Gerlach, Luther P. "Movements of Revolutionary Change: Some Structural Characteristics." In *Social Movements of the Sixties and Seventies*, edited by Jo Freeman. New York: Longman, 1983.

Graham, Richard. *Patronage and Politics in Nineteenth-Century Brazil*. Stanford: Stanford University Press, 1990.

Gross, Daniel R. "Ritual and Conformity: A Religious Pilgrimage to Northeastern Brazil." *Ethnology* 10 (April 1971): 129–48.

Guimarães, Almir R. "Comunidades de base — busca de equilíbrio entre ministérios e comunidade Cristã." *Revista Eclesiástica Brasileira* 38 (1978).

———. *Comunidades de base no Brasil*. Petrópolis: Vozes, 1978.

Halsema, Ineke van. "Religious Developments in a Peasant Village in Rio Grande do Sul, Brazil: Women, Men and Catholicism." Paper presented at the 46th International Congress of Americanists, 4–8 July 1988, in Amsterdam.

Harris, Marvin. *Town and Country in Brazil*. New York: AMS Press, 1956.

Henfrey, Colin. "The Hungry Imagination: Social Formation, Popular Culture and Ideology in Bahia." In *The Logic of Poverty: The Case of the Brazilian Northeast*, edited by Simon Mitchell. London: Routledge and Kegan Paul, 1981.

Hewitt, W. E. "Origins and Prospects of the Option for the Poor in Brazilian Catholicism." *Journal for the Scientific Study of Religion* 28 (1989): 120–35.

———. "Religion and the Consolidation of Democracy in Brazil: The Role of the Comunidades Eclesiais de Base (CEBs)." *Sociological Analysis* 51 (1990): 139–52.

———. "Strategies for Social Change in Brazilian CEBs." *Journal for the Scientific Study of Religion* 25 (1986): 16–30.

Hoffnagel, Judith C. "The Believers: Pentecostalism in a Brazilian City." Ph.D. diss., Indiana University, 1978.

———. "Pentecostalism: A Revolutionary or a Conservative Movement?" In *Perspectives on Pentecostalism: Case Studies from the Caribbean and Latin America,* edited by Stephen D. Glazier. Washington D.C.: University Press of America, 1980.

Hoogen, Lisette van den. "Benzedeiras within the Catholic Tradition of Minas Gerais." In *Social Change in Contemporary Brazil: Politics, Class and Culture in a Decade of Transition,* edited by Geert Banck and Kees Koonings. Amsterdam: Cedla/Foris Publications, 1988.

———. "The Romanization of the Brazilian Church: Women's Participation in a Religious Association in Prados, Minas Gerais." *Sociological Analysis* 51 (1990): 171–88.

Hoornaert, Eduardo. "A distinção entre 'lei' e 'religião' no nordeste." *Revista Eclesiástica Brasileira* 29 (1969): 580–606.

———. *A fé popular no nordeste.* Salvador: Beneditina, 1974.

———. "Catolicismo popular, numa perspectiva de libertação." *Revista Eclesiástica Brasileira* 36 (1976): 189–201.

———. *Formação do catolicismo brasileiro.* Petrópolis: Vozes, 1974.

———. *Verdadeira e falsa religião no nordeste.* Salvador: Beneditina, 1973.

Hoornaert, Eduardo, et al. *História da igreja no Brasil.* 2 vols. Petrópolis: Vozes, 1977.

Howe, Gary Nigel. "Capitalism and Religion at the Periphery: Pentecostalism and Umbanda in Brazil." In *Perspectives on Pentecostalism: Case Studies from the Caribbean and Latin America,* edited by Stephen D. Glazier. Washington D.C.: University Press of America, 1980.

Hutchinson, H. M. *Village and Plantation Life in Northeastern Brazil.* Seattle: University of Washington Press, 1957.

Ireland, Mary Aitken. "Leaseholds on Life: A Study of Land and Lives in Northeast Brazil." Ph.D. diss., La Trobe University, 1982.

Ireland, Rowan. "Catholic Base Communities, Spiritist Groups, and the Deepening of Democracy in Brazil." In *The Progressive Church in Latin America,* edited by Scott Mainwaring and Alexander Wilde. Notre Dame: University of Notre Dame Press, 1989.

———. "The Catholic Church and Social Change in Brazil." In *Brazil in the Sixties,* edited by Riordan Roett. Nashville: Vanderbilt University Press, 1973.

———. "Catholic Clergy in the Northeast of Brazil: An Elite for Modernization?" *La Trobe Sociology Papers* 21 (1976).

———. "Catholics and Politics in Brazil." *Luso-Brazilian Review* 21 (1984): 85–93.

———. "The Prophecy that Failed." *Listening: Journal of Religion and Culture* 16 (1981): 253–64.

Kloppenburg, Boaventura. *Igreja popular.* Rio de Janeiro: Agir, 1983.

Krischke, Paulo José. *A igreja e as crises políticas no Brasil.* Petrópolis: Vozes, 1979.

Lalive D'Epinay, Christian. *Haven of the Masses: A Study of the Pentecostal Movement in Chile.* London: Lutterworth Press, 1969.

Leacock, Seth, and Ruth Leacock. *Spirits of the Deep: A Study of an Afro-Brazilian Cult.* Garden City: Anchor Books, 1975.

Lernoux, Penny. *Cry of the People.* New York: Penguin Books, 1982.

Levine, R. *Pernambuco in the Brazilian Federation 1889-1937*. California: Stanford University Press, 1978.

Levine, Daniel H., ed. *Religion and Political Conflict in Latin America*. Chapel Hill and London: University of North Carolina Press, 1986.

Lima, Vivaldo da Costa. "A família-de-santo nos Candomblés Jeje-Nagos de Bahia: Um estudo de relações intragrupais." Masters diss., Federal University of Bahia, 1972.

Mainwaring, Scott. *The Catholic Church and Politics in Brazil, 1916-1985*. Stanford: Stanford University Press, 1986.

————. "Grass-Roots Catholic Groups and Politics in Brazil." In *The Progressive Church in Latin America*, edited by Scott Mainwaring and Alexander Wilde. Notre Dame: University of Notre Dame Press, 1989.

————. "Grassroots Popular Movements, Identity and Democratization in Brazil." *Comparative Political Studies* 20 (1987): 131-59.

Mainwaring, Scott, and Alexander Wilde, eds. *The Progressive Church in Latin America*. Notre Dame: University of Notre Dame, 1989.

Mallon, Florencia E. "Peasants and Rural Laborers in Pernambuco, 1955-1964." *Latin American Perspectives*, 5 (1978): 49-70.

Mariz, Cecília L. "Igrejas pentecostais e estratégias de sobrevivência." *Comunicações do ISER* 30 (1988): 10-19.

————. "Religião e carnaval num grupo sincretico indo-afro-brasileiro: Os cabocolinhos do Recife." Paper presented at the 46th International Congress of Americanists, 4-8 July 1988, in Amsterdam.

Martin, David. *Tongues of Fire: The Explosion of Protestantism in Latin America*. Oxford: Basil Blackwood, 1990.

Maybury-Lewis, David. *The Savage and the Innocent*. London: Evans Brothers, 1965.

Medeiros, Frei Tito Figueirôa de. "Sincretismo afrobrasileiro-católico numa festa de Padroeira: Consenso e conflito." Paper presented at the 46th International Congress of Americanists, 4-8 July 1988, in Amsterdam.

Melo, Mário Lacerda de. *O açùcar e o homen*. Recife: IJNPS/MEC, 1975.

Melo Neto, João Cabral de. *Morte e vida Severina*. Rio de Janeiro: José Olympio, 1976.

Mesters, Carlos. *Seis dias nos porões da humanidade*. Petrópolis: Vozes, 1977.

Mills, C. Wright, *The Sociological Imagination*. New York: Grove Press, 1961.

Mintz, Sidney W. *Worker in the Cane: A Puerto Rican Life History*. Westport: Greenwood Press, 1974.

Mitchell, Simon. "The Influence of Kinship in the Social Organization of Northeast Brazilian Fishermen: A Contrast in Case Studies." *Journal of Latin American Studies* 6 (1974): 301-13.

Monteiro, Duglas Teixeira. "A cura por correspondência." *Religião e Sociedade* 1 (1977): 61-79.

Motta, Roberto. "Indo-Afro-European Syncretic Cults in Brazil: Their Economic and Social Roots." Paper presented at the 46th International Congress of Americanists, 4-8 July 1988, in Amsterdam.

————. "Renda, emprego, nutrição e religião." *Ciência & Trópico* 5 (1977): 121-54.

Moura, Abdalaziz de. *Frei Damião e os impasses da religião popular*. Petrópolis: Vozes, 1978.

Negrão, Lísias Nogueira. "A Umbanda como expressão de religiosidade popular." *Religião e Sociedade* 4 (1979): 171–80.

Novaes, Regina C. Reyes. "Os escolhidos. Doutrina religiosa e prática social." Rio de Janeiro: Museu Nacional, 1979. (Mimeograph).

————. "Os pentecostais e a organização dos trabalhadores." *Religião e Sociedade* 5 (1980): 65–93.

Oberschall, A. *Social Conflict and Social Movements*. Englewood Cliffs, N.J.: Prentice Hall, 1973.

Oliveira, Pedro Ribeiro de. "Catolicismo popular e romanização do catolicismo brasileiro." *Revista Eclesiástica Brasileira* 36 (1976): 131–42.

————. *Religião e dominação de classe: Gênese, estrutura e função do catolicismo romanizado no Brasil*. Petrópolis: Vozes, 1985.

Ortiz, Renato. *A morte branca do feiticeiro negro — Umbanda: Integração de uma religião numa sociedade de classes*. Petrópolis: Vozes, 1978.

Pang, Eul-Soo. "The Changing Roles of Priests in the Politics of North-east Brazil, 1889–1964." *The Americas* 30 (1973–1974): 341–72.

Perani, Cláudio. "Comunidades eclesiais de base e movimento popular." *Cadernos do CEAS* 75 (1981): 25–33.

Pereira, Nunes. *A casa das minas*. Petrópolis: Vozes, 1979.

Perucci, Gadiel. "Estrutura e conjuntura da economia açucareira no nordeste do Brasil, 1889–1930." Paper given at the Conference on the Northeast of Brazil, 8–10 November 1974, in Racine, Wisconsin.

Prado, Regina de Paulo Santos. "Sobre a classificação dos funcionários religiosos da zona rural da Baixada Maranhense." *Revista Eclesiástica Brasileira* 35 (1975): 59–86.

Prandi, Reginaldo. "Sincretismo afro-brasileiro em São Paulo: Da Umbanda ao Candomblé." Paper presented at the 46th International Congress of Americanists, 4–8 July 1988, in Amsterdam.

Pressel, Esther. "Umbanda Trance and Possession in São Paulo, Brazil," in *Trance, Healing and Hallucination: Three Field Studies in Religious Experience*, edited by Felicitas D. Goodman, Jeannette H. Henney, and Esther Pressel. New York: John Wiley, 1974.

Rabello, Sylvio. *Cana de açúcar e região*. Recife: IJNPS/MEC, 1969.

Ramalho, Jether. "Algumas notas sobre duas perspectivas de pastoral popular." *Cadernos do ISER* 6 (March 1977).

Rolim, Francisco Cartaxo. "Gênese do pentecostalismo no Brasil." *Revista Eclesiástica Brasileira* 41 (March 1980): 119–40.

————. "Igrejas pentecostais." *Revista Eclesiástica Brasileira* 42 (March 1982): 29–59.

————. *Pentecostais no Brasil: Uma interpretação sócio-religiosa*. Petrópolis: Editora Vozes, 1985.

————. "Pentecostalismo de forma protestante." In *A religião do povo*, edited by B. Beni dos Santos and Roberto M. Roxo. São Paulo: Edições Paulinas, 1978.

————. *Religião e classes populares*. Petrópolis: Vozes, 1980.

Romano, Roberto. *Brasil: Igreja contra estado.* São Paulo: Kairós, 1979.

Russell-Wood, A. J. R. *Fidalgos and Philanthropists; The Santa Casa da Misericordia of Bahia, 1550–1755.* Berkeley and Los Angeles: University of California Press, 1968.

Sá, Maria Auxiliadora Ferraz de. *Dos velhos aos novos coronéis.* Recife: PIMES, 1974.

Sader, Eder. *Quando novos personagens entraram em cena.* Rio de Janeiro: Paz e Terra, 1988.

Santos, B. Beni dos, and Roberto M. Roxo, eds. *A religião do povo.* São Paulo: Edições Paulinas, 1978.

Schwartz, Stuart B. "Perspectives of Brazilian Peasantry, a Review Essay." *Peasant Studies* 5 (1976): 11–19.

Schwartzman, Simon. *Bases do autoritarismo no Brasil.* Rio de Janeiro: Campus, 1982.

Sigaud, Lygia. *Greve nos engenhos.* Serie Estudos Sobre o Nordeste, 10. Rio de Janeiro: Paz e Terra, 1980.

Silverstein, Leni M. "'Mãe de todo mundo: Modos de sobrevivência nas comunidades de Candomblé de Bahia." *Religião e Sociedade* 4 (1979): 143–69.

Skidmore, Thomas. *Black into White: Race and Nationality in Brazilian Thought.* New York: Oxford University Press, 1974.

Souto, Anna Luiza. "'Movimentos populares urbanos e suas formas de organização ligadas à Igreja." *Ciências Sociais Hoje* 2 (1983): 63–95.

Strickon, A., and S. Greenfield. *Structure and Process in Latin America: Patronage, Clientage and Power Systems.* Albuquerque: University of New Mexico Press, 1972.

Tamer, A. *O mesmo nordeste.* São Paulo: Herder, 1968.

Tennekes, Johannes. "Le mouvement pentecôstiste chilien et la politique." *Social Compass* 25 (1978): 55–84.

Theije, Marjo de. "'Brotherhoods Throw More Weight Around than the Pᵣpe': Catholic Traditionalism and the Lay Brotherhoods of Brazil." *Sociological Analysis* 51 (1990): 189–204.

Valente, Waldemar. *Sincretismo religioso afro-brasileiro.* São Paulo: Nacional, 1976.

Vallier, Ivan. *Catholicism, Social Control and Modernization in Latin America.* Englewood: Prentice-Hall, 1970.

Velho, Yvonne Maggie Alves. *Guerra de orixá: Um estudo de ritual e conflito.* 2d edition. Rio de Janeiro: Zahar, 1977.

Wagley, C. *Amazon Town.* New York, Alfred A. Knopf, 1964.

———, ed. *Race and Class in Rural Brazil.* Paris: UNESCO, 1963.

Willemier Westra, Allard D. "Paradoxes and Power: Structural Tensions in the Symbolic System of the Candomblé Religion in Alagoinhas (Bahia, Brazil)." Paper presented at the 46th International Congress of Americanists, 4–8 July 1988, in Amsterdam.

Willems, Emílio. *Followers of the New Faith: Culture, Change and the Rise of Protestantism in Brazil and Chile.* Nashville: Vanderbilt University Press, 1967.

————. "Religious Mass Movements and Social Change in Brazil." In *New Perspectives of Brazil*, edited by E. N. Baklanoff. Nashville: Vanderbilt University Press, 1966.

Wilson, Bryan R. *Magic and the Millennium*. London: Heinemann, 1973.

Zald, M. N., and J. D. McCarthy. "Religious Groups as Crucibles of Social Movements." In *Social Movements in an Organizational Society*, edited by M. N. Zald and J. D. McCarthy. New Brunswick, N.J.: Transaction Books, 1987.

Ziégler, Jean. *O poder africano*. São Paulo: Difusão Européia do Livro, 1972.

INDEX

Italic numbers indicate illustrations.

Pitt Latin American Series
Cole Blasier, Editor

ARGENTINA

BRAZIL

Public Policy in Latin America: A Comparative Survey
John W. Sloan

Selected Latin American One-Act Plays
Francesca Collecchia and Julio Matas, Editors and Translators

The Social Documentary in Latin America
Julianne Burton, Editor

The State and Capital Accumulation in Latin America. Vol. 1: Brazil, Chile, Mexico. Vol. 2: Argentina, Bolivia, Colombia, Ecuador, Peru, Uruguay, Venezuela
Christian Anglade and Carlos Fortin, Editors

Transnational Corporations and the Latin American Automobile Industry
Rhys Jenkins